THE EDGE OF ANARCHY

ALSO BY JACK KELLY

Heaven's Ditch

Band of Giants

THE EDGE OF ANARCHY

THE RAILROAD BARONS, THE GILDED AGE, AND THE GREATEST LABOR UPRISING IN AMERICA

JACK KELLY

ST. MARTIN'S PRESS

NEW YORK

www.stmartins.com

Designed by Meryl Sussman Levavi

Maps by Joy Taylor

Artwork:
pg. v: Eugene Victor Debs; George Mortimer Pullman
pg. 1: The White City of the World Columbian Exposition
pg. 85: Service in a Pullman Sleeping Car
pg. 165: Alfred Stieglitz, "The Hand of Man"
pg. 233: Eugene V. Debs speaking

The Library of Congress Cataloging-in-Publication Data
is available upon request.

ISBN 978-1-250-12886-7 (hardcover)
ISBN 978-1-250-12887-4 (ebook)

Our books may be purchased in bulk for promotional, educational, or business use. Please contact your local bookseller or the Macmillan Corporate and Premium Sales Department at 1-800-221-7945, extension 5442, or by e-mail at MacmillanSpecialMarkets@macmillan.com.

First Edition: January 2019

10 9 8 7 6 5 4 3 2 1

Eugene Victor Debs

George Mortimer Pullman

We have been brought to the ragged edge of anarchy.

—U.S. ATTORNEY GENERAL RICHARD OLNEY

Table of Contents

Maps   ix

PART I
May 1893–May 1894

1. Boss Town   3
2. Our Cause Is Just   12
3. More Than a Joke   27
4. A Heart for Others   34
5. The Commercial Value of Beauty   47
6. Well-Wishing Feudalism   55
7. Armies   64
8. The Works Are Closed   73

PART II
May 12–July 3, 1894

9. Nothing to Arbitrate   87
10. Dance of Skeletons   101
11. The Crisis Has Come   108
12. We Mean Business   115
13. Not a Wheel Moving   123
14. Disaster Threatens   133

15. To a Standstill   144
16. Ragged Edge   153

PART III
July 4–July 12, 1894

17. We Shall Have Debs   167
18. Strike Fever   180
19. Pandemonium   191
20. Day of Blood   201
21. I, Grover   209
22. Watching a Man Drown   215
23. Last Resort   226

PART IV
July 13, 1894–October 20, 1926

24. The Poor Striker   235
25. Everything Was at Stake   246
26. Strikes and Their Causes   256
27. The Common Heartbeat   264
28. True to Man   269
29. Solidarity   278

Notes   282
Bibliography   295
Index   301

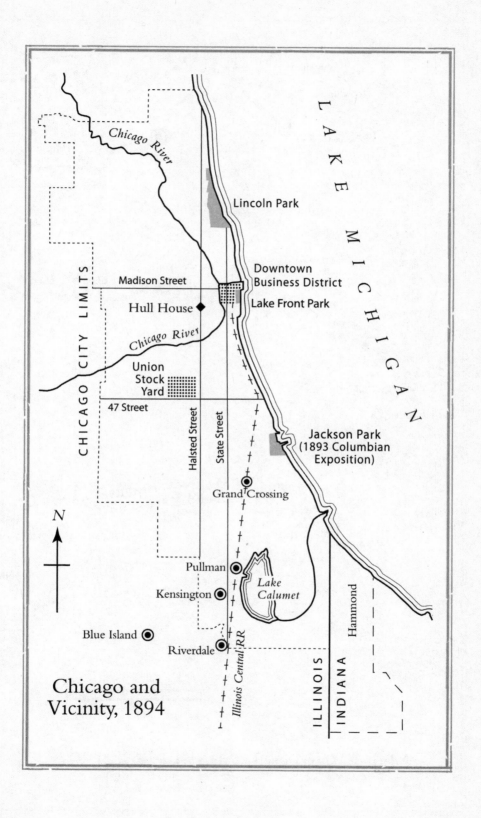

Chicago and
Vicinity, 1894

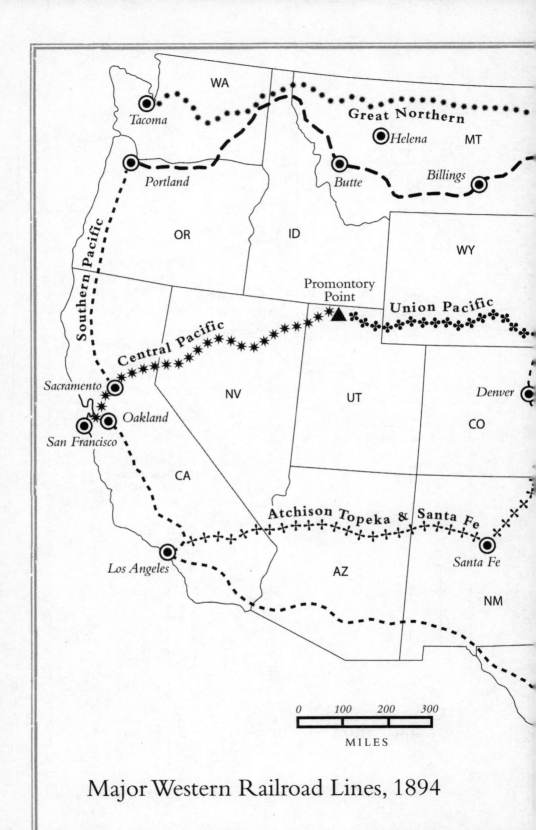

Major Western Railroad Lines, 1894

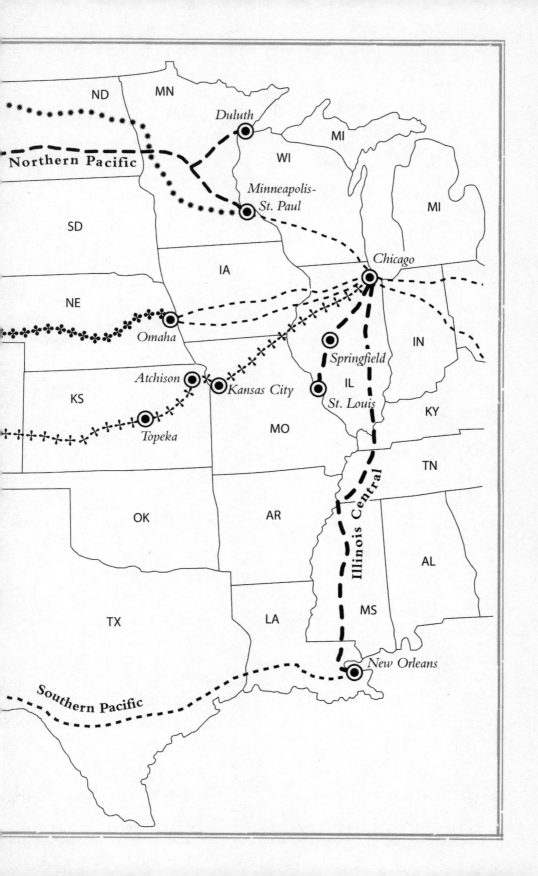

PART I

May 1893–May 1894

1

Boss Town

O N A May morning in 1893, President Grover Cleveland
looked out on the most astounding metropolis ever built, the fab-
ulous White City of the World's Columbian Exposition. Staring
back were the half-million citizens who had crowded into the fairgrounds on Chicago's South Side to view the wonders of the age.

Cleveland was a burly man with a shoe-brush mustache—his
nephews called him "Uncle Jumbo." In his speech, he praised the "stupendous results of American enterprise" and congratulated the nation
for having produced "men who rule themselves." Few in the immense
throng could hear him—they applauded anyway.

A hopeful gleam of sunlight stabbed through the clouds and flashed
from the golden telegraph key in front of the president. Cleveland's pudgy
finger tapped the button, setting in motion a huge dynamo that transformed the fair into a marvel.

Electric fountains made water dance a hundred feet above the heads
of the spectators. Flags unfurled in unison. Salutes boomed and echoed
from the guns of warships. Whistles shrieked. A shroud fell to reveal the
enormous personification of the Republic—a sixty-five-foot gowned
figure in glorious gold leaf that would be known to all as Big Mary. The
mob of onlookers screamed their approval.

They came by the millions and tens of millions. Almost one in every five Americans made the trek to Chicago that summer for the world's fair. Their reaction to the spectacle was summed up by a diarist who wrote: "My mind was dazzled to a standstill."

Almost all who came, came by train. Those who could afford it rode a Pullman car, the epitome of luxurious travel. A Pullman sleeper offered room to spread out, elegant service, and the delicious pleasure of status. Fairgoers were headed to Chicago to shake hands with the future, and in the Pullman car the future seemed to be reaching out to greet them.

Those who had not had the privilege of riding on one could take in all the latest models at a display mounted by the Pullman's Palace Car Company in the fair's Transportation Building. The carved rosewood, Axminster carpets, polished brass, fringed valances, and cascades of curtains and draperies beloved by Victorians all made Pullman travel an adventure in hedonism. By day, a Pullman was a fantastic parlor room on wheels. When night came, a smiling porter turned a pair of facing seats into a bed and produced a second berth from a compartment along the ceiling. He arranged heavy curtains, pristine damask sheets, and mahogany partitions, transforming the car into a comfortable dormitory.

The lucky few, railroad magnates or politicians, might be given a guided tour of the exhibit by the man himself, George Mortimer Pullman. The sixty-two-year-old progenitor of these marvels was one of Chicago's richest entrepreneurs. Many fair visitors could remember the stagecoach days when no man traveled on land faster than the pace of a team of horses. Long train trips had demanded new technology—and Pullman had provided it. The sleeping car had become so closely associated with one company that it was coming to be called simply a pullman. The understated booklet distributed by the company gushed a bit when it called the inception of the Pullman firm, now valued at $60 million, "one of the century's great civilizing strides."

Pullman's name and face were well known across the country—he had made sure of that. His wide, nearly unlined features were those of a tired baby. His hair had gone white and he wore on his chin a goat-like tuft of beard, which boys of the day called a dauber. His imperious eyes were always sizing up.

George Pullman represented a relatively new type in America, a "businessman." He was a man of affairs, a man on the lookout for the new. A businessman's key skill was organizing an enterprise and raising the money to fund it. Pullman knew how to gather resources, command men, and negotiate deals. Early in his career, he had begun to list his profession simply as "gentleman."

The assertion by his publicity machine that George Pullman had invented the modern sleeping car was less than accurate. Most of the credit went to a man named Theodore T. Woodruff, an upstate New York wagon maker. But the mechanics of the car had evolved over decades, and Pullman had introduced his share of innovations.

What was beyond doubt was that Pullman had devised the most efficient system for making money from the sleeper. He saw each car not as a product but as a revenue stream. He retained ownership and allowed the various railroads to haul the cars under contract. The railroads profited because the luxury cars attracted customers. Pullman profited even more as each passenger paid him a hefty fee for the upgrade.

Pullman also understood that monopoly was the path to profit, and by 1893 he was well on his way to absorbing all other sleeping-car manufacturers into his company. A Pullman brochure boasted that the company employed fifteen thousand and ran its cars over enough track mileage to stretch five times around the circumference of the earth.

Pullman asserted that he was free of "the fever of rapid wealth-getting." He could afford to be. He and his wife, Hattie, floated among the highest tiers of Chicago's social heaven. An observer called him a lordly man. Reserved of speech, he let his possessions speak for him.

〰

In 1831, the year George Pullman was born in a remote hamlet in the western end of New York State, a group of Americans at the other end of the state were taking a ride on America's very first steam-powered passenger railroad. It was the beginning of the most stunning transformation in the nation's history. During Pullman's lifetime, private corporations laid more than 175,000 miles of rail, including five transcontinental lines.

"Americans take to this contrivance, the railroad," Ralph Waldo Emerson had observed, "as if it were the cradle in which they were born." In the three decades since the Civil War, the railroads had proliferated into a great tangle of trunk lines and branch lines through the East and Middle West. When builders pounded the golden spike at Promontory Summit, Utah, in 1869, they tied together a continent. The New York Central main line ran from the Atlantic coast to Chicago. The mighty Pennsylvania system extended an arm across the Keystone State and spread its fingers into Ohio, Indiana, Illinois, and beyond. The Southern Pacific, the Union Pacific, and the Santa Fe had erased the frontier. Enormous combines had gobbled individual rail lines, and the railroad corporations had become the most extensive business enterprises in history.

The needs of the railroads had led to an explosion in the production of iron and steel, of coal, copper, oil, and machine tools. The corporations' thirst for capital had established Wall Street as a national money market. The access to far-flung markets that the railroads made possible fueled the rapid growth of other businesses on a scale previously inconceivable.

Chicago was the "Rome of the railroads." Lines converged on the city from every direction. Fair visitors from New York, Philadelphia, and Washington boarded the Exposition Flyer to skim across the continent at eighty miles an hour, barely pausing in the headlong rush toward what trainmen called the "boss town of America."

Chicago's elite citizens had made a mighty effort to win the Exposition for their town. George Pullman had pledged $100,000 to finance the corporation that would mount the fair. Chicagoans were proud of the town's lusty greatness. "Here of all her cities," wrote author Frank Norris, "throbbed the true life—the true power and spirit of America."

Chicago was in a continual hurry. Rudyard Kipling said that its inhabitants swore by the "Gospel of Rush." The city had not existed when the century opened—now it was the sixth-largest metropolis on earth. Its densely packed commercial center pulsed with activity. "Compared to the bustle of Chicago," a visitor said, "the bustle of New York seems like stagnation."

The Columbian Exposition celebrated the acceleration of progress. Fairgoers could hardly wait to get home and describe the technology of tomorrow. They marveled at light bulbs, electric motors, generators, vacuum tubes, neon signs. They made some of the first long-distance telephone calls, listened to a phonograph, rode a moving sidewalk, and gazed in amazement at Thomas Edison's kinetoscope, which displayed pictures that moved.

The fair was an enormous store window on the productivity of American commerce. The nation's output of gold and silver, of telephones and electric lights, lumber and locomotives, sewing machines and pianos, could not be matched.

"The old nations of the earth creep on at a snail's pace," Andrew Carnegie declared, "the Republic thunders past with the rush of the express."

❧

But like the Gilded Age itself, Chicago had a dark side. Urban squalor was spreading there as it was in most American cities. Filth, disease, vice, and abject poverty had become the norm in districts crowded with pestilential tenements. The city, a reporter wrote, was both the "cynosure and cesspool of the world." In 1891, two thousand citizens had died of typhoid.

Entering Chicago by train, travelers saw ugly stretches of smoky factories, slaughterhouses, freight yards, and slag heaps. An English visitor noted the "unrelieved ugliness" of the city. The working-class slums were swept by clouds of coal smoke and intersected by open sewers. The river that ran through the city's heart was caked with "grease so thick on its surface that it seemed a liquid rainbow." A Chicago newspaper complained that the city was permeated by a "solid stink. The river stinks. The air stinks. . . . No other word expresses it so well as stink."

The filth and indigence coexisted alongside the crass opulence of the city's parvenus. George Pullman's home on fashionable Prairie Avenue sat at the center of what a journalist referred to as "the very Mecca of Mammon." Kipling, although impressed by the city's bustle, was put off by the many "terrible people who talked money through their noses."

George Pullman thought he had found an answer to the city's problems. His manufacturing operation was housed in one of the largest factories in the world, which he had built fourteen miles south of Chicago near Lake Calumet. He needed housing to induce skilled workmen to move to the remote location. Rather than leave the matter to the market, Pullman built a planned community that he called Pullman, Illinois.

The all-brick town, a company brochure stated, might be "the culminating product in its enduring benefits to mankind, of the principles on which the entire Pullman fabric is reared." Those principles included the idea that "money could be safely invested in an elaboration of the utilitarian into the artistic and beautiful."

Fairgoers were encouraged to make the fifteen-minute trip to see the unique urban village. They could stroll the grid of streets, take in the neat lines of houses, the town square, the elegant parks, the elaborate Arcade

Building, theater, and library. It was a town where order and cleanliness were sovereign.

The model town was one of Chicago's premier tourist attractions. Like the White City of the fair, it stood as a rebuke to Chicago's squalid tenements. In Pullman, garbage was picked up, sewage pumped away, lawns neatly mowed.

The buildings of the White City were temporary, mere sheds dressed in overcoats of plaster and whitewash. Pullman was built of brick and mortar. Experts confirmed that the model town might well represent a hope-filled future for industrial workers. Yet just as the White City's splendor was a false front, the enchanting surface of the model town hid problems that would, in less than a year, bring about a national crisis.

༄

Although to Chicago's boosters the Exposition was an occasion for unqualified optimism, others were skeptical. The explosion of marvels and conveniences that swelled the exhibit spaces marked the victory of rough-edged capitalism. Most industrial workers, making less than $10 for a sixty-hour week, could not afford to visit the fair. Almost three-quarters of the nation's wealth was in the hands of two hundred thousand citizens.

The skeptical historian Henry Adams commented, "Chicago asked in 1893 for the first time the question whether the American people knew where they were driving." Edward Bellamy, author of the popular utopian novel *Looking Backward*, declared that the motive of the exhibition "under a sham pretense of patriotism is business, advertising with a view to individual money-making." Another observer called the fair a "triumph of materialism."

The coming of the railroads and the instant communication of the telegraph had, in one generation, ruptured the isolation of rural communities. Before the Civil War, America had been a country of small towns with local business owners, local markets, local credit, and local news. Now every village was exposed not only to markets and opportunity but also to the inequality and dissatisfactions of the wider world.

The 1890 census had revealed that the frontier, the line of settlement that had been pushing west since the nation's founding, no longer existed. During the fair, the scholar Frederick Jackson Turner would declare that it was the frontier that had shaped the American character. The availability of free land had allowed pioneers to turn their backs on rapacious landlords or demanding employers and head west. In the process, Turner asserted, they had developed a sense of self-reliance and practicality, along with the confidence, impatience, energy, and egalitarian morality that were distinctly American.

What would shape and inspire citizens now that the West was settled? What would happen to workers who could no longer escape urban slums? Were Americans destined to follow Europeans into a society in which an aristocratic upper class ruled over dependent laborers?

"The free lands are gone," Turner wrote, "the continent is crossed, and all this push and energy is turning into channels of agitation."

Abraham Lincoln had evoked a bygone era when he mused about a "penniless beginner" who at first works for wages, gradually saves a surplus, buys tools or land, and "then labors on his own account awhile, and at length hires another new beginner." This early version of the American Dream was a hollow myth by the waning years of the century.

The labor scarcity of the first half of the century, which had enhanced workers' power and freedom, had been erased by mechanization and mass immigration. The majority of workers were permanent hirelings, not budding entrepreneurs. In the workplace, independence—the defining feature of American society—had given way to the autocracy of bosses.

As industry grew without regulation, the bonds that connected workers to increasingly remote capitalists frayed. Railroad corporations were the first really big businesses in America and have been called "the seedbed of the American labor movement." A series of strikes, beginning with a spontaneous railroad upheaval in 1877, had jolted the country with increasing frequency through the 1880s. During the past seven years, Chicago alone had seen more than five hundred work stoppages. The revolts rattled the moneyed elite. Ordinary citizens found themselves ranked among the "dangerous classes," a common term for workers when they asserted collective rights.

Among those who would later attend and give a speech at the fair was a young union organizer named Eugene V. Debs. Lanky and energetic, the thirty-eight-year-old Debs had spent years promoting the interests of the firemen who stoked the boilers of the nation's locomotives. He had come to see that traditional trade unions were inadequate in the face of consolidated railroad monopolies. Like George Pullman, Debs had a vision of a brighter future for industrial workers, but one that was far more radical than the paternalism of the model town. That summer, he planned to gather all railroad employees into a single, potent union. Once organized, they would demand their rights—he was determined that they would get them.

⌇

Race was another grave issue that troubled the celebration of progress. With the demise of Reconstruction, the nation was reverting to virulent racial hatred. The Jim Crow system condemned black people to permanent second-class citizenship. On the fair's Midway, visitors could watch West African natives enact a dance—"brandishing war-clubs and grinning as only Dahomeans can grin," a guidebook noted. Frederick Douglass condemned the White City as a "whited sepulcher." The ethnological displays, he said, were an effort "to shame the Negro," depicting him as a "repulsive savage."

Douglass understood that the fair was only an image of what Americans wanted to believe about their country four hundred years after the arrival of Columbus. The vision had little substance. The exhibits of the fair offered an empire of things—of technical achievements and the promise of abundance. They kept the nation's festering problems—the fault lines that divided races, religions, and economic classes—out of sight.

⌇

Yet few went home disappointed. They had to be impressed by the forty-six-foot-long Krupp gun that could fire a one-ton shell a mile; by orchestra music transmitted live over wires from New York; by a German-made motor wagon powered by a novel gasoline engine. Hurrying through the exhibits, they marveled at a model of Windsor Castle made of soap, an eleven-ton cheese, a two-headed pig, a map of the United States fashioned from pickles.

On the Midway Plaisance, visitors who had never stood higher than a barn's loft could soar to the height of a twenty-story building aboard the already-famous Ferris wheel. From there, they could look out on the sparkling lake, on all of Chicago's prosperity and blight. What they could not see was the uncertain future.

In February, just before President Cleveland took office, the mighty Philadelphia & Reading Railroad had tottered under its mountain of debt and collapsed. The event had shaken the stock market, but those in the know assured each other that the Reading's failure was a tremor that would quickly pass.

Upbeat predictions could not dispel all worry. Eleven days before the fair opened, a Boston banker wrote to the new attorney general, Richard Olney, to report that "people are in a state to be thrown into a panic at any minute." If the outflow of gold from the Treasury pushed America's reserves below $100 million—a level "held sacred"—he was sure that the country would experience "a panic that will wake the dead." Three days later, on April 23, 1893, the gold stockpile dropped below that holy level.

꙳

On May 1, the fair's opening day, few were thinking of panics, urban problems, disgruntled workers, or anything else that might stand in the path of the headlong express train of progress.

As the crowds rushed into the exhibition halls to view the world's boundless possibilities, the president and several dozen guests took their lunch on the third floor of the Administration Building. Brief confusion broke out when a handful of common folk insinuated their way into the dining room and were found seated at places reserved for dignitaries, who included the Infanta Eulalia, sister of the late king of Spain; John Schofield, commanding general of the U.S. Army; Illinois governor John Peter Altgeld; and Chicago mayor Carter Harrison.

Order was soon restored. President Cleveland dug into his meal of soft-shell crabs, roast filet of beef with mushrooms, hollandaise potatoes, broiled snipe on bacon, and strawberries with cream, all of it washed down with bumpers of champagne.

As the president and his guests enjoyed their repast, the sky cleared and the sun infused the White City with promise. Cleveland basked in the sanguine belief that he ruled over a nation on the verge of a golden age.

What he failed to foresee was the looming conflict between labor and capital, between plutocrats like George Pullman and agitators like Eugene Debs. He could not imagine how that conflict could grow into a violent convulsion that would sweep over the whole nation. Nor did he understand that the bombshell that would set the scene for the catastrophe was only days away.

2

Our Cause Is Just

ON FRIDAY, JUNE 9, 1893, A MONTH AFTER THE OPENING OF the great fair in Chicago, George Pullman and his friend the mustachioed retailer Marshall Field sat down to dinner with two hundred men in the ballroom of the Aberdeen Hotel in St. Paul, Minnesota. At the head of the room a model train fashioned from flowers stretched across a table. The tracks, wheels, and cowcatcher glistened with tin foil.

A newspaper reporter referred to the assembled guests as the "Big Guns of the West"—railroad tycoons, governors, bankers, the tireless strivers of industrial America. In addition to Pullman and Field, they included grocery wholesaler Franklin MacVeagh, flour miller Charles Pillsbury, South Dakota senator Richard Pettigrew, and many prominent railroad men, including John Egan, who had held high positions with the Canadian Pacific and the St. Paul, Minneapolis & Manitoba lines.

The men had come to celebrate the official opening of the Great Northern Railway, whose main line began in St. Paul and now ran all the way to Puget Sound in Washington. Local merchants were confident that the road would make their city a hub for the immense resources of the Northwest, including wheat, lumber, cattle, apples, copper, and iron ore.

They had come to honor one of their own, a big-shouldered, one-eyed man with a full beard and a shaggy fringe of graying hair around his balding scalp. He was the proprietor of the Great Northern, the man known as the Empire Builder, James Jerome Hill.

After a meal served by liveried waiters, a toastmaster predicted that future scholars, reviewing the progress of humanity "from the peak of the twenty-first century," would stand in awe when they contemplated the 1890s, "this wonderful age of iron and electricity." Big Jim Hill then rose to assure his guests that the present era was "as promising as any time in the past ten years." Thunderous applause and the waving of two hundred handkerchiefs signaled the big guns' approval.

In fact, Hill had completed his railroad in the midst of an economic crisis of bewildering proportions. One of his main Wall Street backers, J. Kennedy Tod, was too busy coping with the economic catastrophe to attend. A colleague reported to Hill that "Tod has been p-s-ing down his leg for the last month."

Businessmen and speculators across the country had reason for high anxiety. Four days after the great fair opened in Chicago, the bottom had dropped out of the U.S. economy.

One of the first affected was Stephen Van Cullen White, Wall Street's most daring speculator. Known as Deacon White for his somber dress, he had invested heavily in shares of the National Cordage Company. Managers of that rope manufacturer had gobbled up competing firms and tried to corner the market in hemp imports. It was one of the many business trusts of the day, legal conglomerations of companies that allowed investors to exercise virtual monopoly control over industries like sugar, lead, and whiskey.

Cordage was the very definition of a high flyer. During February 1893, the stock was selling for $75 a share. In April, corporate managers made investors smile with a generous 12 percent cash dividend. Then the firm began to wobble. Rumors reached traders' sensitive ears. Cordage shares dropped precipitously. By the beginning of May, they could be had for less than $19. On Thursday, May 4, Cordage failed.

Deacon White's brokerage company went down with it, along with two other prominent Wall Street firms. The next day, traders gave in to panic. Some rushed to liquidate. Others scrambled to snatch up bargains. The stock exchange erupted. "The floor might have passed for a morning in Bedlam," an observer noted.

All day, brokers swung from "wildest excitement" to lulls when they seemed to sink into apathy. Then, hearing a rumor, spotting an opportunity, fearing the worst, they again sprang into a frenzy, pushing their fellows out of the way to grab at a trade. Gossip hissed incessantly across the floor. The sugar trust was going to rescue the market. Vanderbilt money would be arriving soon. Shares that had been prostrated at least climbed back to their knees.

"The most remarkable day Wall Street has had in twenty years," the *New York Times* declared. Comparisons of the trading floor to a madhouse and descriptions of "wild scenes" were everywhere. Like bedlamites, the brokers, now sure that the worst was over, broke into raucous cheers at the closing bell. Some, no doubt, were simply relieved that the pressure was off—at least until Monday.

One broker said it was the worst day he had ever seen. "While there may be a God in Israel," he stated, "we need him on Wall Street." Forced optimism prevailed during the weekend. The panic might have been a blip. But traders would wait in vain for Jehovah to visit the stock exchange. May 5 was only the beginning.

On Tuesday, May 9, the Chemical National Bank of Chicago failed, leaving depositors dumbfounded. Two days later, Columbia National Bank, an affiliate of Chemical that had been established on the fairgrounds, also declared itself insolvent. Gone were the deposits of many of the exhibitors. Fair officials rushed to George Pullman and several other wealthy Chicagoans and begged them to put their fingers in the dike. Their guarantees headed off an even more disastrous run.

The causes of the national calamity were complex and ultimately mysterious. Economists who had recently foreseen the "steady development of a prosperous period" now looked backward and detected warning signs galore. Construction had been in decline all year; consumption of everything from cotton to rubber to coal had been dropping; cycles of overproduction and bad harvests had ravaged farmers. Democrats traced the causes back to the Republicans, who had held power during the past four years. Their economic sins, it was said, were legion.

Nervous European banks and governments were now rushing to redeem American notes for gold. U.S. reserves of the precious metal evaporated. American banks, equally spooked, stopped making loans. Depositors, fearing the loss of their funds, rushed to convert their bank accounts to cash. Consumer spending dried up.

A mind more subtle than Grover Cleveland's would have been hard-pressed to identify all the forces that were coming together to accelerate the downturn. Overinvestment in railroads, the manipulation of tariffs, and sheer psychology each played a role.

Nervous denizens of Wall Street pressed Cleveland to do something—anything. Caught up, like many Americans, in the mystique of precious metals, the president preached the gospel of gold. An unsound currency, he said, was the root of all evil. As soon as the magnitude of the problem became clear, he called a special session of Congress for August to repeal the Sherman Silver Purchase Act, which had obligated the government to buy all the silver mined in the United States. During the summer, Cleveland endured a painful and hazardous surgery for oral cancer while tied to a chair on a swaying yacht in New York Harbor rather than make the disease public and risk further panic.

In Chicago, the business generated by the fair buffered the effects of the collapse. Americans desperate not to miss the chance of a lifetime mortgaged their homes and sold their furniture to bankroll a trip to Chicago. The railroads discounted rates to encourage visitors. Hotels and eating places, taverns, barbershops, and blacksmiths, all basked in the influx of tourist dollars.

In other areas of the country, it became clear that America was sliding into an economic slough of despond unparalleled in its history. The *Commercial and Financial Chronicle* noted that there had never been "such a sudden and striking cessation of industrial activity." In September, New York governor Roswell P. Flower described men and women deprived of work and facing destitution. "How vast this army of unemployed is nobody can accurately estimate."

A New York City street preacher said that "one could hear human virtues cracking and crumbling all around." In Boston, historian Henry Adams observed that "everyone is in a blue fit of terror, and each individual thinks himself more ruined than his neighbors."

In towns and cities across America, commerce came to a virtual standstill and citizens were "approaching beggary." Half the workers in Paterson, New Jersey, were idle. Schoolchildren in New York City were urged to bring a cold potato to share with their hungry classmates. In Colorado, desperate silver miners flooded into Denver seeking relief. The government there arranged for trains to take them east for free just to get rid of them. Armies of unemployed men tramped across the country looking for nonexistent work. Poorhouses went bankrupt. Public schools closed for lack of funds. Five thousand Polish immigrants in East Buffalo, New York, were reported in "imminent danger of starvation."

With desperation came anger. The big guns who cheered for Jim Hill and his Great Northern line that night in June could scarcely imagine that less than a year later they and the celebrated Empire Builder himself would be vilified as greedy plutocrats. Hill would receive a letter suggesting "it would be a fitting climax if you should be taken by your employees and *hung* by the neck till dead, from one of the triumphal arches so recently erected at the expense of the very people you are now defrauding of their hard earnings."

⟋⟍

Twelve days after the St. Paul feast, on Wednesday, June 21, 1893, Chicagoans opened their papers, eager to read the big news. A Fall River, Massachusetts, jury had decided the fate of thirty-two-year-old Lizzie Borden, who had been accused of the hatchet murders of her stepmother and wealthy father. The two-week trial had offered just the right stew of innuendo, ambiguous evidence, and horrific detail—including the courtroom display of the victims' skulls—to set readers' curiosity ablaze. Citizens across the country had followed the trial with breathless interest. Many were stunned to read that the jury had found Lizzie not guilty.

Those digging deeper into the *Tribune*, among ads for Hood's Sarsaparilla and Schenck's Mandrake Liver Pills, came across a short item announcing, RAILWAY UNION PLAN: NEW AMERICAN ORGANIZATION MAKES ITS FORMAL ENTRY. It was an announcement of the birth of the American Railway Union, known as the ARU.

Fifty railroad men had attended a meeting at Ulrich's Hall on Clark Street in Chicago to ratify the organization. They wore the sack suits and tightly buttoned vests of fashion, but no one would have mistaken them for businessmen. They were men who knew work. Their blunt fingers had performed the crude, precise, dangerous tasks of transforming iron and coal and high-pressure steam into locomotive power.

Their mustaches disguised the excitement they felt as they listened to the tall, angular orator who stood before them. He had the lean, clean-shaven face and nearly bald skull that suggested a bone-hard intensity. His blue eyes burned with sincerity. So energetic was the spirit packed into his rangy frame that the air around him seemed to crackle with electricity.

Everyone knew Eugene V. Debs as Gene. He had served the roads as a fireman, shoveling coal into the maw of an engine while riding a rocking locomotive across the Indiana prairies. He had spent almost two decades organizing railroad employees, building the Brotherhood of Locomotive Firemen (BLF) and other fraternal groups.

But the traditional railroad trade unions, he now declared, were too anemic to confront the corporations of the 1890s. For the financiers who operated those companies, maximizing the return on their investment trumped the welfare and traditional prerogatives of their employees. The brotherhoods represented the various railroad trades—engineers, conductors, firemen, brakemen. They had cooperated with the owners of smaller rail lines. The larger corporations were now playing one brotherhood off against another to break strikes and drive down wages. Workers, Debs insisted, had to meet power with power, consolidation with consolidation. The companies would have no choice but to reckon with a group that represented *all* railroad men. His plan, he declared, meant hope for the 750,000 toilers on the nation's railroads.

"Our cause is just," Debs had told his followers. Their purpose was not to war with the railroads but to bring about a new era for the workingman. "Strikes as labor weapons are obsolete," he said. "We have advanced to a higher scale."

That higher scale would include more than labor relations. Debs was troubled by the "mad chase for the 'almighty dollar'" and spoke against the "debasing greed for gain which pre-eminently distinguishes the age." He advocated "a quiet but ceaseless protest against isolation." Americans were independent, but they were also interdependent. Their hearts throbbed with "divine aspirations for the welfare of their fellow men."

The American Railway Union was a gamble. Almost all of the labor organizations of the day were trade unions, in which workers with specific skills came together for mutual benefit. Debs was proposing an industrial union, which would join highly skilled engineers with unskilled track laborers in a single organization. The idea drew on some of the principles of the Knights of Labor (KOL), a semisecret group that had gathered workers from all professions into a large organization in the 1880s but had lost membership and influence in recent years. If the ARU succeeded, it would mark an epoch in the history of labor in the United States.

Debs said he was tired of hearing the question: what can we do for labor? That was what one asked about a slave. The modern query was to be: what can labor do for itself? The answer was not difficult. "Labor can organize," he said, "it can unify, it can consolidate its forces. This done, it can demand and command."

The hard times presented both difficulties and opportunities for Debs and the infant organization. Many an unemployed man would prefer to have a job, even if he had to become a strikebreaker and take it from a fellow worker. But many others might see the ARU as their last hope before pay cuts and privation erased for good their rights and their dignity. They would join out of desperation. Among those who proved eager to sign up were the disgruntled employees of Big Jim Hill's Great Northern Railway.

⁓

In trying to consolidate power, Debs and his fellow organizers came head-to-head with a small group of men one generation older than most of those at the ARU meeting. Born in the 1830s, they were not, for the most part, the heirs to fortune or family connections. Their forebears were farmers, mechanics, immigrants. With strong wills and abundant imagination, they had come into their prime years during the explosion of technology and commercial opportunity that followed the Civil War.

James J. Hill was one of them. George Pullman and Marshall Field were also among the group. So were Andrew Carnegie, Philip Armour, Jay Gould, and John D. Rockefeller. Each had been able to grasp a new technology: an innovative railroad car, a new retail system, an efficient way of processing hogs or steel or petroleum. Each understood the abstract realm of finance and was adept at putting capital to work. They were the earliest masters of the corporate form of enterprise.

By the 1870s, they were rich, the heroic businessmen of the postwar boom-and-bust years. By the 1890s, they were far richer. Hated by some, venerated by others, they were the personification of Capital. Increasingly, they were coming into conflict with the toilers who constituted Labor.

Their wealth made the men conspicuous. They lived in manor houses and traveled on the private railcars manufactured by the Pullman's

Palace Car Company. They owned sumptuous summer homes, sent their children to exclusive schools, and attended elegant churches to hear sermons on the virtues of wealth. They contrasted sharply with the laborers who worked for them, especially the growing hordes of immigrants, who found themselves trapped in urban poverty.

"The time was when none were poor and none rich," Texas politician John Reagan noted in 1877. That same year, Cornelius Vanderbilt died and left an estate of $90 million. Money, according to Walt Whitman, was becoming "a sort of anti-democratic disease" dividing America. The fondness of these men for luxuries, their ruthless business practices, and their overweening arrogance led to them being dubbed "robber barons."

Nineteenth-century Americans loved to hate the rich. In 1893, with the country gripped by the worst hard times in living memory, the disparity between the dollar-a-day laborer and the millionaire businessman was becoming stark. George Pullman would soon follow Big Jim Hill in the wild swing from emulation to infamy.

༄

For months following their organizing meeting, Debs and his fellow ARU directors crisscrossed the country recruiting railroad men and organizing locals. It was a duty that Debs knew well from his decades as an official of the firemen's brotherhood.

Now he turned his enormous energy, charm, and powers of persuasion to building the new union. His congenial, talkative nature and easy laugh quickly broke the ice with strangers. His enthusiasm was contagious—he converted as much as convinced his listeners. He was never averse to taking a drink or two, telling a joke, quoting poetry, or showing a man in plain language where his best interests lay. Every railroader knew his name, and he was said to have "more friends than any man who ever occupied a like position."

During these months, Debs rarely spent two consecutive nights in the same city. He organized one lodge after another, offering the men gathered in pine-board halls the gutsy rhetoric of a man who knew their work. He emphasized that the hundreds of railroads in the country had been conglomerated into only twenty systems and that "organized railway labor in its present condition has shown that it is unable to cope successfully with such large organizations."

He went about the effort of building the ARU with a sense of urgency.

Debs aimed for harmony with the corporations, but he knew it was likely that the railroad companies would test the new union. Asserting his members' rights would, sooner or later, require a show of force.

⌒

During that summer of 1893, as the increasingly ferocious depression crippled commerce, Jim Hill told his chief lieutenant to "take whatever steps are necessary to reduce track, machinery, station, and other services to the lowest point possible." Cutting wages was part of the strategy for coping with the alarming economic downturn.

Hill avoided dramatic cuts to the pay of the engineers and firemen whose talents he valued, focusing instead on the poorest of his workers, those who possessed minimal skills. He ordered his subordinate to reduce section men to a dollar a day. "There will be plenty of men to work at those rates," he said.

These lowly workers were not members of any of the railroad brotherhoods, whose leaders were cooperating with Hill and advising their men to accept his pay cuts. But many of the unskilled section men, who maintained a stretch of track, were signing up with the American Railway Union. They asked how a man who worked sixteen hours a day could support his family on a monthly paycheck of less than $30. Coal cost $11 a ton. Rents could be $20 a month. What about food and clothing for himself, his wife, and his children? Hill's answer was that the men were lucky to have a job at all in hard times.

In adjusting his men's pay, Hill cooperated with managers of the Northern Pacific Railway, the other trunk line that ran across the states of the Northwest. The two companies coordinated wage reductions, obscuring their illegal collusion by cutting rates by slightly differing amounts.

Jim Hill had built a railroad strong enough to sustain hard times. A bumper wheat crop in 1893 along with improved efficiency on the line and lower prices for equipment and supplies all added to Great Northern profits. As he saw many of his competitors slip into bankruptcy, Hill took pride in his achievement.

Hill's employees knew that the Great Northern's efficiency had been built on their sweat and hardship. Through the spring of 1894, engineers, firemen, and brakemen joined their less-skilled colleagues in signing up with the ARU. When the railroad's managers announced yet another wage reduction in March, the workers wrote to union officials complaining of deteriorating working conditions and relentless pay cuts.

Debs sent organizer James Hogan to St. Paul to represent the ARU. Alarmed Great Northern managers secretly ordered the dismissal of all active union supporters. Learning of the move, Debs could not allow the affront to stand. With Hogan reporting overwhelming support by the men on the line, Debs threatened a strike to "break the chains that are being forged to reduce us, not only to slavery, but to starvation."

On the morning of April 13, 1894, American Railway Union representatives sent a message to Charles Whipple Case, general manager of the Great Northern. Case was told that he had until noon to rescind the draconian pay cuts. He refused.

At twelve o'clock, a message was wired to workers down the line: "Stick together and God bless you; success is sure." The men stopped working. Trains along the Great Northern, the artery that supplied life to hundreds of towns and cities across the Northwest, came to a halt.

⁓

Two years earlier, Jim Hill had crushed the railroad brotherhoods whose members had dared to strike his railroad. Now, in an effort to crack the workers' unity, Hill issued an order to his "faithful employees" promising that any who continued to work would be rewarded. Some engineers, the aristocrats of the labor hierarchy, remained on the job and tried to persuade others to return. Frank Sargent, leader of the firemen's brotherhood, informed Hill that if any firemen joined the strike, "they have violated the rules of the organization and will be expelled." The conductors' brotherhood took a similar stance. An official of the engineers' union said Hill was too tolerant of the "ARU rabble."

Debs seethed at this betrayal of workingmen by their own brothers. He had come to see this tendency as the fatal flaw of unions organized around a single trade. This was the type of intramural rivalry that he hoped to prevent by forming his inclusive union.

The strike put this notion of solidarity to the test. An engineer gained his position through hard work, experience, and learning. Would he sacrifice pay, maybe risk his job, to help an engine wiper or track maintenance man gain a higher wage?

The question was quickly answered. The nine thousand Great Northern employees overwhelmingly backed the ARU. The strike held. On

April 18, five days after the action began, Debs arrived in St. Paul to take command. He and his younger brother, Theodore, along with ARU vice president George W. Howard, set up a strike headquarters in the Sherman House, a prominent St. Paul hotel. He heard reports that all the employees—engineers and section men alike—were standing as one.

Debs vowed "to go over the Great Northern in person; hold popular mass meetings at every point; appeal to the whole people to stand by us in this unholy massacre of our rights." His rallies along the line took on the tone of revival meetings. Workers felt the strength of their unity and stood firm in the face of increasing destitution.

～

For a week, Debs and Hill sparred through exchanges of notes. Determined not to afford the union recognition, Hill said he would only negotiate with men who were in the company's employ. Debs pointed out that Hill had fired employees who were ARU men and that it "does violence to their common intelligence" to agree to meet only with men still working. Debs assembled a committee to represent workers from all Great Northern departments. Both sides finally agreed to talk.

By this time, Debs was accustomed to dealing with powerful railroad executives. In his years of representing the Brotherhood of Locomotive Firemen, he had become a widely known and respected labor leader. But sitting across a table from a legend in the business, a man of formidable will and intelligence, was an experience to remember. Jim Hill had lost the vision in his right eye in a childhood archery accident. Meeting his icy, slightly skewed gaze could be unnerving.

The tall, blue-eyed Debs, on the other hand, was described by a reporter as "somewhat awkward, with an embarrassed gentleness of manner." At the same time he had "a gift of explosive profanity." He was a fluid talker who could employ a disarming bonhomie to charm adversaries.

At the meeting, the Empire Builder offered to submit the matter to the arbitration of "three disinterested railway men." All unions, the ARU and the brotherhoods, would be allowed to make their case. His aim was to undermine the strikers' solidarity by including the trade unions, whose leaders did not back the strike. The ARU president was determined to thwart this tactic.

In this tense game of poker, Debs took the risky move of raising the stakes. He flatly rejected the offer and asserted his determination to continue the walkout. The brotherhoods, he pointed out, were not party to the strike. "If the other organizations represent the men," he told Hill, "get them to set your wheels turning." He would settle on the ARU's terms and "no others."

"It will be to no avail to attempt to divide us into factions," he insisted. The fight would continue. The meeting ended on a strained note. "We understand your position," Debs told Hill. "You understand ours."

Reaction to the strike was mixed. Minnesota governor Knute Nelson summoned Debs to his office and lambasted him as an agitator, an anarchist, and a foreigner, who was "stirring up strife among peaceful and contented workingmen."

But railroad managers were surprised that either from sympathy or fear, the people along the line were "upholding the strike and sympathizing with the men, even to the extent of joining them in their Meetings."

Debs received telegrams expressing support for the strike from mayors of affected cities, including Great Falls, Butte, and Helena. These towns were cut off by the stoppage, yet their leaders warned Great Northern managers against employing strikebreakers. Local businessmen and merchants extended credit to strikers. They considered these men who were their neighbors and customers the "life of the town." At the same time, they resented the monopoly power of Hill and other railroad barons, who used their control of vital lines of transportation to maximize profits in the unregulated marketplace.

Why did Jim Hill not reduce dividends, maintain pay levels, and wait out the economic storm? Why slash the wages of men who could barely subsist on their current pay? To succeed in uncommon ways requires uncommon qualities. A driven man, Hill had a hair-trigger temper and a vindictive instinct. He had pushed himself—once he had walked across the state of Minnesota on snowshoes—and he would push others. Obsessive and frugal, he kept detailed records of the price of his groceries and the size of fish he caught. He was determined to maintain his empire. Yet this was also a man who, when his private car was stuck along a snowed-in rail line, had climbed down, hefted a shovel, and allowed men who had been working in the cold to take a breather by his stove.

With no end in sight, Hill began to feel the pressure of the strike. On April 28, he wired President Cleveland to complain of "turbulent mobs" in North Dakota and Montana. He claimed that the strike was interfering with the U.S. mail, even though the men were scrupulous about letting mail trains proceed down the line. He asked the president to send federal troops to break the strike. The workers, he said, were "misled and misrepresented."

Cleveland turned to his attorney general, Richard Olney, for advice. Olney was a railroad industry insider, but he disliked Hill and warned Cleveland not to interfere in a dispute "in which the employees may possibly be right." The president sent no troops westward.

The strike had now gone on for more than two weeks. Townspeople along the Great Northern line were suffering. Residents ran out of kerosene for lamps and had to rely on the flicker of candles. Unable to obtain materials or ship products, businesses were closing. In Butte, shuttered copper mines left a thousand men out of work. Yet merchants there expressed sympathy with Great Northern workers and many called for a restoration of the men's wages.

Hill appealed to the St. Paul Chamber of Commerce. The town's merchants and businessmen, as well as those from nearby Minneapolis, were cut off from markets and sources of supply. Hill assumed they would support him. Forming a committee, they asked Debs to explain the workers' point of view. He laid out a persuasive case. The businessmen suggested that the Minnesota Supreme Court appoint a panel of arbitrators, their decision binding on both sides. Hill did not like having the matter decided by non-railroad men. But in order to strike a conciliatory pose, he agreed. If Debs again rejected arbitration, Hill would gain the moral high ground. But he had misread his man. Debs also accepted.

The man selected to head the panel was Charles Pillsbury. The fifty-one-year-old capitalist had been milling wheat in Minnesota for more than twenty years. He had introduced new methods and machinery, positioning his "Pillsbury's Best" flour as the dominant brand in the country. A shrewd businessman, he had introduced profit sharing for his employees and had never suffered a strike at his mills. The railroad tie-up was pinching him severely. He and the other arbitrators would hear only from Debs and Hill, excluding the representatives of the railroad brotherhoods.

Appearing before the arbitration panel, the union leader had an advantage over the gruff railroad president. Debs had a gift for making issues clear in human terms. His genuine sympathy for the most destitute of the Great Northern workers was apparent to his listeners. After less than an hour of deliberation, the arbitrators found in favor of the men. As a newspaper report put it, they "gave the strikers nineteen-twentieths of their demands."

Debs's personal charisma had contributed to the victory, but the workers' determination to stand together had won the day. It was the capitalists' united front that had cracked. Debs had played his cards just right. Even Jim Hill congratulated him on his "shrewd management" of the affair. Years later, Hill said, "Gene Debs is the squarest labor leader I have ever known. He cannot be bought, bribed, or intimidated. . . . I know. I have dealt with him and been well spanked."

The settlement came on the first of May 1894, a day traditionally dedicated to the workingman. Eugene Debs had just won the greatest victory of his life. It was a feat that vindicated the enormous risk he had taken in starting the American Railway Union. Having put his reputation and the well-being of thousands of men on the line, he had triumphed.

〜

Charles Pillsbury suggested that the principals celebrate the resolution of the strike at a lavish banquet. Debs declined. The money would be better spent on calico for the wives of the section men, he suggested. In any case, he was dead tired. Because the ARU locals had yet to develop experienced leaders, the burden of managing the strike, which included warding off the very real possibility of violence, had fallen on Debs and his small cadre of union officials. There were, Debs noted, "so many interests to be considered."

He was immensely proud of his achievement. It was not only a victory over a railroad but the opening of a new way for industrial capitalism to coexist with American democracy. "For the first time," Debs told a reporter, "we have demonstrated that it is possible to conduct a strike of such magnitude without violence." Now, he said, he wanted to go home and rest.

As his train pulled out of St. Paul, Debs looked out the window at a surprising sight. Workers were standing at attention along the track, many of them section men with shovels in hand. The eyes of some were filled with tears. As the train passed, they removed their hats to honor the young man who had restored their salaries and their dignity. The recognition from these men "whose frames were bent with years of grinding toil" moved Debs profoundly.

"The greatest tribute that was ever paid to me," he would later remember, "was that of the section men after the Great Northern Strike." The demonstration was "more precious to me than all the banquets in the world."

3

More Than a Joke

DURING THE LAST WEEKS OF APRIL 1894, NO AMERICAN could pick up a newspaper without reading unsettling news. Journalists detailed an alarming "wave of industrial unrest." On April 21, while the Great Northern Railway was still tied up by the ARU strike, bituminous coal miners from Pennsylvania to Illinois and beyond ceased working. Rail and river transportation depended on the fuel. So did heat, electricity, gas lighting, and most manufacturing.

John McBride, president of the United Mine Workers of America, declared that the men were not striking. This was a "suspension" of work intended to reduce the current glut of coal. Higher prices would allow mine operators to raise the miners' abysmal pay to a "living wage."

The walkout succeeded in squeezing the nation's coal supplies. "It will not be long," McBride said a week into the action, "until there will not be coal enough left in the general market to boil a tea kettle with." Railroads felt the pinch immediately. Some engineers had to fuel their locomotives with wood. Streetcars were forced to shut down. Coal became scarce in many communities.

As mine operators brought in strikebreakers, miners fought against them with clubs and rocks, then with pistols and rifles. The killing of four miners near Pittsburgh fueled anger. Parts of the coal fields grew chaotic as local sheriffs found it impossible to keep order or arrest lawbreakers. Illinois saw widespread violence—Governor John Peter Altgeld sent National Guardsmen to enforce the law in one community after another.

The work stoppage went on through May. Miners grew desperate. Their wives and children, lacking flour and meat, subsisted on spring dandelions. By late June, members' indigence, combined with the flow of coal from anthracite mines where workers were not on strike, forced the union to accept a rate of pay lower than the one in effect before the strike. Wildcat strikes and sporadic violence continued into the summer of 1894.

⎰

That wasn't the only trouble brewing that spring. On a blustery Easter Sunday morning, a band of unemployed idealists had marched out of Massillon, Ohio. Their goal was to walk to Washington, D.C., and petition the government to take concrete steps to address the lack of work.

All along the route of the five-week hike, farmers stood at fences and townspeople lined streets, alternately nodding and shaking their heads at the peaceful, patched army, whose troops a journalist called "sandwichmen of poverty." Local people, glad for the diversion and inspired by the men's determination, were generous with meals and gifts of old clothes and shoes.

As it proceeded, this mass appeal to the nation's lawmakers increasingly grabbed the attention of the nation. People traveled for hours to see a group of ragged men and a brass band marching the dusty roads. Crowds near Pittsburgh became so dense that police officers were "swept away and lost in the crush."

Many members of the working class agreed with a Terre Haute, Indiana, man, who said, "They may be wrong. They say their scheme is only an experiment. If it succeeds, every laboring man will be benefitted." With the depression still sapping the nation's spirit, the march offered Americans hope.

The organizer of this "petition in boots" was an Ohio businessman named Jacob Coxey. His goal was to induce the federal government to prime the economic pump by pouring millions of dollars into improving the nation's roads. There was nothing militant about the protest. In fact, Coxey had added some religious trappings to the movement and deemed the protesters the Commonweal of Christ. Yet reporters insisted on labeling them Coxey's Army and endowing their mild-mannered leader with the title General Coxey. Over time, the military metaphor helped to stoke the anxiety of newspaper readers, who envisioned armies reminiscent of Mongol hordes sacking cities.

The forty-year-old Coxey was not himself a workingman. He had made a small fortune in scrap metal and the mining of silica sand and had spent a good deal of it on his passion for racehorses. He had applied a businessman's logic to the nation's problems. Roads in America had always been atrocious. With the coming of the railroads, even the improved national roads had fallen into disrepair. Farmers struggled to get their crops to towns and to railheads. Work to improve roads would create jobs, alleviate the pervasive unemployment in the country, and leave behind a valuable economic resource.

So convinced was Coxey of the soundness of his solution that he bankrolled a movement to bring a hundred thousand—perhaps half a million—unemployed men to the capital to demand action. In the process, he teamed up with Carl Browne, a journalist, labor agitator, and carnival barker. In contrast to Coxey's gold-rimmed glasses, conservative suit, and stiff white collar, Browne dressed in fringed buckskin with Mexican silver dollars for buttons and a ten-gallon sombrero. It was a costume, a reporter noted, that a bad actor would don to play the role of a cowboy.

Although he was the type of rambunctious character that Mark Twain might have dreamed up, Browne had a genius for igniting a movement. He possessed a penetrating mind, an overabundance of energy, and a mad sincerity that won over skeptics.

Both contemporary observers and many later historians emphasized the outlandish qualities of those who accompanied Coxey. They commonly depicted the movement's leaders as classic American cranks.

The sensationalism hid the truth that Coxey was a serious political organizer and that most of his followers were unemployed factory workers with legitimate grievances, not tramps or buffoons. They were living proof of the dysfunction of the unregulated industrial system.

Coxey's plan for temporarily expanding the money supply and stimulating the economy—a scheme that predated the theories of John Maynard Keynes—suited the stagnant, deflationary times better than the hard-money instincts of Grover Cleveland. The president's fetishizing of the gold standard did little to restore confidence but much to deprive businesses of the cash needed for recovery.

For reporters, the Coxey movement was a boon. The march was novel, colorful, and it turned the grim news of mass unemployment into a daily melodrama. Would the men reach the capital? Was the march the beginning of a nationwide revolt by the unemployed? Or was the whole thing a massive humbug?

The press had their pick of eccentrics. The ever-present Carl Browne was an avowed Theosophist with theories about reincarnation. Cyclone Kirtland was a Pittsburgh astrologer. Oklahoma Sam, a genuine cowboy, became a particular hero of boys along the way. So did Honoré Jaxon, who posed as a Métis Indian, wearing a blanket and carrying a hatchet. In fact, Sam had been a worker on Coxey's horse ranch. Jaxon was a college-educated Canadian who had fought against the oppression of both Native Americans and industrial workers.

Another who joined the march was a handsome, thirty-five-year-old dressed in an expensive coat and patent leather boots. He said he would be known as Louis Smith, although that was not his real name. "I am the Great Unknown," he declared. "The Great Unknown I must remain." This was irresistible fodder for reporters. The Unknown, along with his veiled female companion and his collie, Nero, was featured in all accounts of the march. Reporters knew he was actually a Chicago patent medicine seller known as E. P. Pizarro and by several other names, but the "Unknown" sold papers.

As the march progressed, some journalists began to appreciate the seriousness of the effort. Ray Stannard Baker of the *Chicago Record* saw it as "a manifestation of the prevailing unrest and dissatisfaction among the laboring classes. . . . It seems to me that such a movement must be looked on as something more than a huge joke."

Coxey had spent $2,000 to print and mail out pamphlets and circulars in the run-up to the event. He knew that plenty of observers, including his ex-wife, considered him crazy. He averred that "it doesn't hurt me to be called a lunatic."

The success of his plan, Coxey said, would allow "peace and plenty to take the place of panic and poverty." A reporter wrote that Coxey "leaves a trail of new thought in the minds of many." For all its outlandish aspects, the march of the Coxeyites made Americans think. Coxey was talking about new ways to create and distribute wealth.

"Is there anything foolish or anarchistic or wild in the demand for good roads?" a union official asked. Like many, he thought the plan was legitimate, practical, "and above all, American."

To others, Coxey was a threat. A military man declared the Coxey phenomenon "a symptom of the dreadful unrest that is just now, like the effects of a fever, afflicting and weakening our whole people." New York City police superintendent Thomas Byrnes labeled the Coxeyites a serious danger to American society. These "idle, useless, dregs of humanity," he wrote, were intent on "intimidating Congress." He went further: "I think this movement is the most dangerous this country has seen since the Civil War." He was sure that if Coxey's march was successful, the country would "fall into a chaos in which mobs will be fighting mobs everywhere."

Among those spooked by Coxeyism were Grover Cleveland and his attorney general, Richard Olney. Olney imagined that Coxey could be the initial wave of a general insurrection. The commander of the U.S. Army, John Schofield, stated, "There is no telling to what proportions the movement may swell."

Cleveland assigned two Secret Service agents to join the Coxeyites in disguise. He put troops on alert at Fort Myer in Virginia and at the Washington Barracks. Fearful that the industrial "army" might sack the Treasury Building, whose creaky vault was stuffed with the nation's currency reserves, Cleveland ordered that rifles be handed out to department employees.

༄

Even as the high command worried about the Ohio recruits due to arrive in Washington at the beginning of May, they grew even more concerned about the "industrial armies" following in their wake. These men were setting off for the capital from the West and were in a far more militant mood. They were generating a mixture of sympathy and fear as they moved across the country.

"General" Lewis C. Fry of Los Angeles, inspired by a Carl Browne manifesto, announced that he would have a million men with him by the time he reached the East. The written constitution of his group cataloged some of the widespread grievances that prevailed across the country. "The evils of murderous competition; the supplanting of manual labor by machinery; the excessive Mongolian and pauper immigration," the members complained, "have centralized the wealth of the nation into the hands of the few and placed the masses in a state of hopeless destitution." Fry suggested a ten-year ban on immigration. His men were determined that "something must be done and done quickly."

Charles T. Kelley led one of the largest armies, departing San Francisco with well over a thousand men. The thirty-two-year-old printer looked like a divinity student but had a magnetic personality. He was hoping to get his men to Washington to present a scheme similar to Jacob Coxey's good roads idea. His plan was to employ the jobless to dig irrigation ditches in the West, providing both jobs and productive land for farmers. "We Demand Nothing but Justice," was the group's motto.

Like the other western contingents, Kelley and his men had no practical alternative for reaching the nation's capital except to ride the rails. Lacking funds, the men would have to beg, borrow, or hijack trains.

Other armies marched in Kelley's and Fry's wake. In Portland, Oregon, men led by an unemployed stonemason named S. L. Scheffler marched out of town and then appropriated a locomotive. They were halted by U.S. cavalry troops 120 miles down the line. Frank T. "Jumbo" Cantwell, a Tacoma saloon keeper, gathered seven hundred men for the journey to the nation's capital. "We ain't too good to steal a train," he declared. "Congress broke the law, why can't we?" His motley crew made it all the way to Chicago before Cantwell plundered their treasury and fled to South America.

"General" Henry Carter formed an army in Utah as a "protest against plutocracy." His men made it to Denver, where hundreds more joined them in the largest Coxeyite camp in the nation. An attempt to float down the South Platte River ended in disaster as more than forty inexperienced boatmen drowned.

Another army of protesters, who followed Kelley's contingent out of San Francisco, was led by Anna Ferry Smith. She had been a nurse in the Civil War, had studied law, and had found her calling as a reform lecturer. "I'm not afraid of anything," she said. "I have a woman's heart and a woman's sympathy." The men had chosen her so as to have an effective speaker on hand "when we get to Washington." The group never made it out of California. They commandeered a fruit train but were captured in Barstow.

During that chaotic spring, as citizens found themselves out of work, short of coal, and haunted by armies of the unemployed stalking the countryside, real fear began to grip the populace. Those who had lived through the Civil War knew that a divided society could give rise to bloody conflict. Across the country, many came to agree with Henry Adams that Americans no longer knew where they were driving.

4

A Heart for Others

As he left St. Paul after his victory over Jim Hill's Great Northern, Eugene Debs relaxed to the *clack-clack* of the train wheels and the deep breathing of the locomotive, familiar sounds to a man who had spent his life working and traveling on the rails. His eyes followed the bounce of the drooping telegraph wires and took in the blur of wildflowers the trains had sown along the right-of-way. He was supremely happy.

Debs had ridden a thousand trains. He would still rather be traveling up front in the engine cab than in a coach car. Organizing for the Brotherhood of Locomotive Firemen, he had often hitched rides in the locomotives of freight trains to save money. The rushing wind, the metallic bitterness of burning coal, the throb of steam, the perpetual vigilance, the sheer sense of speed—he remembered it all with excitement in his blood.

Terre Haute lay on the Wabash River in west-central Indiana. Pulling into the town, Debs was astounded to find an enormous crowd gathered around the station. Three, maybe four thousand of his fellow townsmen—workingmen and prominent citizens alike—had turned out to greet him.

He stepped down onto the platform amid the chant: "Debs! Debs! Debs!" He greeted his wife, Kate, his parents and sisters. All of them were beaming, proud that Terre Haute's native son had become a national figure, the victor in what a local paper called "one of the completest tie-ups in the history of labor troubles." When he spoke to the crowd, Debs praised the heroism of the workers. They had "stood up as one man and asserted their manhood."

The outcome of the Great Northern strike was a signal of the American Railway Union's growing power. Out of power would come harmony. "An era of close relationship between capital and labor, I believe, is dawning," Debs told his audience.

Debs's neighbors were enormously impressed with the young man whom many had known as a store clerk, railroad hand, and small-time politician. The minister of the First Baptist Church, a skeptic about labor matters, noted Debs's magnanimity. The fact that he did not attack his defeated opponent showed him a "born leader."

The shout "Our next Governor!" brought a "hearty response," a reporter noted.

"What has occurred tonight seems to me like a dream," Debs said after this gratifying homecoming.

⚭

For Debs, now thirty-eight, railroads, locomotives, and steam power were the shining relics of his youth. As a boy, he had watched the men in dirty denim climb down from their huffing, naked machines and swagger through town, lords of power, speed, and distance.

Gene's father, Jean Daniel Debs, had fallen in love with Marguerite Bettrich, a laborer in one of the Debs family's mills in the Alsace region of eastern France. When Daniel's people objected, he gave up his patrimony and the couple fled to America. In 1851, they purchased a tiny frame house in Terre Haute.

After this fairy-tale beginning, the young immigrants faced a rugged existence in the raw western town. Men in Terre Haute still carried guns routinely. A stench wafted through the town from the fifty thousand hogs that were butchered there every year. Daniel worked in a slaughterhouse and laid track on the new Terre Haute & Indianapolis Railroad, later known as the Vandalia line. He barely eked out a living. Marguerite, always known as Daisy, took forty dollars that she had saved and bought stock for a grocery store she opened in the front room of their home. The shop made money. A year later, in November 1855, their first son, Eugene Victor, was born.

While not religious, Daniel and Daisy embraced a high idealism. The atmosphere in the house was one of gaiety and an appreciation for the small things in life. The joie de vivre left a permanent mark on Gene. He would remain devoted to his parents until they both died in 1906.

Sunday nights, Daniel read in French to his children and the house was filled with talk. The couple had named their son after Eugène Sue, who, like Charles Dickens, had written serialized melodramatic tales of the common people. Gene's middle name was an homage to Victor Hugo, the great romantic poet, whose novel *Les Misérables* was published when Gene was seven. The book would always remain his favorite—he was drawn to Hugo's extraordinary sympathy for the working class and his devotion to social justice.

While going to school, young Gene clerked in his parents' store. He gained a reputation for giving generous weight and easy credit rather than keeping a close eye on the shop's profits.

The forests of tulip poplars and elderberry along the riverside became his playground. He went hunting with his father for woodcock and squirrels. He watched uniformed soldiers marching through town on their way to the war that broke out when he was five. He became a hero to the younger children, helping them build kites and construct rafts on the river.

The Debses soon moved to a larger house as their family grew to four girls and two boys. Gene's parents imagined their son climbing the ladder of education to reach a secure position in society. Yet they were understanding when, at the age of fourteen, he left school to pursue a railroad career. Gene's father asked a favor of another Alsatian immigrant, landing his son a position with the Vandalia line, which now extended from Indianapolis to St. Louis.

Out of his fifty-cents-a-day wages, Gene had to purchase a scraper for removing caked grease from the engines in the Vandalia roundhouse. He would keep the implement until he died, an emblem of his passage to adulthood. The tedious scraping and washing with caustic potash was hardly the work of his dreams, but Debs was an able and willing laborer. He was soon promoted to the paint crew, renewing the finish on engines and freight cars. He also used his skill to paint signs for neighbors.

Debs had the good fortune to enter the business during the boom years that followed the Civil War. The Vandalia was expanding, and labor was in short supply. A week before Christmas in 1871, a fireman reported for his shift drunk. The supervisor called on the sixteen-year-old Debs to assume the man's duties. He soon became a regular fireman. Stationed on the left side of the cab, he learned all there was to know about the intricate tasks of operating a steam engine. "The locomotive was my alma mater," he would later declare.

Running flat out, a fireman might heave two tons of coal into the firebox in an hour, all the while maintaining his balance on the swaying footplate. It was exhausting work, swinging like a pendulum to scoop and lift and toss. Muscles protested, then screamed. In summer, he sweated. In winter, icy air clawed through the cab.

Besides spreading coal across the blazing grate, the fireman had to monitor the water in the boiler. Allowing it to drop below the top of the firebox could result in a catastrophic explosion. He had to keep alert for rock slides, misaligned switches, or straying cattle approaching on his side of the engine. The job offered little respite—Debs sometimes worked six sixteen-hour shifts in a week.

The teenager took pride in his work-hardened hands. He loved the sense of movement. He came to know America's midlands by heart, the names bearing down on him in dreams: Plainfield, Cartersburg, Bellville. Next stop Clayton, Pecksburg, Cincinnatus. He continued his education by fitting in classes at a local business school. He was participating in the most dynamic enterprise of the age and felt that his prospects could not be brighter.

⚘

Reality brought him up short. Years of overinvestment in rail lines had created a shaky financial foundation for the industry. In 1873 the house of cards collapsed. Fifty-five railroads went bankrupt. The country plunged into an economic depression. Gene Debs was laid off.

He went on the tramp, joining the tens of thousands of unemployed men who hopped freight trains and chased rumors. Debs's journey took him south through Illinois and finally to East St. Louis. He found a job there as a substitute night fireman in a rail yard. The work was sporadic and disappointing, but it was a job. "I have a little company," he wrote home. "But sometimes I am all alone and I am so homesick, I hardly know what to do."

He observed firsthand the extreme poverty of which Victor Hugo had written. "It makes a person's heart ache," he wrote, "to see men women & children begging for something to eat." He yearned for home, for the familiar certainties of Terre Haute, but he was reluctant to trudge back in disgrace. He would stay long enough "to prove that I can act manly when must be."

His youth and natural resilience sustained him. In his spare time, he studied books on railroad economics and technology, making himself an amateur authority on the industry. He read French and German classics. He shared a room with an engineer who said Debs was a "damn fool" to spend so much time reading. Thirty years later, the engineer observed, "I still believe there was a damn fool in that room, but I know now that it wasn't Debs."

Gene's mother had a single concern: the danger. No job in the nineteenth century involved more bodily peril than railroad work. When one young man signed on as a switchman, his sister "kept one clean sheet for the express purpose of wrapping up my mangled remains."

Railroad men knew that many American lines had been built cheaply. Steep grades, tight curves, wobbly trestles, and questionable engines made accidents commonplace. So did loose or spread rails, defective switches, ice, landslides, and cattle wandering onto the unfenced tracks.

In the year 1890, when statistics began to be compiled, 2,451 railroad employees were killed on the job, more than the Union deaths at the bloody battle of Antietam. Another 22,000 men were injured. Debs would write that he understood "the ceaseless danger that lurks along the iron highway."

The engineer and fireman were subject to head-on collisions: many lines ran on single tracks, and the switch and signal systems to prevent crashes were primitive. Boilers sometimes exploded with catastrophic force. Derailments were all too frequent, train wrecks a popular spectacle.

In order to slow a freight train, a brakeman had to climb onto the roof of a boxcar and turn a horizontal wheel. Then he ran along the top of the car and hopped to the next one to apply the next brake. The process "took nerve, coordination, timing and a perfect sense of balance," one brakeman said. "Wary feet, an alert mind, and chilled nerves were needed every instant." At night or during a sleet storm, the danger multiplied. A fall usually meant death.

Rail yards, like the one where Gene was working, held serious dangers, too. The cars of early trains were joined by link-and-pin couplers. One of the jobs of a switchman was to position an iron chain link that dangled from the front of one car to fit into a slotted drawbar attached to the rear of the next. He then dropped in an iron spike to hold the two together. If his hand accidentally came between the unforgiving iron parts, flesh and bone could be crushed. The switchman often had to keep pace with rolling cars. If he caught his foot in intersecting rails and tripped, the wheels might slice off a leg or worse.

Automatic couplers and George Westinghouse's air brake system were available in the 1880s and would have protected workers against some of these perils, but railroads were slow to adopt the new technology. Critics accused them of economizing at the expense of workers' safety. But issues of competing technology and standardization across systems also played a part in the delay.

The dangers were accepted by workmen and railroad managers alike as natural hazards. Losing a finger, a worker reported to a government commission, had "never been considered serious by the trainmen." Veteran railroaders could often be spotted by their missing digits.

Many of the men who worked on the roads during the era had fought in the Civil War. They had learned the nobility of facing risk, bearing pain, and accepting inevitable casualties. The danger on the roads gave their jobs a soldierly dignity and reinforced the esprit de corps among comrades.

☙

Mothers saw it differently. According to one biographer, Debs witnessed the death of a friend under the wheels of a freight car in the East St. Louis yard. Certainly he was aware of the grim reality of bodies crushed and dismembered. So was Daisy.

He finally gave in to his mother's pleas. In October 1874, he returned to Terre Haute, "that sacred little spot." The Debs grocery remained prosperous. His father again stepped in, landing Gene a job with Herman Hulman, who operated one of the largest wholesale outfits in the West.

Debs put his business education to work as an accounting clerk. Working amid the aroma of coffee and spices, he quickly mastered his clerical duties. With his amiable personality, he made friends with everybody, including Hulman. He had the satisfaction of contributing to his family's finances.

He hated the job. "There are too many things in business that I cannot tolerate," he wrote. "Business means grabbing for yourself." What was second nature to men like George Pullman was foreign to Debs. He found himself wandering down to the rail yards, watching the engines come and go, greeting old pals. He spent evenings in saloons where railroad men told stories of adventures on the iron highway.

In February 1875, he mounted the stairs of a Terre Haute meeting hall to hear a speech by Joshua Leach, the Grand Master of the Brotherhood of Locomotive Firemen. The encounter set his life on a new path.

Debs was impressed by Leach's "rugged honesty, simple manner, and homely speech," but the Grand Master had as yet only managed to organize thirty-one lodges with six hundred members. Leach was surprised that a billing clerk from a wholesale company would apply, but he was happy to accept the nineteen-year-old Debs as an associate member.

Debs continued to work his white-collar job, but his heart was more and more captured by his union duties. He devoted all his free time to the BLF. He looked on his initiation into the brotherhood as "the obligation that is to bind me to my fellow-firemen to the end of my days."

Like other organizations of skilled railroad workers, the brotherhood was more a fraternal society than a labor union. It helped unite far-flung members into a community. The meetings of the local lodge were occasions for male camaraderie and fellow feeling. Since the railroads did not compensate injured workmen, providing accident insurance and death benefits at a reasonable cost was one of the BLF's principal functions.

Debs was conservative in his view of the developing conflict between workers and their employers. He opposed the massive, disorganized, and violent railroad strike that swept from Baltimore to Chicago in 1877.

The firemen's brotherhood, like organizations representing engineers, conductors, and other skilled trades, restricted membership to those who possessed the required technical skills. Running a train was an intricate and demanding task involving immense responsibility. "Benevolence, Sobriety and Industry" was the motto of the BLF. Members whose drinking interfered with their duties were reprimanded by the union and might be reported to their employers.

When Debs won election as Terre Haute city clerk in 1879, his victory was touted as "the triumph of the *laboring* man." A local paper called Debs "the blue-eyed boy of destiny."

Debs pursued his political career as far as the Indiana state legislature but grew frustrated with that stodgy body. Turning away from a career in government and giving up his clerk's job with Hulman, Debs became a full-time officer of the Grand Lodge of the BLF, the brotherhood's national organization. He edited the brotherhood's periodical, the *Locomotive Firemen's Magazine*, building it into a national publication read by influential people outside the industry.

The *Firemen's Magazine* fulfilled many of the functions of what we now call social media. It offered space for firemen to air their opinions about everything from technical railroad questions to matters of health and politics. It was a networking tool, allowing far-flung lodge members to keep up on the activities of friends in the business. Debs included articles about mathematics, chemistry, coin collecting, and international politics. He urged members to gather new knowledge and to expand their horizons.

Admired by working people, Debs was also friendly with men like William Riley McKeen, a prominent Terre Haute banker and organizer of the Vandalia Railroad. Debs admired McKeen for treating his employees with respect. "Mr. McKeen," he declared, "is absolutely adored by his men."

In Terre Haute, the idea of community was palpable. The town's elite—the merchants and factory owners—were not outsiders. Bonds of family and affection tied them to a wide swath of townspeople. Older residents could remember Terre Haute's frontier roots. The egalitarian values that had governed the lives of pioneers still prevailed.

As a rising labor leader, Debs organized other workers, including Terre Haute's carpenters. He advised groups of coopers and printers. He helped gather these local organizations into a Central Labor Union in the city. He even formed an organization for the youngsters who were the city's newsboys and bootblacks. He traveled, sometimes paying his own expenses, as far as Oklahoma and Texas to organize firemen, conductors, brakemen, and telegraphers. His name became well known in labor circles around the country.

Again and again in *Firemen's Magazine*, Debs came back to the theme of manhood, a prevailing idea in nineteenth-century America. Elements of traditional masculinity and patriarchal authority were part of it. Women's roles in work and society had been increasingly abridged by Victorian mores and the industrialization of labor. But self-reliance and personal dignity were important elements of manhood as well. To be possessed of manhood was to be *somebody*. It meant earning a living and winning respect. It meant, Debs said, to be able to approach bosses on a basis of "perfect social equality, and state our grievances like men." He still held to the republican notion, increasingly a myth, that there were no classes in American society.

"One of our fundamental doctrines," Debs wrote in *Firemen's Magazine*, "is that labor and capital are brothers." Money could do nothing without labor, which he called "muscle capital." Owners and workers could only prosper in a "harmonious alliance." He insisted that the role of the brotherhoods was to provide the corporations with "a class of honest and intelligent laborers, men upon whom they can depend."

These were a young man's ideas, looking up to authority, deferring to power, stressing education and uplift for workingmen. They were ideas shaped by his boyhood in a town where business owners and employees shared a sense of community. His early years had imbued him with hopes and ideals that he would never entirely relinquish.

෴

Debs's world was changing by the second half of the 1880s. Terre Haute was losing its small-town qualities, and the precious idea of social harmony was becoming an anachronism. Consolidation meant that business owners no longer had a personal connection with workers. Shared interests disappeared.

The large railroads, run by management bureaucracies, employed executives who were not personally familiar with the work of the roads. Responding to demands from on high, they stripped the men of their long-established privileges. Work rules and hours grew more onerous.

The changes angered workers and made Debs reconsider his opposition to confrontation. He supported BLF delegates when they rescinded their vow never to strike and when they set up a fund to support members involved in job actions.

"Our fundamental principle is justice," Debs now declared. Men should receive a fair share of what they produce. He came to see employers' paternalism as demeaning, not generous. Men must have the right to join a union. "Strike down that idea," Debs declared, "and the idea of *personal* liberty disappears."

෴

In spite of his relentless travel to attend to BLF duties, Debs found his emotional sustenance along the lazy Wabash River. His ties to Terre Haute were tightened when in 1885 he married Katherine Metzel, a handsome woman two years his junior. Kate's stepfather owned the largest drugstore in Terre Haute. The marriage joined two of the town's middle-class families. Five years later, when Kate came into a small inheritance, she helped finance a Queen Anne–style home for the couple in a fashionable Terre Haute neighborhood convenient to the train station.

Critics pointed to the house and to Kate's taste for diamonds and furs as evidence that Gene was drifting from his working-class bearings. Kate's inability to conceive children and Gene's frequent travel led to persistent rumors that the marriage was a loveless formality. The idea was given credence by Gene's brother, Theodore, who referred to Kate as "a self-adorning clotheshorse."

In fact, the couple enjoyed a stable marriage that lasted more than forty years. Kate—Gene usually called her Ducky—fully shared her husband's ideals. Highly self-sufficient, she was able to cope with his frequent absences and almost obsessive work habits, while at the same time responding to his emotional neediness when he returned home after long trips. At times Kate helped Gene with his work and sometimes she accompanied him on his travels. She compiled a voluminous scrapbook as a record of Gene's accomplishments.

Always, she played the crucial role of gatekeeper to screen the many visitors who clamored for his attention. Gene's health was not robust— he needed the periods of recuperation at home that his wife made possible.

⧫

During these years, a series of shocks pushed Debs toward an ever more radical view of the world. In 1886, he supported the broad coalition of workingmen fighting for an eight-hour day. May Day rallies to support the movement led to violence two days later near the McCormick Harvesting Machine plant in Chicago. The next night, as police moved to break up a demonstration in the city's Haymarket Square, a bomb exploded. The blast and the barrage of gunfire that followed killed seven officers and at least four civilians.

The result was the first red scare in America, a wave of repression aimed at anarchists, immigrants, and labor advocates. Membership in the Knights of Labor had ballooned in recent years. Because of the group's involvement in the eight-hour movement and the fact that two of those arrested for the crime were KOL members, the organization saw its membership plummet.

A rigged trial convicted eight men on little or no evidence. It was their fiery speeches and anarchist sympathies rather than guilty actions that convicted them. Four of the men were hanged; one committed suicide. Debs, like many labor leaders, took a stand against the hysteria and the injustice. To him, the activism of American workers was rooted in Jeffersonian principles and evoked the independence and self-worth enjoyed by farmers and craftsmen in the early Republic.

Two years after Haymarket, members of the Brotherhood of Locomotive Firemen joined engineers in a strike against the Chicago, Burlington & Quincy Railroad, a major western line that ran through Burlington, Iowa, and on to Denver. Burlington president Charles Elliott Perkins took a hard stance against union demands for a pay increase. The failure of workers on other railroad lines to support the Burlington strikers doomed the effort. Employees turned on each other and the strike collapsed. Brotherhood members returned to work with no gains.

The Burlington fiasco hardened Debs's views. "The strike is the weapon of the oppressed," he wrote. "The Nation had for its cornerstone a strike." It was a radical departure from his younger views.

Hoping to build unity among the members of the various rail crafts, Debs spent several fruitless years trying to cobble together a federation of the existing railroad unions. He failed. The brotherhoods were built on exclusion. Engineers, conductors, and firemen felt that their power was in their unique skills. They eschewed alliances with less-skilled track workers and shop men.

In early 1892, switchmen in Buffalo walked off the job to pressure state authorities to enforce a law mandating a ten-hour day. They appealed to the other brotherhoods, but none agreed to help. State militiamen put down the strike. A railroad industry publication, noting the recent Indian wars against the "red savage," declared that "the white savage needs his lesson" as well. Debs saw that something more than a federation of existing unions was needed.

That same year one of the most violent labor battles of the century exploded at Homestead, Pennsylvania, outside Pittsburgh. Members of the Amalgamated Association of Iron and Steel Workers failed to come to terms with the Carnegie Steel Company for a new contract. Both union and non-union workers voted to strike. Andrew Carnegie, vacationing in Scotland, left the dirty work to his company president, Henry Clay Frick. Frick ordered a wall built around the massive plant on the Monongahela River. Refusing to negotiate, he locked out the workers and barricaded the factory. Union picket lines shut down the operation.

On July 6, 1892, Frick sent a private army of three hundred Pinkerton detectives down the river on barges to open the factory. Strikers broke into the grounds and both sides began shooting. During the twelve-hour gunfight that followed, the trapped strikebreakers fired from inside their barges and workers used dynamite and burning oil to try to dislodge them. Nine strikers and five Pinkerton men died in the melee.

Then the government stepped in. State authorities sent 8,500 National Guardsmen to take control of the plant. The company immediately filled positions with replacement workers. On July 23, anarchist Alexander Berkman strode into Frick's office and shot him twice in an unsuccessful assassination attempt.

In the aftermath of the strike, the Amalgamated Association was barred from the plant. Carnegie enforced longer hours and lower wages, as did other steel companies.

After watching one of the nation's most powerful trade unions go down in defeat, Debs became determined to devise a new and more comprehensive approach to labor organizing. He wanted a union that would bring the workers of an entire industry into a single organization. He jettisoned his relationship with the BLF, telling members he was no longer "in harmony" with the brotherhood. What had worked a generation earlier did not answer now.

It did not mean he was giving up on working people. "I have a heart for others and that is why I am in this work," he said. "When I see suffering about me, I myself suffer, and so when I put forth my efforts to relieve others, I am simply helping myself."

His new vision took shape as the American Railway Union, the industry-wide organization that he and other railroad men formed in 1893. The ARU grew rapidly. The showdown on James J. Hill's Great Northern line—what Debs called the "only clear cut victory of any consequence ever won by a railroad union in the United States"—inspired more workers. Men, especially the unskilled who had been ignored by the brotherhoods, began signing up with the ARU at a rate of two thousand a day.

Many of the new local unions consisted of a few dozen members and a post office box. What they lacked in organization and experience, they made up for in enthusiasm. Debs gave them what guidance he could by telegram and letter and during frequent organizing trips around the country.

By the summer of 1894, the union had gathered in a remarkable 150,000 members, more than all the railroad brotherhoods combined. The group now rivaled in size the American Federation of Labor, which drew members from a wide range of crafts. Eugene Debs had, almost overnight, become the single most powerful labor leader in the country.

⬡

American Railway Union bylaws allowed the employees of any company that operated a railroad line to become members. On Chicago's South Side, George Pullman's enormous manufacturing facility needed short rail lines to move cars onto and off of the roads. His employees were therefore qualified for ARU membership, even though they followed none of the traditional railroad trades.

George Howard, the ARU vice president, knew of the growing discontent among the Pullman workers. During his career, he had served on the Atchison, Topeka & Santa Fe and half a dozen other roads, in every function from gandy dancer to superintendent of transportation. He was a respected organizer and a persuasive speaker. That spring he had been circulating among the Pullman men, talking up the idea of the industrial union. The discontent at the factory prompted many of the employees to take a chance on the new organization.

Largely in secret, men and women from the various departments began to form ARU locals in the Pullman shops. By late April, an organizing meeting in Kensington's Turner Hall, a German health club, drew an overflow crowd. Soon, a large portion of the four thousand employees had cast their lot with the union and formed themselves into nineteen locals. Elated by the results of the Great Northern strike, these workers began to wonder if, like Jim Hill, George Pullman could also be induced to pay a fair wage. With the might of the American Railway Union behind them, they hoped to stand up to one of the premier industrialists of the era.

5

The Commercial Value
of Beauty

GEORGE PULLMAN GREW UP BREATHING THE AIR OF THE FADing frontier on a farm south of Lake Erie in western New York State. Like Eugene Debs, he quit school at fourteen and learned the value of a dollar clerking in a retail store. But while Debs did not take to the work, Pullman was said to have had an uncanny knack for calculating costs and turning a profit.

After his family moved to the Erie Canal town of Albion, New York, George became the chief troubleshooter in a business his father, Lewis, operated to lift and move buildings. Although fastidious about his clothing, George did not hesitate to scramble into the mud beneath a raised structure to adjust rollers and yell: "Check 'er" or "Go ahead." In 1853, when George was twenty-two, he took over the business following his father's death. He began moving warehouses and other buildings to facilitate an enlargement of the canal. He soon employed a dozen men. After work he often "promenaded in all his glory, with high top hat and longtailed coat."

In 1859, Pullman learned of a project in Chicago to raise buildings. The city's swampy location was cramping its growth, and its open sewers were breeding cholera, tuberculosis, and other diseases. Officials had decided that they needed to build up the perpetually mud-clogged streets and install proper sewers and drains. That meant that every downtown building would have to be lifted at least six feet.

Pullman hurried to the city to investigate. He won a contract to elevate the Matteson House on West Randolph Street, one of Chicago's premier hotels. It would be the largest building yet raised. He hired men to break into the foundation and position hundreds of screw jacks beneath the building. They eased the wooden structure upward, levitating it inch by inch until it reached its new elevation.

Settling permanently in Chicago, Pullman soon became one of the leading players in the business. He acquired a partner, bought out a rival firm, and called on his older brother Albert to help him manage the operation. Within a year, he joined two other moving firms to raise an entire city block on Lake Street, between Clark and LaSalle. So deft was the operation that "not a pane of glass has been broken nor a crack in masonry appeared," the *Chicago Daily Press and Tribune* reported.

Pullman knew that his business in Chicago would decline as fewer buildings remained to be raised. He continued to be on the alert for new opportunities, and he naturally turned his attention to the booming railroad business.

But the lessons he had learned in his early trade were not lost on the young entrepreneur.

When young Pullman had a five-story hotel perched on screw jacks, he commanded his workers to act in unison with short blasts from a whistle. The man in charge of maneuvering such a massive burden needed imagination, an eye for detail, a commanding presence, and steady nerves. These qualities would serve Pullman throughout his career. More than anything, a building mover needed to be in control. A miscalculation, a moment of confusion, or a slip of discipline invited disaster. For Pullman, remaining in control of himself and his work became an obsession.

The young entrepreneur could be a martinet in the office, but he was never frivolous, never timid, never soft, never uncertain. Notably short-tempered and often irritable, he was never dishonest or slapdash. As he gained success, he acquired a hauteur that made some roll their eyes, but he was no buffoon. He never cut corners or dealt in shoddy merchandise.

❧

Early in his career, George Pullman had dealings with a man his own age who shared his ambition. Andrew Carnegie had started his career as a telegraph operator with the Pennsylvania Railroad and quickly worked his way up. He discovered that Pullman was interested in taking control of the Central Transportation Company, the sleeping-car operation that serviced the Pennsylvania system. Carnegie suggested a deal that would benefit both parties.

It was an exciting meeting of minds. Each man saw that the other intuitively understood the delicate balance of caution and daring needed to master the age. Carnegie acted as midwife for Pullman's takeover of his rival. He said of Pullman: "He was one of those rare characters who can see the drift of things, and was always to be found, so to speak, swimming in the main current where movement was the fastest." The men became lifelong friends.

Pullman's nostrils were always open to the scent of a deal. During the early 1860s he already had enough money to hire a substitute to take his place in the Union Army. Unlike the class of men who would later man the railroads, Pullman avoided the lessons about duty and brotherhood taught in the crucible of war. Instead, he followed the gold rush to Colorado—not to prospect for the yellow metal but to pursue a surer path to profit by providing services to miners. Reaching that remote region from the most western railhead at St. Joseph, Missouri, entailed a jolting stagecoach journey of nearly six hundred miles. On arrival, he set up a lucrative crushing mill, charging a fee to extract gold from hard rock.

Colorado served as Pullman's business school. He soon employed fifteen men. He started a general store, a saloon, another mill. He raised cattle, speculated in real estate, and set up a quasi bank that dealt in gold dust. He displayed the keen memory and grasp of detail that were invaluable assets for a man of affairs. He had a knack for taking risks. He wrote his mother that he had "pitched in *pretty deep*" in his Colorado ventures. After three years of sharp dealing, he had accumulated a hefty chunk of capital. It was time for him to focus on the sleeping-car business that would make him famous.

What he really invested in was quality. The principle that guided all his dealings, Pullman said, "is that the people are always willing to pay for the best." His strategy was to "improve upon the best."

᧖

Then as now, conducting business required personal contact. Pullman traveled up and down the country selling and trading. On these frequent trips he recognized the inadequacy of early sleeping cars. They were uncomfortable and dirty, noisy and poorly ventilated. "Like sleeping on a runaway horse," one traveler complained. With transcontinental travel

on the horizon, quality sleeping cars represented a ripe opportunity. Pullman formed a partnership and hired a mechanic to construct a coach
car that could be converted to a sleeper.

The luxurious Palace Cars that Pullman developed during the 1860s
were variation on a rapidly developing technology. Patent wars were common. Pullman was not to be outdone when it came to riders' comfort.
While most railcars rested on eight wheels, Pullman's sleepers ran on sixteen. This made for a far smoother ride over America's rugged rail system. Rubber-dampened springs and lighter wheels with laminated paper
cores further curtailed rocking and vibrations. Double-glazed windows
and doors provided a hushed interior. A modern ventilation system fil-
tered out soot. Gas chandeliers with deflecting mirrors provided bright
illumination.

Pullman extended his ideas of luxury and innovation to other cars.
He introduced a dining car, which he named the Delmonico after the
nation's most famous restaurant. Trains would no longer have to make
stops to allow passengers to bolt a meal at a station restaurant. The car's
compact kitchen allowed chefs to offer passengers more than eighty
dishes, ranging from Saddle Rock oysters to grilled mutton kidneys, Lob-
ster Newburg, and local game like loin of elk, golden plover, and blue-
winged teal.

His hotel cars offered both buffet dining and individual staterooms.
He developed a plush parlor car described as a "hotel lobby on wheels."
Pullman's goal was to allow middle-class customers to upgrade to a far
more luxurious rail experience than was available on standard coach cars.
He charged them twice what a common laborer might make in a day,
but he gave them value.

The ultimate in opulence and status was the custom-made car available only to the moneyed elite and to corporate executives. The elegant
appointments of the so-called private varnish took a visitor's breath away.
Each featured a unique arrangement of staterooms, parlor, smoking
lounge, and kitchen, as well as an open observation platform at the rear.
Wealthy Americans outfitted these mansions on wheels with gold-filled
plumbing, marble baths, jewel safes, and Venetian mirrors.

⌇

During the time Pullman was consolidating his company, he was also
courting his future wife. Harriett Amelia Sanger, known as Hattie, was

a twenty-five-year-old beauty, the daughter of a prominent Chicago rail-road and canal builder. At thirty-six, Pullman was an elegant, rising busi-nessman well on his way to a great fortune. Hattie's parents were impressed by George's devotion to his widowed mother. The couple mar-ried in 1867 at the bedside of Hattie's dying father.

After a honeymoon in Niagara Falls and Canada, the Pullmans joined the social set of Chicago's young elite couples. They both loved to enter-tain, and George never stinted on lavish parties or household luxuries.

The couple had four children over the next seven years. Florence, the firstborn, was always her father's favorite. When he later objected to her marrying the man of her choice, she told her future husband to acquiesce to George's moodiness. "He will feel his position has been maintained with dignity, and there will be nothing that he will not do to promote my happiness."

Harriett, a year younger than her sister, found herself less in the sun of her father's affection. Her flitting from one beau to another did not sit well with her Victorian parents. After her 1892 marriage, she settled with her husband in San Francisco.

The Pullmans' youngest were twins George Jr. and Sanger. As did many wealthy parents of the time, the couple left the rearing of their children largely to governesses and tutors. All attended exclusive board-ing schools. The boys, pampered and ignored, indulged in the high life to excess. Neither ever settled into a solid career. Self-indulgent fops, they were a heavy disappointment to their father.

The marriage of Hattie and George was marked by mutual sympa-thy and affection but was weakened over the years by frequent absences. George traveled continually for business. Even when the couple were stay-ing in New York City, he often lived in his mother's apartment, while Hattie resided at a hotel. She became a hypochondriac and took frequent sojourns to fashionable resorts in Hot Springs, Arkansas, and upstate New York. George's irritable nature sometimes erupted in bitter scenes and recriminations with his wife and children.

༄

In his business, Pullman pioneered many features of the modern corpo-ration. He experimented with techniques of mass production. He aggres-sively built a monopoly position in his industry. He integrated the business vertically, building his own foundry, rolling mill, paint-making factory, and knitting mill. A brickworks on the site made the materials from which his factory and town were constructed. The company became an early multinational firm, with offices in Italy, France, and England.

Two forward-looking insights guided him. First, he regarded his company as a service business, not just a manufacturing operation. Rather than sell cars to the railroads, he convinced most of them to haul his sleepers as a concession and split the fee. Passengers paid the standard fare to the railroad and an extra charge of $2 to ride in a Pullman car. The Pullman Company provided linens, cleaned the cars, and employed the trained porters who converted the car from coach to sleeper mode and back.

The arrangement saved the railroads the cost of a new class of cars and meant that passengers did not have to change cars when transferring from one railroad to another. Most importantly, it allowed Pullman to retain complete control over quality. The system proved immensely profitable.

The second idea that sustained George Pullman's success was an understanding that promotion and public relations, although intangible, were critical elements of a modern business enterprise. The identification of a person with a "brand" is a modern trope, but George Pullman was among the earliest entrepreneurs to consciously build a brand in all aspects of his business.

Pullman understood the value of being talked about. He invited reporters on elaborate, champagne-drenched sojourns to view his latest cars. He lent the fanciest ones to presidents and potentates. He featured his products at fairs and expositions—his grand display at the Columbian Exposition was typical. The standard dark-olive color and prominent Pullman name made the cars easily identifiable on any line. The *Chicago Tribune* noted that anything with the name Pullman was accepted "as the fashion."

The opening of the first transcontinental railroad ignited the sleeper-car business. Coast-to-coast travel time suddenly shrank from a month to a week. But seven days on a train could be an ordeal without the provisions for comfort that Pullman's cars provided.

In 1870, the company hauled the members of the Boston Board of Trade and their families to San Francisco aboard the first chartered train to cross the continent. The travelers were astounded by the comfort and speed of the all-Pullman train. The tour generated publicity at every stop.

On returning, the members expressed the hope "that there will be no delay in placing these elegant and homelike carriages upon principal routes in the New England States." They were not disappointed.

A prime example of a Pullman public-relations coup was the story that emerged about one of his earliest sleeper cars, the luxurious Pioneer. The car, which incorporated many of the innovations that made Pullmans rolling palaces, cost $20,000 to build—twice the cost of a locomotive and four times as much as a typical sleeper.

Pullman promoted the notion that the Pioneer had carried President Lincoln's body from Chicago to its interment in Springfield. There could be no more valuable endorsement. Elaborations of the tale stated that Lincoln's wife, Mary, had demanded the Pioneer be used so that she could ride in luxury to the funeral. It was said that stations and bridges along the Chicago & Alton Railroad had to be urgently enlarged to allow passage of the oversized Pioneer.

It is possible the Pioneer carried some dignitaries from Chicago to Springfield for the 1865 ceremony. The rest of the story was pure fantasy. Mary Todd Lincoln was too distraught to attend the burial and had never seen the car. Nor did the Pioneer at any time carry the martyred president's body. The notion that Pullman had constructed a car that could not fit on standard rail lines made little sense, nor was there any evidence of hurried construction work on the Alton. Yet so skillfully managed was this bit of publicity that the story is repeated in railroad histories even today.

⁓

The enhancement of his brand was one factor that prompted Pullman to build his model town outside Chicago. Like many endeavors in Pullman's life, it brought together practicality, idealism, self-aggrandizement, and an instinct for making money.

The idea was born when, in the late 1870s, Pullman decided to become a player in the booming market for freight and streetcars. To build all his cars, he created one of the largest production plants in the world on a tract of farm and wasteland fourteen miles south of Chicago. The town that Pullman built beside it was intended to attract carpenters, wood-carvers, and other craftsmen to the remote location. It would also prove an idea that had intrigued George Pullman.

"I have always held that people are greatly influenced by their physical surroundings," Pullman observed. He wanted to prove "that decency, propriety and good manners are not unattainable luxuries for them."

This notion had been reinforced by his experience with the sleeping cars themselves. Critics had predicted that passengers would ruin his cars with their muddy boots and liberal spitting of tobacco juice. Pullman held that the cars' elegant interiors would instill decorum in riders. He was right. He likewise felt that the orderly town would yield civilized employees with efficient work habits, thus making his investment profitable.

The notion ran against the standard thinking of the day, which held that a person's character was a fixed quality. That idea was fertile soil for prejudice, as various classes and races were assigned particular characteristics thought to dictate their proper stations in life. Industrial workers were mindless drudges, blacks naturally servile, Irishmen given to drink, Jews miserly.

Company towns had a long history. As early as 1792, Alexander Hamilton had hired Pierre Charles L'Enfant to design an industrial town on the Passaic River. Some New England mill towns were constructed from scratch according to idealistic plans. George Pullman certainly knew of planned communities like the one near the Krupp works in Essen, Germany, and Saltaire, the model town built by British wool tycoon Sir Titus Salt. Pullman's own town would be the largest and most modern ever built.

Pullman recognized that a skilled, reliable workforce was critical to the success of a manufacturing operation. The town, "from which all that is ugly, discordant and demoralizing is eliminated," would attract the highest class of employee. The Pullman workingmen, a company brochure declared, not only had "clearer complexions and brighter eyes," but were "forty per cent better in evidence of thrift and refinement."

In addition to the town's uplifting effect on his employees, Pullman expected it to turn a neat profit. It had to. Pullman did not intend it merely as a charitable gesture. He wanted it to serve as a model for the future of industrial operations.

"Capital will not invest in sentiment," Pullman insisted. But once other business owners observed the results at Pullman, "we shall see great manufacturing corporations developing similar enterprises, and thus a new era will be introduced in the history of labor." Pullman was out to prove the "commercial value of beauty."

6

Well-Wishing Feudalism

I N THE AUTUMN OF 1884, ECONOMIST RICHARD ELY, COMBINing business with pleasure, spent his honeymoon in the town of Pullman. The thirty-year-old scholar had been hired to write an article about the town. With his bride, he checked into the elegant Hotel Florence in the center of town.

Named for George Pullman's eldest daughter, the rambling building resembled a "large gingerbread country villa." Standing on the hotel's porch, Ely could see, immediately to the north, the ornate clock tower of Pullman's huge factory. The town itself stretched to the south in a neat grid of streets named for inventors like George Stephenson, the "Father of Railways"; Robert Fulton, of steamboat fame; and, of course, George Pullman himself.

Along those streets, Ely heard a variety of languages spoken. A majority of the employees at the Pullman factory were immigrants— Scandinavian, German, and Dutch workers were predominant. Although the town was a well-established community of more than eight thousand residents when Ely arrived, it still had a new feel. The shade trees, whose leaves were beginning to show splashes of yellow and orange, were saplings. The brick buildings seemed to be standing at attention.

As Ely strolled through the town, he encountered parks and squares bright green with mown grass. The houses were mostly attached two-story bungalows interspersed with small apartment buildings and

multifamily homes. Although built in the country, the town had an urban look. A variety of designs prevented visual monotony.

The housing mirrored the company hierarchy. Attached cottages for
workers, freestanding houses overlooking the main square for company
foremen, elegant homes to accommodate executives. Tenement buildings
offered housing for the lowly workers at the company's brickworks.
Mrs. Duane Doty, the wife of the town's manager, wrote in a brochure:
"We have never had any patience with the oft repeated dream of Rous-
seau, that 'All men are created equal, etc.' . . . The first great law of nature
is in the inequality of man."

Ely found in the town an "all pervading air of thrift and providence . . .
of general well-being." He noted that the company allowed housewives
to choose low-cost wallpaper and then hung it for them without charge.
This small act marked for many of the women the first time that they
were able to "exercise taste and consider the beautiful."

The scholar toured the block-long Arcade, the Middle West's first
shopping mall. The dry goods purveyors, barbershops, and other businesses were leased by independent merchants. George Pullman emphasized that he ran no "company store," a notorious device by which
employers fleeced their workers.

"What is seen in a walk or a drive through the streets," Ely observed,
"is so pleasing to the eye that a woman's first exclamation is certain to
be, 'Perfectly lovely!'"

Ely mounted the stairs of the Arcade to examine the town library,
which embodied George Pullman's faith in learning—he had personally
donated five thousand books. The journalist walked over to Lake Calumet to inspect the athletic facilities along its shore—playing fields, a
tennis court, boating facilities, and, in winter, an ice rink. An annual
fifteen-mile cycling race from downtown Chicago to Pullman attracted
thousands of spectators in that age of bicycle mania.

The town's ornate theater was said to be the finest showplace west
of the Hudson River. The public school was exemplary, the kindergarten free. Immigrants could study English and take classes in art and
music appreciation. Human waste was processed and pumped a few miles
away to fertilize a company vegetable farm, the produce sold in the town
market.

"High honor is due Mr. George M. Pullman," Ely wrote. Another reporter speculated that George Pullman "might be the Messiah of a new age."

As much as he sought favorable publicity, Pullman was reticent to put himself forth as a man of vision. Interviewed a year earlier, he had said that he saw the town "simply as a matter of business. I have little of the sentimental in my nature."

〜

In February 1885, Richard Ely's article appeared in *Harper's Weekly*, one of the most popular periodicals of the day. As he began to read, George Pullman was gratified by the professor's glowing description of the model town. But Ely was not finished.

The author's tone changed when he referred to "a needless air of secrecy" that pervaded the town. Residents were strangely reluctant to talk to him. When he was able to strike up a conversation, he found that townspeople were worried about company "spotters."

A substantial town "where not one single resident dare speak out openly" gave Ely an eerie feeling. In spite of the tidy streets, parks, and flower beds, "one feels that one is mingling with a dependent, servile people."

As he found more residents willing to talk, Ely began to accumulate a laundry list of complaints. Few of the inhabitants were happy with the fact that the company owned all the buildings and administered all aspects of the town. George Pullman, Ely wrote, was offering his workers a "gilded cage as a substitute for personal liberty."

To make sure that he retained complete control, Pullman had decided to rent the houses in the model town rather than sell them to their occupants. If he had sold homes to his workmen, he later commented, he would have risked "seeing families settle who are not sufficiently accustomed to the habits I wish to develop."

In each lease, he included the provision that the company could evict the occupants on ten days' notice for any reason. He was worried about "baneful influences" such as brothels or gambling dens that might be established if he could not dislodge troublemakers.

"Nobody regards Pullman as a real home," Ely noted. A resident told him: "We call it camping out."

George Pullman set the rents at a level that would pay a return of

6 percent on the capital invested. The prices ranged from as little as $4.50 to as much as $75.00 a month, averaging about $14.00. Rents were higher than those in nearby towns, but company officials pointed out that residents' homes were of better quality and included access to all the amenities of Pullman. There were no flower beds or tennis courts in the neighboring village of Kensington.

The town had no municipal government. Company officials made all decisions. The school board was loaded with Pullman executives. Foremen sometimes accompanied workers to the polls to make sure they voted the Pullman line.

The sole church in the model town was a magnificent structure of green limestone. George Pullman imagined that various denominations would rent the sanctuary on a shared basis. But the $300 monthly tab was more than any congregation could afford, and the church sat empty for years.

"It was not intended so much for the moral and spiritual welfare of the people," a clergyman pointed out, "as it was for the completion of the artistic effect of the scene."

Notices posted in residences admonished tenants to "always enter or leave the building quietly" and warned them against "boisterous conduct," the "use of musical instruments after bed time," and "entering the halls with muddy feet." For a grown man who performed hard labor ten or more hours a day, such childish commandments quickly became an irritant.

Saloons were the common living rooms of working-class life, but the only bar in the model town, at the Hotel Florence, was intended only for visitors and company executives. One worker reported that he "looked at but dared not enter Pullman's hotel."

One of the reasons George Pullman had located his factory far from the center of Chicago was to protect his workers from the influence of labor organizers. Pullman loathed unions. He had handled the few strikes at his works by adamantly refusing to negotiate and by threatening workers with mass dismissals. Labor advocates were not allowed to speak in his model town. Employees had to schedule meetings in nearby Kensington and brave the possibility of company spies just to attend lectures by union proponents.

"It is not the American ideal," Ely wrote. "It is benevolent, well-wishing feudalism." His verdict: the town of Pullman was "un-American."

A proud patriot, George Pullman was stung by this critique of his pet project. His initial reaction to Ely's article was to order his managers to track down and punish the employees who had dared to share their grievances with the visiting professor.

∽

Critics could carp, but the Pullman's Palace Car Company thrived. In 1889 Pullman acquired the Mann Boudoir Car Company and the Woodruff Sleeping and Parlor Coach Company, eliminating competition and bringing even more of the industry under his control. Business soared in the years leading up to the 1893 Columbian Exposition as railroads contracted for sleepers, dining, and parlor cars to bring visitors to the fair. Pullman investors were gratified by their 8 percent annual dividend and the growing value of the company. Its three thousand shareholders included the British monarch, Queen Victoria.

But the depression that followed the May 1893 panic hit the Pullman factory hard. Orders had already dropped off. Now sales and leases plummeted. The company fired workers and reduced the wages of those remaining. Managers changed work methods to increase productivity and minimize costs.

During the first week in December 1893, steamfitters and blacksmiths at Pullman called a strike to protest a 25 percent reduction in pay. George Pullman gave them a choice: work for what the company offered or quit. What could they do? Almost all returned to their jobs. This was typical when workers' discontent came up against George Pullman's adamant hostility toward unions. In earlier strikes against the Pullman's Palace Car Company, employees were routinely fired and replaced.

During the difficult winter and spring of 1894, the grievances of the workers at Pullman grew to desperate levels. They wanted answers from company officials. Those officials occupied the imposing Pullman Building in Chicago's business district. George Pullman showed his face in the shops only six times that winter. The company had no formal system by which the men could file grievances or communicate with upper managers. Workers who had once admired George Pullman no longer knew him.

∽

The Pullman workers' complaints fell into three categories. The first was pay. Wage cuts had ranged from 20 to 35 percent. Reduced working hours cut further into compensation. The take-home pay of some skilled mechanics, among the most severely affected employees, had dropped by 60 percent.

Thomas Heathcoate, whose job was to finish the insides of cars, found himself laboring for less than half of what he had been earning a year earlier. Carpenter R. W. Coombs worked on refrigerator cars, gondolas, and cabooses. By March he was making only 68 cents a day, less than the unskilled section men on Jim Hill's Great Northern line.

Nineteen-year-old Jennie Curtis worked as a seamstress. "We made all the carpets," she later remembered, "and all the silk, satin, plush, and velvet drapings for the dining cars . . . and all such work as that." The company had cut her pay from $2.25 for ten hours of work to 70 cents. Less experienced girls made only four cents an hour. In part, this was the result of the common—and for the company profitable—notion that women's wages were only a supplement to those of the head of the household. Yet many women, including Curtis, were the sole providers in their homes.

During the 1890s, the Pullman Company had turned increasingly to piecework until almost all the factory employees were paid in this manner. Not only did piecework usually mean less pay for more effort, but it introduced a set of decisions for foremen and supervisors. What was a fair rate for a task? Should it be based on the performance of an expert worker or of an average one? If the rate allowed hard workers to make more than a typical wage, should it be lowered?

George Pullman called piecework an "educational tool in that it offered incentive to the worker to improve his skills." In reality, it was demeaning, particularly for skilled craftsmen, such as wood-carvers, marquetry artisans, and car builders. They felt a continual pressure to increase their output even as they saw their take-home pay fall, often to levels below those of common laborers.

The second category of complaints revolved around rents in the town of Pullman. The employees' income had diminished but rents remained "exorbitant." Unable to pay what they owed, workers became debtors to the company. Those caught between slack pay and high rent were "afraid to complain for fear of dismissal."

Steep rents forced many residents to take in boarders. The crowding counteracted the benefits of the carefully planned town. In small flats, it destroyed family privacy.

Of George Pullman, workers would later say, "The wages he pays out with one hand . . . he takes back with the other." When he first opened the model town, this was literally true—the company collected rents by simply deducting them from workers' pay. After Illinois banned that practice, Pullman began to give each worker two checks, one equal to his bimonthly rent, the other for whatever remained from his pay. The paymaster pressured the employee to endorse the former to the company to satisfy his debt. If he instead tried to cash it at the town bank, which was owned by Pullman, he was questioned and harassed.

Some men ended up, after paying rent, with little compensation left. Walter Easton had to support a family of four on the $3.56 paycheck he received for two weeks' work. They survived on bread and water, and when he grew too weak to work, his wife borrowed fifteen cents to buy a soup bone and some liver sausage to sustain him.

Although Pullman's church remained unoccupied, clergymen held services in spaces rented in the town's commercial buildings. Reverend William Carwardine, who served as minister of the Methodist Episcopal congregation in Pullman, observed: "One man has a pay check in his possession of two cents after paying rent. He has never cashed it, preferring to keep it as a memento. He has it framed."

When a man earned only a few dollars with which to feed his family for two weeks, hunger became a reality. "I have known men to drop down by the side of a car when they were working for want of food," said Thomas Heathcoate.

Workers who considered leaving Pullman to find cheaper housing in a nearby village thought twice about the move. The company naturally wanted to keep its houses rented so that wage payments flowed back to the firm's coffers. Although some employees did live in surrounding communities, most were convinced that moving out of the model town put their jobs at risk. There were no recorded cases of dismissal for leaving the town, but the workers' fear of such a consequence was real.

The final area of workers' discontent was the steady erosion of their rights in the factory and the abuse they suffered at the hands of the bosses. During George Pullman's youth, American industrialism had followed a template laid down when most manufacturing was conducted in shops run by craftsmen. The factory at Pullman was referred to as "the shops."

Originally, the master—a carpenter, blacksmith, or shoemaker— hired journeymen and took on apprentices who wanted to learn the trade. The system, which had roots back to the Middle Ages, fostered a sense of teamwork and offered traditional rights to workers. Hours were flexible. Masters viewed their employees as colleagues. They expected deference, but they knew the men. They wanted them to learn and improve their skills.

Elements of this older system were retained into the 1890s. Informal rules maintained workers' prerogatives. But managers increasingly wanted a free hand. Work rules put the company "in a position subordinate to the men," one railroad executive declared.

The various departments at Pullman were run by foremen and subforemen. These supervisors were allotted a budget for the completion of a job, such as building a batch of cars. They were given latitude in how they allocated work and how they distributed pay among their crew.

But rather than accommodate workers, the system put power in the hands of the foremen, who resorted to favoritism and petty despotism. "It was only the friends of the foreman" who would be paid by the day rather than for piecework, Thomas Heathcoate pointed out.

The harassment by foremen further impinged on the longstanding privileges of men at work to control their lives on the job. Theodore Rhodie, a painter in the shops, said the foremen would "talk to the men as though they were dogs." Worse, when an inexperienced foreman made a mistake that required repair, the men had to "do the work for nothing or quit." Jennie Curtis complained of "the tyrannical and abusive treatment we received from our forewoman." This woman "seemed to delight in showing her power in hurting the girls in every possible way." She would not let the workers take time off, even when they fell sick.

⌁

In March 1894, George Pullman, his hair snow white, had turned sixty-three, an age when birthdays start to bring intimations of mortality. A lifetime of impatient striving had taken its toll. Pullman suffered from relentless fatigue and frequent minor illnesses. He worked with dogged determination, putting in ten or eleven hours at the office most days. His older brother Henry warned him to slow down. His wife, Hattie, noted in her diary of March 9, 1894, that "George is feeling very tired and disinclined to do anything but rest."

Pullman had a cantankerous streak, and the pressure of guiding his company through the most serious economic slump of his lifetime had taxed his nerves. Occasionally his mood grew so irritable that he lashed out at Hattie and other family members. The previous December, his brother Albert, an even-tempered man who for years served as trouble-shooter for George's business, had died. The loss removed another stone from Pullman's emotional foundation.

News of unrest among his employees troubled Pullman. He had formed his view of his workers back when he hired gangs to raise build-ings. A realtor who knew him then said "he was always quick, ready, and wanted his men to work fast." When Pullman tooted his whistle, his em-ployees did their job. Unions complicated the process unnecessarily.

His employees saw things differently. Pullman had not lowered his own salary in response to the hard times, nor had he reduced the pay of the company's executives. It was well known that the Pullman's Palace Car Company was hoarding $25 million in surplus profits and had con-tributed another $4 million to this fund during 1893 alone. Even in 1894, the company as a whole had turned a healthy profit, though the car-building operations were supposedly losing money. Pullman continued to pay shareholders the generous dividends to which they were accustomed.

As more and more employees signed up with the American Railway Union, the emboldened members elected a general committee of forty-one men and five women to approach the company about their grievances. In early May, the committee members called on Harvey Middleton, the plant manager, hoping for some relief. He told them that he had no au-thority to deal with the matter. They would have to go see Thomas H. Wickes, second vice president of the corporation.

ARU organizer George Howard had contacted Eugene Debs in Terre Haute to report his progress at Pullman. He related the employ-ees' discontent and said there had been liberal talk of a strike. Debs wired back that Howard should "do all in his powers" to prevent a strike. If the workers presented a united front to company managers, Pullman would likely arbitrate the dispute. Their case was solid. But to strike in the midst of a depression would involve grave danger for the employees and the union itself.

On May 7, the committee of common laborers traveled to company headquarters for a rare meeting with a top Pullman executive. They knew the odds were stacked against them. They understood that speaking out might well cost them their jobs. But desperation and determination gave them the courage to take a stand.

Armies

THE DISCONTENT OF WORKERS AT A MANUFACTURING PLANT in Chicago was not yet news. During the period when Pullman employees were demanding to be heard, Americans were focused on other crises, including the widespread strikes in the coal fields and the militant action of the Great Northern employees. The most frightening development for many was the progress of Jacob Coxey's industrial "armies" marching across the nation.

Members of the large battalion that unemployed typographer Charles Kelley had led out of San Francisco were making good progress toward their goal. They had managed, with the complicity of railroad officials, to secure train passage all the way to Council Bluffs, Iowa. Chicago was only a day's train ride away. Iowans were friendly and supportive. The men, however, found themselves stranded. A spokesman for the Chicago & North Western Railway said, "If these tramps and bums try to capture one of our trains, there will be trouble."

Kelley rejected the idea of having his men steal a train outright. If they had to walk, they would walk. They soon set out on the 130-mile trek to Des Moines, where they hoped to arrange for passage from a more cooperative railroad.

Even more alarming were the audacious actions of a rough crowd of miners and railroad men in Montana. Their leader was a thirty-four-year-old Butte teamster named William Hogan. A slender, even-tempered Irish immigrant, Hogan was a gregarious sort who occasionally delivered lectures explaining Shakespeare to his fellow workers. Like many miners in the region, he had lost his job when metal prices had collapsed at the onset of the depression. Now he and his companions, desperate to reach the nation's capital, were about to become the quarry in one of the great train chases of American history.

The thirty-five hundred members of the Butte Miners' Union had come together around the compelling, democratic idea of carrying their complaint directly to their representatives in Washington. Hogan emerged as the man who would take them there. Like all the Coxey armies, the men crafted their own set of demands. They hoped that their congressmen would make a priority of restoring the federal silver purchases they had curtailed in 1893, thereby reviving western mines.

The third week in April, more than five hundred of them gathered in the Butte rail yards, which were nestled in a valley of the western Montana mountains. Hogan negotiated with officials of the Northern Pacific to provide transportation eastward. He found the railroad's managers eager to rid themselves of the threatening mob. But then he ran into a roadblock.

Following the panic of 1893, many heavily indebted railroads, including the Northern Pacific, were unable to pay their obligations. Typically, they were placed under the control of a federally appointed receiver until their finances were reorganized, a process similar to today's Chapter 11 bankruptcy. The receivership of the Northern Pacific was being overseen by Judge Hiram Knowles. He wired Attorney General Olney that "a dangerous mob sentiment still prevails" in western Montana, with thousands of miners idle. "May have further trouble here."

Olney refused to allow any accommodation to Hogan's men. He and President Cleveland were determined to clamp down on the dangerous Coxey movement before it gained even more adherents. The government's authority over railroads in receivership gave them the power to act. Olney contacted U.S. Marshal William McDermott in Butte, who replied: "Public sympathy strongly in their favor." The attorney general ordered McDermott to hire more deputies and quell the threat of the Coxeyites.

On April 24, with an armed force gathering around them, the miners took matters into their own hands. Led by the railroad men in their ranks, they broke into the Northern Pacific roundhouse, fired up engine No. 512, and coupled on six coal cars to hold the men and a boxcar for provisions. With nearly five hundred men aboard, they chugged up the thousand-foot grade to Homestake Pass, then picked up speed on the downslope. Their means of transport was, in railroad lingo, a "wild train," meaning one not on the schedule.

Marshal McDermott assigned Deputy M. J. Hailey the unpleasant task of catching up to Hogan's renegades and stopping them. Hailey had to scour Butte saloons to round up sixty-five men desperate enough to go after the protesters. By the time they got under way at six the next morning, Hogan's men had ridden their stolen train all the way to Bozeman, another mining city eighty-five miles east of Butte.

The people in Bozeman warned Hogan of the posse approaching from behind. They added the news that railroad superintendent J. D. Finn was ahead of them on the tracks with a crew of maintenance workers. Finn had suggested to railroad executives that they simply give the men a train and be rid of them. Now he complained to his superiors: "How in hell do you expect one Irishman to stand off the whole of Coxey's army?" Nevertheless, he was determined to do what he could to obstruct the tracks down the line.

He was in luck. A landslide had already blocked the track just beyond a long tunnel twelve miles east of Bozeman. Finn told section men who had begun to clear the tracks to leave the rocks, earth, and trees in place.

The obstruction brought the wild train to a halt there. Hogan's men began digging, knowing that Hailey's deputies were gaining on them. They decided the work was proceeding too slowly. The volunteer engineer and fireman were told to get up a head of steam. They backed the train into the tunnel, then roared out. They crashed into the pile, used the cowcatcher as a plow, and forced a way through. The train continued down the line.

At five that evening, the men stopped at Livingston, thirty-five miles east of Bozeman. They gave speeches to enthusiastic townspeople and took on more recruits. While the men changed engines, residents supplied them with food, blankets, and words of encouragement. A festive, comradely atmosphere prevailed, with local people happy to see workingmen getting the better of the railroad.

Ahead, Finn had used dynamite to create a number of additional landslides. Hogan's men dug through each one. In some cases, they "thoughtfully replaced the obstruction" to make things harder for

Hailey and his deputies in pursuit. Finn's squadron spiked switches, a procedure that normally kept the switch from being thrown toward a deactivated side spur. They drained the water from tanks along the way. Hogan's men struggled forward, barely keeping ahead of Hailey's contingent. They formed bucket brigades to replenish the locomotive's water supply from streams.

The next morning, Hailey and his men caught up with the renegades near Young's Point, west of Billings. Hogan ordered his engineer to stop with the rear cars resting on a bridge that spanned a steep canyon. Hailey deployed armed deputies along the banks and demanded the Hoganites' surrender. The protesters waved the flag of the Butte Miners' Union and dared their pursuers to shoot. The deputies backed down. The hijackers continued eastward.

Halfway across the state and beyond the high peaks, the Coxeyites pulled into the town of Billings late in the morning. They were "met with enthusiasm and supplies," a newspaper reported. Hundreds of townspeople rushed to the depot to witness the novel event.

Hogan's men were still there when their pursuers arrived. Hailey stopped his train up the tracks and his men climbed down. Wary of the large, cheering crowd that surrounded the stolen train, the deputies sauntered toward the depot and casually mixed with the locals. They slowly worked their way forward. Two of them suddenly pulled revolvers, jumped into the cab of the wild train, and confronted the men's leader. "Shoot and be damned," Hogan barked.

They hesitated. The crowd jeered. Suddenly one of their fellow marshals gave in to nervousness and fired his rifle. The crashing sound set off a fusillade of two dozen more shots. Several men of the industrial army were wounded. One bullet tore through the chest of Billings tinsmith Charles Hardy, who was watching the action. He dropped down dead.

The enraged crowd tore the rifles from the deputies' hands. The local sheriff arrested several of them for the shooting. It took Hailey seven hours to resume his pursuit of the Hogan train, which was now chugging through eastern Montana.

BLOOD FLOWS FROM COXEYISM, the *New York Times* bellowed. BATTLE BETWEEN LAW AND ANARCHY.

The *Billings Weekly Gazette*, on the other hand, proclaimed it a wonder that the town did not "crucify every slinking cur of a deputy." The federal marshals, the paper said, were "the scum of the great mining camp, mercenary ruffians who would assassinate their brothers if there was a dollar in it."

Montana governor John E. Rickards wired President Cleveland that the deputy marshals were proving ineffective. State militiamen were unreliable because of their sympathy with Hogan and his men. Only federal troops could stop the rampage.

Cleveland called an emergency meeting of his cabinet. They decided that a federal judge had authority to issue an injunction against interference with any railroad in receivership. Whoever disobeyed could be jailed for contempt without trial, circumventing sympathetic local juries. Federal judges in the West began to issue a flurry of such injunctions. If U.S. Marshals were unable to enforce the edicts, Cleveland decided, the army would be called out.

Army commander Schofield was not enthusiastic about using his troops for domestic law enforcement. Attorney General Olney, who had spent most of his career as a lawyer for railroads, and Secretary of War Daniel S. Lamont, along with other cabinet members, urged Cleveland to act.

Cleveland shared Olney's concern that Coxeyism might grow into a dangerous mass movement. Visions of a mob marching toward Washington unnerved him. He ordered Schofield to call out his troops. The general sent a message to Colonel J. H. Page at Fort Keogh in eastern Montana to hurry down the line and stop Hogan.

The *Times* trembled at the possible confrontation between the troops and "the 500 miners, who are known to be desperate characters." In fact, Hogan had wired ahead the message that his men would surrender peacefully if confronted by United States soldiers.

Superintendent Finn sped eastward to pick up Colonel Page and five hundred soldiers from the Twenty-Second Infantry Regiment. Just before dawn, while Hogan's train stealers took a needed respite for some sleep, the soldiers emerged from the darkness, rifles in hand.

The unemployed men surrendered without incident and were found to be armed with only a few pistols. The 350-mile chase was over 1,900 miles short of the nation's capital. More than a hundred of Hogan's men slipped away through the early morning gloom. Judge Knowles sentenced Hogan to six months in jail for contempt and gave his followers lesser sentences.

As the soldiers relaxed after their easy victory, they directed their contempt not at their prisoners but at the railroad managers and the politicians in Washington. These were the men who had forced them to bear arms against their fellow citizens, "whose only crime," a newspaper said, "has been to help themselves to boxcars."

∽

Jacob Coxey noted that although Hogan's men were in the wrong for stealing a train, "questions of ethics do not carry much force with hungry men, and these men are starving for lack of employment."

Coxey's own band of eccentrics had been trudging eastward along dirt roads for five weeks. At the end of April, the weary men finally arrived at Brightwood Riding Park in the District of Columbia, seven miles north of the Capitol. Mobs of curious citizens crowded streetcars to ride out and view the famous corps of protesters. Congressmen, senators, and diplomats also made the trip.

On May 1, under an ultramarine sky and a gleeful sun, the Coxey Commonweal, reinforced by a contingent from Philadelphia and numbering perhaps six hundred marchers, lined up for the walk from their camp to the Capitol building. A crowd estimated at as high as thirty thousand souls crowded the streets to watch the bedraggled men march past.

Following a brass band, Jacob Coxey rode in an elegant open phaeton with his wife and their four-month-old son, named Legal Tender in support of the cause. Following him was his titian-haired teenage daughter, Mamie, who portrayed the Goddess of Peace. Perched sidesaddle on a white palfrey and overwhelmed by the attention, she beamed with youthful ardor. Carl Browne rode behind her, decked out in his Buffalo Bill buckskins. Then came a color guard and the ranks of marchers.

This stalwart band of mountebanks and determined men trudged along the city streets, which through the outskirts were still unpaved. "Such a fantastic aggregation," the *Baltimore Herald* judged, "never paraded itself in seriousness before the public."

In 1882, Congress had passed a statute—an ironic one in the eyes of some—that made it a crime to deliver a "harangue or oration" on Capitol property. Citizens were also prohibited from parading or standing in a group on the grass. Neither the nation's representatives nor

President Cleveland would make an exception for these earnest petitioners who had come so far.

Congress had as yet taken no effective action to ameliorate the harsh economic conditions that in 1894 had already gripped the country for a year. The government effort to shore up the nation's gold reserves and cut tariffs had done little to relieve the widespread suffering.

Public spending on infrastructure projects to relieve unemployment was anathema to the politicians' view of small government. They equated Coxeyism with an objectionable paternalism. Coxey's schemes would encourage citizens to "lean on the government instead of standing upright on their own two feet," the *Chicago Record* said. This view ignored the government's paternalistic handouts to businessmen, including land grants and generous subsidies.

Washington remained something of a sleepy southern town, and residents had little firsthand familiarity with factories or the hardened workers who manned them. For many, the approach of an industrial army had presented a menacing prospect. The press had predicted that the Coxey movement would mean class warfare. The *Portsmouth (Ohio) Daily News* reported that Coxey was "bringing terror to the national capital" and warned of "predatory gangs." National Guard troops in the District of Columbia had been conducting emergency riot drills for days.

One source of fear was the fact that the capital was home to eighty-five thousand African Americans, the nation's largest urban population of blacks. More than half of them were now unemployed. They turned out in large numbers to cheer Coxey's legion. The city's police chief pronounced himself more afraid of "colored people than he was of Coxey's Army."

As the march threaded through the streets, the men were outnumbered by almost a thousand city policemen, many of them mounted on horseback. When the parade arrived at the eastern side of the Capitol building, confusion became general. With little provocation, the police charged into the crowd, setting off a panic. Mounted police blocked Browne, who tried to scramble up the Capitol steps with a flag. Browne's shirt was ripped as he was knocked down and beaten. When the parade's standard-bearer, a black youth named Jasper Johnson Buchanan, tried to come to Browne's aid, he was roughed up severely enough to need hospitalization.

Coxey himself, in starched collar and gold-rimmed glasses, had tripped climbing over a low retaining wall. He regained his feet and made it partway up the steps. A police lieutenant told him he could not speak and officers pushed him back down.

Coxey instead handed reporters copies of the statement he had wanted to read. "Up these steps the lobbyists of trusts and corporations have passed unchallenged," he pointed out. "We, the representatives of the toiling wealth-producers, have been denied."

Coxey climbed back into the carriage with his wife and son. The police, warming to their work, again charged into the mass of onlookers, beating citizens indiscriminately. The members of Coxey's Commonweal, still assembled in ranks, marched away toward a vacant field in an African American neighborhood, where they would make a new camp. The Goddess of Peace still led the way as crowds of onlookers cheered the conquered army.

⸙

The march turned into an occupation. Coxey's followers, with nowhere to go, would linger in two District camps through much of the summer as additional recruits from across the country straggled in.

On May 2, Coxey appeared in court to see about Carl Browne and another Commonweal member who had been arrested. Police took Coxey into custody as well. A trial was set for May 21. In court, Coxey's claim of a constitutional right to free speech was ignored. He was charged with having walked on the lawn of a public building.

"I appreciate," Coxey stated, "that the preservation of the grass around the Capitol is of more importance than saving thousands from starvation."

The judge labeled him a "dreamer." Coxey answered, "Twenty million people are hungry and can't wait two years to eat. Four million people idle for nine months. That is what Grover Cleveland has cost this country."

Others concurred. Samuel Gompers, who had founded the American Federation of Labor eight years earlier, looked favorably on the Coxey movement. "Clubbing may subdue Coxey or Browne," he said, after meeting with Coxey in the wake of the demonstration, "but it will not drive thought out of the people's minds. A club will subdue one man, but it will recruit one hundred for the cause he represents."

During Coxey's three-day trial a prosecutor asked a witness if the cheering crowd at the Capitol was disorderly. "Oh no," he said. "They had a right to cheer. They were American citizens."

The judge found Coxey guilty. The sentence was twenty days in prison and a $5 fine.

The Works Are Closed

IN THE LAST DECADES OF THE 1800S, THE DISTINCTION BETWEEN wealthy Americans and the mass of citizens became stark. The men and women who toiled in factories faced long hours, harsh conditions, meager wages, and frequent bouts of unemployment. The tiny cohort who controlled the nation's capital enjoyed refined leisure, attentive servants, and mansions modeled on castles. They were no longer embarrassed to consider themselves members of a privileged class.

George Pullman helped set the tone for the era Mark Twain had labeled the Gilded Age. His home on Chicago's fashionable Prairie Avenue, "the sunny street that held the sifted few," proclaimed his status. It included a two-hundred-seat theater, a billiard room, a bowling alley, a pipe organ, and a palm room with a leaded-glass dome. Among the most extravagant spenders of the age, he and his wife, Hattie, threw parties there for four hundred guests.

Hoping to bring some East Coast sophistication to the Middle West, Hattie sponsored lectures and readings to introduce society women to Shakespeare. She arranged for dance lessons in her ballroom. Among those practicing the waltz, polka, and quadrille there were Robert Todd Lincoln and Frederick Dent Grant, both the sons of presidents, and Civil War hero Philip Sheridan, who repeatedly stepped on his partner's toes.

In the 1870s, during the administration of President Ulysses S.

Grant, the Pullmans spent two weeks in the White House, where Hattie helped First Lady Julia with a formal reception. George had hired Grant's secretary, General Horace Porter, as a Pullman vice president. He took on Robert Lincoln as his personal lawyer. President Benjamin Harrison had paid Pullman the enviable compliment over lunch of asking the name of his tailor.

The cultivation of politicians was another facet of Pullman's business acumen that anticipated the practice of modern corporations. He hired ex-military men, hobnobbed with presidents, and lent private cars to influential government figures for a purpose: to cultivate goodwill and attract favors for the Pullman's Palace Car Company.

Although congenial with friends and a polished salesman, the sleeping-car magnate had a reputation for being remote and dictatorial. He liked to spend time alone—he kept a suite at the Hotel Florence in his model town as a retreat. One of his office workers noted that "I never knew a man so reserved." Pullman, he felt, would have liked to treat people as friends, "but he couldn't. He just didn't know how."

A neighbor called Pullman "one of the most frigid, pompous autocrats I have ever seen." When riled, Pullman addressed underlings with a sneer of cold command, "about as hot," one said, "as an ice crusher in the winter out on the lake."

An exaggerated correctness suited Pullman. He wore a dark Prince Albert coat even in summer, a vest, striped trousers, and patent leather shoes. Every morning he arrived at the Pullman building in a polished Victoria pulled by blooded horses and driven by a coachman in livery.

For lunch he typically repaired to the Chicago Club, two blocks down Michigan Avenue from his office. His companions often included his good friend Marshall Field, the meat tycoon Philip Armour, and other grandees of Chicago commerce. They occupied what came to be known as the "millionaires' table."

Armour once gave a summary of his outlook on life that would have drawn nods from his colleagues. "I have no other interest in life but my business . . . I do not love the money. What I do love is the getting of it. All these years of my life I have put into this work, and now it is my life and I cannot give it up."

Embracing the customs of the nation's moneyed upper classes, Pullman maintained a seasonal residence in Long Branch, New Jersey. This home on the Atlantic shore was not far from President Grant's own summer cottage. Pullman built another vacation home on one of New York's Thousand Islands, a stone bastion he named Castle Rest and dedicated to his mother.

During the spring of 1894, in the midst of the Coxey movement and the Great Northern strike, Pullman boarded his private car to seek a brief respite in the East. From the seashore he was able to commute to his New York office and in the evenings listen to the whisper of the surf from his "cottage," a palatial pagoda festooned with porches, porticos, and awnings.

When he returned to Chicago, talk of aggrieved employees and a possible strike erased whatever ease Pullman had found at the shore. On May 4, he and his wife went out to Pullman to tour the model town. He saw nothing amiss. The few men he had contact with were respectful, as usual. Works manager Harvey Middleton expressed no alarm.

ॐ

On Monday morning, May 7, 1894, forty-one men representing the Pullman employees put on Sunday suits and bowler hats and rode uptown through a pristine spring day. They were accompanied by Jennie Curtis and four other women who represented the females employed in the company's sewing and laundry departments. ARU organizer George Howard came along as an adviser. They all filed into the unfamiliar, fortress-like Pullman Building on Michigan Avenue opposite the Art Institute.

Thomas Wickes, the company's second vice president, was a cultured Englishman with steel-gray hair, an imperial mustache and chin patch, and an affable manner. At forty-nine, he was one of a new breed of professionals who specialized in managing a corporation. He had worked with George Pullman for twenty-six years and knew instinctively what his superior wanted. His suave manner and reputation for honesty and good judgment made him well liked within the company.

Needing a pattern to emulate in constructing management bureaucracies, the owners of corporations had modeled them on the military. They formed a hierarchical chain of command and separated line and staff functions. The managers at each level were answerable to and sought the approval of those higher up. The system rewarded decisions that maximized profits and discouraged those based on sentiment. The ultimate "boss" was capital, and capital had no tears to flow.

The workers who sat down with Wickes told him that their principal complaint was pay. Car builder Thomas Heathcoate, now the spokesman for the employees, told Wickes that the men saw no reason why they should not receive the same scale that had been in effect a year earlier. The work was the same; the output was the same. Their rents, too high to begin with, had not changed. They wanted double time for working on Sunday. And why was a wall being erected along the east side of the shops? Why was the company said to have hired extra guards?

Wickes listened. His manner was conciliatory. He was sorry, he said, but the car-building operations were not making money. The company was only keeping the plant open in order to give the men work. With the severe slump in business, it would have been more profitable to close the works over the winter. If he gave in to their pay demands, the firm would lose $20,000 on the recent Long Island Rail Road contract alone. It was impossible.

Heathcoate replied that if the plant had closed, the men could have moved out of Pullman, avoided its steep rents, and found jobs elsewhere. Wickes said the residents owed $70,000 in back rent and had not been "pushed" to pay it. One man spoke up and said he had been pushed. After deduction of rent, he had earned only $2 for two weeks' work. Two dollars to feed eight children.

Heathcoate emphasized the seriousness of the situation. He was himself fifty-eight years old—the gray in his hair and mustache testified to his thirty-five years as a car builder. He paid $17 a month for a five-room house that he could have had for $8 in a village just outside Pullman. He could barely afford to feed his family. Buying clothes was out of the question. The well-dressed Wickes pointed out that the times were extraordinary—the company had $4 million invested in idle Palace Cars that were depreciating in the company's yard.

One man suggested that the matter be decided by arbitration. Some of the others, suspicious of the process, frowned him down. Arbitration inevitably meant compromise. The idea of a strike was raised. George Howard jumped in to discourage such talk. No, the purpose of the American Railway Union was to prevent strikes, not foment them.

Some of their grievances were personal. Heathcoate complained about the foremen in the plant, many of whom were incompetent, wasteful, and tyrannical toward the men. Plant manager Middleton did nothing to rein them in. The men declared that they had trusted the former manager, H. H. Sessions, who understood the business. If he had been forced to bid low to get a job, they said, they were willing to "work for lower wages to help him, but we can not help the present management."

Wickes said that it was hardly in the company's interests to retain abusive or inefficient supervisors. The employees knew Mr. Pullman's reputation for fairness. The company would be glad to investigate any allegation of abuse. All the committee had to do was to put in writing the incidents they wanted looked into and he would personally see that each was examined. The meeting ended on this positive note. Wickes invited the representatives to return in two days, bringing their written complaints.

∽

On Wednesday, the Pullman employees repeated their trek to the city center. In the corporate offices, Vice President Wickes was joined by plant manager Harvey Middleton and several department heads. For two hours, Heathcoate and the other representatives documented their complaints about the shop supervisors. They said that foremen routinely used foul language, showed favoritism, and set arbitrary piecework rates. Wickes took notes, asked questions, and promised to investigate. He again dismissed talk of any pay increase. No, that was impossible. Nor could rents be adjusted.

One man said if the company was actually operating at a loss to keep them employed "we will stand by it through thick and thin." But the workers doubted it was true.

Finally, executing a bit of stagecraft, Wickes announced that Mr. Pullman would join them. The men's eyes widened as the potentate who controlled from a distance virtually every aspect of their lives strode into the room. Jennie Curtis examined with practiced eyes his impeccable clothing, the fine sewing and rich fabric. His manner combined the congenial with the imperious. He was a supremely self-assured man, a confidant of presidents.

Pullman first read a prepared statement. The entire matter, he said, could be reduced to dollars and cents. He reiterated in more detail Wickes's assertion that the company was losing money on car building. Refrigerated cars were being constructed at $15 more than what customers were paying. The car-building business was competitive. If he gave them the wages they wanted, the company would win no contracts. The plant would have to close.

As for the rents in the model town, the committee members could surely see that his role as employer was entirely separate from his role as landlord. A landlord did not set rents based on the income of prospective tenants. He had not raised rents during the boom of business leading up to the fair. Why would he lower them now?

His white goatee bouncing, he talked numbers. He mentioned the 3.82 percent return on capital the company received in rents, less than the 6 percent he wanted. He pointed out that the company removed their garbage for nothing. Kept the streets clean. Mowed their yards. He had made no legal effort to collect overdue rents. Why? Because the town's well-being was important to him. Because he thought of his employees as his "children."

He praised himself for keeping the shops open, even as the operation lost money. He would allow them to examine the company's contracts and books if they wanted. They could see for themselves the impossibility of his raising wages. They declined. The books were just paper, they could be made to show anything.

One man put their demand succinctly: "Mr. Pullman, we want more pay."

Pullman stared at him. A veteran of a thousand business deals, he knew how to make his look go hard without perceptibly changing his features. He slowly enunciated his answer in the form of a question: "Is there a man here, who, knowing that we took in the two hundred cars we are now working on at a loss of twelve dollars a car, would say he wants more?"

The man who had spoken up licked his lips and made no reply.

Pullman said he had heard loose talk of a strike. He told them to consider well before deciding to quit his employ. The unstated implication hung in the silence while dust motes danced in the late afternoon sunlight.

Before the meeting ended, George Howard asked Pullman if he would confirm the promise made by Mr. Wickes that the company would not retaliate against any of the members of the committee. It was not a casual request, given Pullman's staunch opposition to labor organizations, which had led to dismissals of union men in the past.

Pullman gave his word that there would be no reprisals.

At 6:00 p.m., the meeting ended. Pullman and Wickes congratulated themselves for defusing the situation. The newspapers reported relief throughout the city that the hard times were not likely to be made worse by the disruption of one of Chicago's largest manufacturing plants. NO STRIKE JUST NOW, the *Tribune* reported the next day. PULLMAN IS SERENE.

⸎

Immediately after the meeting with Pullman, members of the grievance committee hurried to Kensington, the village across the Illinois Central tracks from the model town. ARU members crowded into Turner Hall to hear the company's answer. George Howard told them that "the committee was received in the fairest spirits, on the part of Mr. Wickes."

When a group of women entered, he called for three cheers. "I am glad they are being encouraged by their fellow-workmen in the Pullman shops," he said. "We have not given the girls the credit they ought to have in the days gone by."

Howard advised the employees to take no action at present. "You may have to be a little patient for a while." They should do nothing rash. He was convinced that "six inches of foresight is worth a thousand miles of hindsight."

He warned that in spite of its spectacular growth, the American Railway Union was still young. "You cannot expect us to do too much." The employees should give the company time to prove its good faith by investigating the complaints of abuses in the shops.

Theodore Rhodie, a thirty-nine-year-old painter, stood up to say that if Howard and Debs advised it, they were willing to wait. "We cannot afford to strike, we do not want no strike." But he also said his fellow painters were tired of their low pay and bad treatment. "We cannot be any worse off than we are. We are ready to stand up and be knocked down."

Howard said the union was a democracy and the decision up to them. "My advice is to go back to the shops tomorrow." They need not worry about retaliation. "I guarantee myself tonight, from the assertions I got from Mr. Wickes, that not one of the committee will be allowed to suffer for serving on this committee."

At six thirty the next morning, Pullman employees did go back to work. But in the iron department, two men were told that there was no work for them. They should come back in a week. A third man worked for an hour and a half and then was also laid off. All three were members of the grievance committee.

Word of these dismissals shot through the plant. Having revealed themselves as sympathetic to the union, the men were likely to be blacklisted from all future employment. George Pullman had gone back on his word. He had taken revenge on the committee members. Anger began to percolate through every department.

The company later denied that the dismissals had had anything to do with the union negotiations. Neither Wickes nor Pullman knew about the moves. Perhaps a foreman had gotten word that the men had complained about him to the boss and was taking his personal revenge. Perhaps nothing more than a ripple in the flow of work had cost the men their jobs. Whatever the case, the dismissals pushed a volatile situation one step closer to a breaking point.

In the afternoon, Vice President Wickes came down to the factory. Along with other executives, he questioned some two dozen men about their complaints of mistreatment in the shops. Plant manager Middleton insulted and intimidated some of the witnesses, but Wickes vowed to get to the bottom of every issue.

That evening about 150 women employees met in the Arcade Building of the model town to hear Thomas Heathcoate speak. He was interrupted by word that a strike was being discussed at a union meeting in Kensington. He hurried off to take part.

The teenage Jennie Curtis took charge. A company spy reported that she made remarks "of the same impudent nature as has characterized her actions from the first." She spoke of company officials as "Middleton" and "Wickes" and "the other fellows," leaving off the deferential "Mister." In her anger, she had found a voice—in the coming weeks, she would speak at rallies all over Chicago.

The grievance committee was meeting in a back room at the Dewdrop Tavern in Kensington. George Howard and ARU director Louis W. Rogers sat in for the union. No one was happy. The Pullman employees immediately began to talk about a strike.

Cigar smoke circled the astringent gaslights. Howard said he understood the frustration, the sense of having reached a limit. But the time was not right to bet on a strike, not when the Pullman Company held all the good cards.

He told the men that Eugene Debs had asked him to convey a message. They needed to remain patient, to consider carefully, to act prudently. Debs knew they were disappointed, but it was best to wait until after the shop complaints had been investigated.

The men were in no mood to submit. The layoffs were the last straw. As the night wore on, the employee representatives vented their anger. How much were they supposed to take? Where would it end? Eugene Debs advised patience, but Eugene Debs had also spoken of manhood. Was it manly to allow your wages to be slashed until you could not buy food for your family? Was it manly to be sworn at and cheated in the shops?

Strike. The word kept returning to every tongue. A strike resolution was submitted to a vote. Forty-two in favor, four opposed. More talk. They were determined to fight for higher pay and lower rents, yet they were afraid of joining the desperate masses of the unemployed. They had to take a stand, but they had to be careful. Their honor was at stake, their jobs were at stake.

Strike. Another vote. Support had to be overwhelming—a strike would not work if every department did not agree. More talk, more anger. The thick air was now giving way to the first gray light of a spring dawn. Manhood. Security. Dignity. Danger. Strike. The third vote was unanimous. Strike.

It was four thirty in the morning. George Howard again emphasized the democratic nature of the ARU. Each local within the plant must decide, he said. He told them they should go back to the plant and poll their members. It would not do to walk out unless they knew the men would overwhelmingly back their actions. Everyone had to be willing.

Agreed. The men set no date to walk off the job. They hurried home to wash up and get to the works before the shift started. The members of the locals would decide.

The men reported to work as usual on the morning of Friday, May 12. Everyone wanted to know what had gone on during the all-night meeting. Would there be a strike? The atmosphere was rife with rumors. It was whispered that the company had sent spies to the union gathering. It was said that the executives, knowing of the intended strike, had decided to preempt the action by closing the works at noon. A Western Union messenger had seen the orders. Was it true?

No one knew for sure, but distrust of company officials now colored every man's mind. They should strike now, before the company had the chance to lock them out. At ten thirty, word began to circulate. Strike. Prearranged signals were given. Mechanics began to return their tools to their chests. Department by department, they ceased working. They turned their backs on their only source of sustenance. They walked out of the shops in a disciplined and orderly fashion. They congregated on Florence Avenue in front of the entrance to the plant.

Feelings ran high. For those who had labored from a young age, many hours a day, six days a week, year after year, with no vacations and few holidays, an unexpected break generated a strange and unfamiliar euphoria. The release from routine was exhilarating. Only when they set down their burden did they appreciate its great weight.

They were stunned to find themselves, for once, free men and women. Even more exciting was the heart-swelling sense of solidarity with each other. They felt themselves transformed from struggling, beaten-down individuals to a community standing together against their oppressors. Men and women who had worked together, lived together, endured humiliation and privation together, were now taking their fate into their own hands. Together.

As groups from different departments appeared, they were hailed by those already out. When Jennie Curtis and four hundred young women from the embroidery and laundry departments emerged, the plaza in front of the gate erupted in cheering. Before the clock on the tower struck noon, three thousand workers had left their jobs. The Pullman works, one of the largest factories in the country, fell silent.

Soon a notice appeared on the gates: "The works are closed until further notice."

The strike was on.

⁓

George Pullman refused to speak to reporters, but Thomas Wickes expressed baffled surprise. The company had not fired any of the committeemen in retribution, nor had there been a plan to close the works. It was all a misunderstanding.

George Howard, in his initial enthusiasm, told reporters that ARU members might boycott Pullman cars, spreading the job action to most of the nation's railroads. It was rumored falsely that workmen on the

Cleveland, Cincinnati, Chicago & St. Louis Railway, known as the Big Four, had already cut Pullman cars from the trains. Illinois Central trainmen, it was said, were also refusing to handle the company's sleepers.

That Friday afternoon, the workers, astonished by the action they had taken, elated by the sudden sensation of freedom, went home and donned their best clothes. They congregated at the baseball field on the edge of Lake Calumet. They talked in small groups. Some lay on the grass, their faces bathed in sunshine.

That night, they packed a meeting at Turner Hall to overflowing. When he rose to address them, George Howard had regained his cautious tone. He advised the strikers not to threaten, intimidate, or use force of any kind. The men should ignore any provocations from the company. They should let liquor alone. Of George Pullman he said, "It is so long since he has done any work that he has forgotten what ill-usage means." If Pullman had come down and listened to the men, he asserted, the strike might have been avoided.

Thomas Heathcoate, now head of the strike committee, told the crowd that he had once respected his employer, but now he did not trust the man. He scoffed at the idea of examining the company's books. Numbers could be altered. A hungry child was not a number. He was trying to feed his family on eight cents a meal. How would George Pullman get along on such fare? The men laughed.

Theodore Rhodie stood to say he could not believe that the company took any contracts at a loss. George Pullman had given a hundred thousand dollars to the museum in Jackson Park. The money "came out of us and Pullman got the credit." The men jeered.

When Pullman finally did face reporters, he said the action was a "most unpleasant surprise for me." His workers were the best paid in the world. "We have made no preparations for riots," he said, "for we do not anticipate there will be any."

That evening, Pullman abandoned Chicago. He boarded his private car and journeyed overnight to Long Branch, New Jersey. He found his oceanfront estate besieged by reporters. He took another train to the Saint Lawrence River. Anxious and worn out, he at last found quiet at Castle Rest.

Thomas Heathcoate was resigned. "The boys were bound to go out anyway," he said. He summed up the workers' stoic feelings: "We do not expect the company to concede our demands. We do not know what the outcome will be, and in fact we do not care much."

The employees realized that they were working for less wages than they needed simply to feed their families. "And on that proposition," Heathcoate said, "we absolutely refuse to work any longer."

PART II

May 12–July 3, 1894

9

Nothing to Arbitrate

WITH THE STRIKE UNDER WAY, EUGENE DEBS TRAVELED TO the model town. Over the next few days, he spent more time listening to Pullman workers than George Pullman had in years. He heard their complaints about pay and rents, about restrictions on political activity, dictatorial foremen, piecework.

The workers at the car shops were only a fraction of the growing American Railway Union membership. Debs was determined to advise and support them, but he did not intend to throw his still-fragile organization into a larger fight. He did not need to point out to the strikers the headwinds they faced. They well knew that legions of unemployed men in Chicago were eager to take their jobs.

Four days after the workers walked out, directors of the Pullman's Palace Car Company declared their customary 2 percent quarterly dividend. Debs was furious. Years earlier he had hammered "King" Pullman in the *Firemen's Magazine*, grouping him with "codfish, coal oil and bucket shop snobs." Now the "palace car nabob" was divvying up among a small group of capitalists the $600,000 in profit that had been accumulated in just three months from the labor of his employees.

Unable to meet in Pullman, a central strike committee with Thomas Heathcoate as chairman gathered daily across the tracks at Turner Hall. Heathcoate had advised the men to keep away from the plant, to avoid congregating in public, and to abide by the law. Knowing that employees would be blamed for any damage, the committee had assigned three hundred strikers to surround the plant and keep it safe from saboteurs and other intruders. This force, which the company chose to regard as a picket line, stood guard around the clock.

Debs addressed a large meeting of employees. "I am with you heart and soul in this strike," he said. In general, he told them, he was against a work stoppage. But if the only alternative was "the sacrifice of manhood," he preferred the strike.

At another rally two days later, he declared: "I believe a rich plunderer like Pullman is a greater felon than a poor thief." He felt he had a duty to "strip the mask of hypocrisy from the pretended philanthropist and show him to the world as an oppressor of labor." He proclaimed the company's actions "a terrible illustration of corporate greed . . . which for years has prevailed in this country." Pullman workers would win the strike, he insisted, if they held together.

Privately, Debs worried. The Pullman's Palace Car Company was not the Great Northern Railway. George Pullman was in a financial position to keep the plant closed for months. Now the prestige of the American Railway Union was tangled in the dispute. The railroads might try to pull the young, unprepared, and virtually penniless organization into a wider dispute in order to hobble or destroy it. Debs would have to tread a fine line between appearing weak and plunging into a contest he could not win.

Neither the local unions nor the entire ARU could support four thousand workers and their families for any length of time. They appealed to the public for relief. Laundresses and seamstresses from Local 269 went around Pullman to determine the most urgent needs. Help started to arrive. Sympathetic police officers from Chicago's South Side solicited aid from shopkeepers. The *Chicago Daily News* offered a downtown storefront rent-free as a place in the city to accept contributions. Many Chicagoans sympathized with the strikers' courage and gave what they could.

The workers had a friend in the Springfield statehouse. Governor John Peter Altgeld, who had risen from the working class himself, was an avid reformer. Last September, as the depression was tightening its grip, he had declared that "it will be the duty of all public officials to see to it that no man is permitted to starve on the soil of Illinois." The statement was revolutionary. The idea that government officials were responsible for citizens' well-being was widely rejected on principle by politicians.

The most generous donations came from Chicago mayor John Patrick Hopkins. Born in Buffalo just before the Civil War, Hopkins had arrived in Chicago in 1879 and taken a job at the Pullman works. He started as a lumber shover, unloading boards at the waterfront. Sharp of mind, he quickly ascended to timekeeper, then to paymaster. He opened a shoe store in the town's Arcade, expanding it to a general dry goods emporium.

During the 1888 election, Hopkins, a Democrat, rented the theater in the town of Pullman for a party rally. The staunchly Republican George Pullman was not amused. After Pullman employees backed Grover Cleveland in his losing bid for reelection, Pullman fired his paymaster. Hopkins went on to form a prosperous mercantile partnership, the Secord-Hopkins Company, in nearby Kensington.

The thirty-five-year-old Hopkins won a special election in December 1893 after the assassination of Mayor Carter Harrison by an aggrieved office seeker. He took over leadership of the city in the midst of the crippling economic depression. Well liked, respected by his own employees, quick to remember a man's name, Hopkins struck what newspapers described as an "Apollo figure." His glossy black hair fell into ringlets, a ready smile winked from beneath his mustache.

His business success allowed him to provide generous aid to the strikers. Through his store, he donated $1,500 in produce, including twelve tons of meat, and another $1,000 in cash. Early in June, the Chicago City Council asked the mayor to appeal to the public on behalf of the Relief Committee at Pullman. Hopkins set aside a day to encourage all city residents to contribute money, clothing, and food.

Physicians and druggists donated their services. Members of the Chicago Fire Department gave $909.75. A German singing society chipped in $140. A supply of tobacco was donated "to solace the minds of anxious strikers."

It was not enough. On May 22, Pullman workers received their last paychecks. Few had been able to maintain savings during the depression. Many fingered overdue butcher and coal bills as well as demands for back rent. Malnutrition began to haunt the town.

Yet it hardly seemed like a strike. As May wore on, a newspaper noted the "absence of excitement" in the town. A *Chicago Inter Ocean* reporter wrote that the town was "as quiet as a New England village, and there was nothing to indicate that the workers in the car shops were in the throes of a strike fever." After a month of strife, "it is rather as though each day was a Sunday." Strikers took to wearing white ribbons as an emblem of solidarity.

On Sunday, May 27, members of Chicago trade unions attended a mass meeting at Pullman to boost morale and to gather contributions for the relief fund. Debs told the assembled workers that George Pullman's "specious interest in the welfare of the 'poor workingman' is in no way different from that of the slaveowner of fifty years ago. . . . You are striking to avert inevitable slavery and degradation."

The crowd took advantage of Pullman's park for a picnic. In the evening, they attended a dance upstairs in the Market Building. Jennie Curtis, now president of the "girls' local," enjoyed the first promenade with Mayor Hopkins himself.

Picnics and dances belied all common notions of an industrial strike. But the question on the minds of anxious town residents as they entered the third week of the walkout was simple: when will it end?

⚬

Among those who took a keen interest in the Pullman strike was Jane Addams. At thirty-three, the young woman from rural Illinois had already acquired an international reputation as a social reformer. During the world's fair, thousands of visitors had stopped by Hull House, the settlement house she had founded in the middle of the city's slum-clogged West Side. There, working with her close friend Ellen Gates Starr, Addams dispensed aid and moral uplift to the poor at a time when public assistance was minimal.

At the time, three of every four citizens of Chicago were foreign-born. Many worked in factories or in sweatshops scattered throughout the neighborhoods. Hull House offered them a chance to learn English and to socialize with each other. Volunteers taught classes in everything from dietetics to the philosophy of Plato. Mothers were especially appreciative of the innovative kindergarten, nursery, and daycare opportunities. Playgrounds were a rarity then—Hull House had one of the first.

The work of Jane Addams was one sign of an awakening of middle-class citizens to the egregious conditions in urban slums. But the 1893 depression had shaken Addams's faith in the efficacy of her strategy. A third of Chicago's factories had closed. Nearly half its working population was unemployed. Now she was seeing that real poverty, "dire poverty," meant starvation, homelessness, and despair. "We are sunk under a mass of the unemployed morning, noon, and night," Ellen Starr observed in August 1893.

The panic that had swept Wall Street was nothing compared to the mental anguish of those who shouldered the real economic burden. Already engulfed in poverty, they grew confused as their livelihoods disappeared. Mental depression turned to terror. The fears of the people Addams saw every day were not abstract. She found that residents were especially terrified of three things: debt, the shame of appearing as paupers to their children, and dying of hunger. Addams had been impressed by the resilience and generosity of the poor. Now she saw that extreme poverty could break the spirit, that anxiety could drive a person mad.

She and her colleagues kept asking if they were doing enough. The soul of the worker was put "in a state of siege" by the brutality of urban life, Starr wrote. "It is merciful and necessary to pass to him the things which sustain his courage and keep him alive (i.e., art, music, etc.) but the effectual thing is to raise the siege."

Yet Addams was wary of radical action. She preferred to apply reason and conciliation to social problems. Her efforts at Hull House bore some resemblance to George Pullman's at his model town. He had contributed funds to help further her work. Each of them was making an attempt to change people by changing their environment, giving citizens access to order and beauty. Each offered courses and facilities intended to teach working people middle-class values. Each emphasized an appreciation of art. Each had organized a kindergarten and a playground.

The year before, Addams had joined some of the city's middle- and upper-class reformers to found the Chicago Civic Federation. The group was headed by the prominent banker Lyman Gage and included merchants, lawyers, professors, and union leaders. The members worked to maintain labor peace and urged employers to heed the grievances of their workers. In May 1894, they formed a conciliation board to look into the Pullman strike.

Addams had taken the initiative early in the strike to consult with Thomas Heathcoate and the union's relief committee about providing for the desperate strikers. While at Pullman she had eaten supper with some of the women and gone around to look at their homes. She spoke with

George Howard and learned that the ARU might be open to arbitrating a settlement to the dispute. But no talks could begin, he told her, until company officials expressed their own willingness to negotiate.

Addams took this information back to the federation. When they procrastinated, she went to see Pullman vice president Wickes herself. She cooled her heels in the Pullman Building lobby for an hour before being told Wickes was "not in." She persisted, returning on Saturday, June 2, with another committee member. Although Wickes finally agreed to see them, he said the company could not allow third parties to become involved in something that was "not their issue." Nor would the company negotiate with "ex-employees." Mr. Pullman, he said, was convinced that there was "nothing to arbitrate." The phrase became a Pullman mantra throughout the strike and would haunt George Pullman to his grave.

∾

As the strike wore on into June, time began to work against the employees. The strikers could be sustained only so long by the union's frantic relief efforts. Some workers who could manage it had already left the model town, seeking lower rents and the chance of work elsewhere. Most were too destitute to move away.

While the press and public admired the David-and-Goliath nature of the contest, few newspapers gave the strikers much chance of winning. Some called the action a stupid blunder. The strike was "a grave mistake," the *Chicago Record* declared, "at a time when mistakes are dear and dangerous." The workers were simply joining the already-crowded ranks of the unemployed. The *Evening Journal* said that those who encouraged the strike were "almost criminal in their disregard of the consequences." The *Tribune* called the strike "wanton, causeless, and suicidal."

The Pullman's Palace Car Company was well able to endure a long work stoppage. The firm still enjoyed a steady stream of revenue from its operation of sleeper, diner, and parlor cars on railroads all over the country. Its war chest, unlike that of the strikers, was enormous.

But George Pullman understood that publicity was important—and his "brand" was being damaged by the strike. His model town had drawn favorable attention to the firm and had become an emblem of its enlightened, forward-looking operations. The strike had turned it into a symbol of his autocratic disregard for his workers.

Pullman was on his way to becoming the sole competitor in the industry and he knew that "monopoly" was an increasingly dirty word. The strike amplified the talk that was already circulating about government regulation of sleeper-car fares, a move that could seriously crimp Pullman's enormous profits.

The strike also tarnished Pullman's personal reputation. Even the newspapers that opposed the strike, which were the majority, had taken to referring to him as "Baron" or "Duke" and comparing the town to a feudal manor. On May 30, the *Chicago Inter Ocean* noted that for the Marquis de Pullman to become a proper tyrant "there is nothing needed but the knout, a liberal supply of shackles, and cheap transit to Siberia." Editors of the *Chicago Times*, the only Chicago paper that consistently defended the strike, found the situation in the town "almost deplorable," and declared on June 9 that the overwhelming majority of Chicagoans supported the strikers.

Yet George Pullman was determined not to give in. He owed it to his shareholders, he said. He had run his company and the town on business principles, and he would stand on those principles.

∽

There the matter stood on Tuesday, June 12, when four hundred delegates from American Railway Union locals all over the country met in Chicago. This would be the first national convention of the burgeoning organization. The agenda included writing a formal constitution and setting up the union's administrative structures. All knew that the Pullman strike would also be prominent on the agenda. All looked to Eugene Debs for guidance and inspiration.

The first morning of the convention, Debs stood on the podium in Ulrich's Hall to welcome the delegates. He noted that in the nine months since the first ARU lodge was formed, 425 locals had come into existence, an astounding reception for the new organization. This was a different type of railroad union. Its purpose was not to quarrel with the brotherhoods of engineers, firemen, or conductors. The ARU had another purpose. It would represent *all* railroad men, particularly those "left in the cold to endure the pitiless storms of corporate power." It would set out to create a balance between labor and capital.

"When men accept degrading conditions and wear collars and fetters without resistance," he declared, "when a man surrenders his honest convictions, his loyalty to principle, he ceases to be a man."

Throughout the speech, Debs mixed caution with enthusiasm. The convention had serious work ahead. Delegates needed to promulgate thoughtful policies. "There is danger in extremes," he warned. The organization "must be built for war" but not provoke war. They had to choose their battles, to avoid "continuous embroilment," to exercise "patience and forbearance." They were meeting at a time of unprecedented demoralization of workers. The "cyclonic disturbances" of the depression "fall with crushing force upon labor."

He vowed to stand up for the adherents of the Coxey armies, many of them still on the road. He criticized Grover Cleveland for his harshness toward these "victims of a greedy and heartless capitalism." The ARU must continue to push for the eight-hour day, not only to give hardworking Americans leisure, but to expand employment to those idled by layoffs.

Turning to the Pullman strikers, he shaped a verbal effigy of George Pullman and proceeded to bash it. He compared the industrialist to the "proprietor of the lake of fire." George Pullman was as "greedy as a horse leech." He had "a soul so small that a million of them could dance on the little end of a hornet's stinger."

"The boys all over the country," Debs said, "are clamoring to tie up the Pullman cars." A boycott was a logical move. It did not make sense for ARU members to handle the sleepers that supplied Pullman with his profits, while their brothers and sisters were locked in a battle with the company. But Debs stopped conspicuously short of advocating direct action by the larger union. "Nobody ever knew how hard I tried to prevent that strike," he said later. For now, he acknowledged that the strike at Pullman "will, I doubt not, engage the attention of this convention."

He quickly moved to other issues. "The time is approaching," he said, "when the government will be required *to own* the railroads, to prevent the railroads from *owning* the government." He welcomed women members to the ARU and affirmed that the union would insist that "when a woman performs a man's work, she ought, in all justice, to have a man's pay." It was an idea so far ahead of its time that it left many of the male delegates with puzzled grins.

Workers, Debs declared, must "march together, vote together and fight together." Returning to a perennial theme, he foresaw a "reign of justice" in which there would be no need for strikes, "an era of good will" between labor and capital.

Committees were formed, and the men got down to work. They needed to decide issues of leadership and finance. It was crucial that they continue to organize additional members—only a fifth of the nation's 750,000 railroad employees had signed up with the ARU so far. Workers on most of the eastern roads remained to be brought aboard. Debs felt the urgent need to strengthen the organization and to build a war chest before taking on any further struggles with the railroads.

Delegates rode trains or streetcars down to the model town to look over the situation and talk to the strikers. The Pullman employees became emblems of the fact that workers were being asked to bear the burden of hard times, while plutocrats continued to revel in their wealth.

The business before the ARU convention was consequential, but the men also needed to get to know one another. Many delegates were new to the labor movement. Informal talk and serious drinking would lubricate the wheels of the organization. And for men from the hinterland, this was an opportunity to take in the sights of Chicago—the stockyards, the skyscrapers, and the fleshpots of the vice district that the boys back home would be asking about.

❧

Members of the Civic Federation, concerned about how the Pullman strike was harming Chicago, decided to make another try at convincing George Pullman to arbitrate. Banker Lyman Gage suggested that the conciliation board approach the strikers and focus strictly on the rents in Pullman. Just as the ARU convention was getting under way, Jane Addams and activist Ellen Henrotin arranged a meeting with Eugene Debs to suggest this starting point for the arbitration process.

Debs jumped at the chance. He had surveyed the mood of the convention delegates and found them leaning toward a nationwide boycott of Pullman cars. The Civic Federation effort could be a last opportunity to avoid the risk that such an action would pose for the union.

In Addams, Debs recognized a sympathetic spirit. A reporter described her face as "a window behind which stands her soul." She was pale, with deep-set eyes, a mellow voice, and a manner at once gracious and deadly serious. Debs agreed to set up a meeting between the conciliation board and the strike committee.

Addams was the only board member to turn up for the meeting with about sixty representatives of Pullman locals. They were skeptical, worried that considering arbitration at this point would make them look weak. But her sincerity convinced them to trust her. She acknowledged that the workers had many demands, but she felt that examining the rent issue first would be a productive step away from conflict.

Debs, whose cagey use of arbitration had won the victory over Jim Hill's Great Northern Railway, applied his influence. The strikers agreed to arbitrate not only rents but all issues. Addams was delighted to report to her board that "we had made a beginning toward conciliation."

It was a one-sided beginning. George Pullman agreed to listen to the proposal but would talk only with the male members of the board, excluding Jane Addams. He met in his office with the group only to tell them that the situation had not changed. He would not arbitrate. He would not adjust employees' rents. He would not raise their pay. "It was impossible to come to any understanding with the Pullman Company," Addams said. "We considered the effort a failure."

A few days later, speaking to the female graduates of Western Reserve University, Addams warned of the "narrow individuality" of those who lacked "that broad conscience which takes in those around them."

As the strike continued, Addams grew increasingly nervous. She told English newspaper editor William Stead that Chicagoans were feeling "unrest, discontent, and fear." She sensed that they were "on the edge of some great upheaval but one can never tell whether it will turn out a tragedy or a farce."

⁊

Contentious issues split the ARU delegates at the convention. The most bitter was the question of whether to include African American members. The original statement of principles hammered out by Debs, Howard, and the other founders a year earlier had not mentioned race. It left membership criteria to the locals. All of them had followed the pattern of the railroad brotherhoods, which had confined their rolls to men who were "white born . . . and able to read and write the English language," barring blacks and most new immigrants from competing for jobs. Now, as the massed delegates considered a constitution, some proposed that the preamble specify that only railroad employees "born of white parents" be eligible for membership. This raised a pressing and thorny problem.

The abolition of slavery had left four million newly freed black Americans in need of subsistence. Now, three decades later, the relationship of the races remained a fraught subject. Northern white workers asserted that blacks were incapable of the skills that the railroad trades entailed. But blacks had already performed these and other skilled jobs in the South, disproving the claim. Whites saw a threat to their jobs and wages. They excluded African Americans from fellowship. Very few blacks had been hired by northern railroad companies.

George Pullman was an exception. As a Republican, he was touched by the spirit of Lincoln and felt a responsibility to provide for the slaves whom the Great Emancipator had freed. He donated to Negro causes. He hired a black coachman and black household help—most wealthy Chicagoans preferred English servants. He allowed black customers to ride his cars, much to the consternation of Southern whites. Arthur A. Wells, a black man who served as the porter on Pullman's private car, was a trusted assistant and would be the beneficiary of a generous $5,000 legacy in the magnate's will.

For Pullman, the idea of employing former slaves fit neatly into his conception of making a profit while doing good. The Pullman Company furnished conductors to take tickets on its cars and porters to attend to passenger needs. The porters performed the vital duty of making up berths, a complicated chore that transformed a daytime coach car into a sleeper at night.

Pullman began to hire black workers as sleeping-car porters soon after he started in the business. Many were indeed former slaves. The benevolent effort to give these men jobs turned Pullman into the largest employer of African Americans in the country. There was, of course, a catch. The position of porter was the only one open to blacks at the Pullman Company. None were allowed to work in manufacturing. None could advance to become conductors.

The racial distinction served Pullman well. The porters were forced to work for pay that white workers would not have tolerated. At first, Pullman paid them nothing at all—they worked for tips. By 1879, they were making $10 a month for a ninety-hour week. The fact that they continued to rely on gratuities shifted the cost of their services to Pullman customers and encouraged the porters to feign cringing deference and to perform additional duties such as shining passengers' shoes. Conductors, all of them white, earned $65 a month.

The other advantage of employing black porters was the fact that the social distance between the races allayed any suspicion that porters would overstep boundaries while waiting on patrons who might be in a state of undress or intoxication. Small children were entrusted to their care. Pullman, the porters noted, wanted to hire the "blackest man with the whitest teeth." Since few northern whites had black servants at home, they saw the porters' services as an exotic bit of luxury.

Eugene Debs had spoken about the injustice laid on the porters in the pages of the *Firemen's Magazine*. "Everything is in the line of degradation," he wrote. The use of company spies was particularly reprehensible. The honesty of both porters and the white conductors who supervised them was tested by company agents, "spotters," who tempted them to cheat the company. "It is such detestable practices," Debs said, "that breed the unrest and vindictive spirit abroad in the lands that furnish anarchists and socialists with the raw material for their diatribes against law and social order."

George Pullman's operation demeaned African Americans in many of the same ways that it denied dignity to industrial workers. Work rules could be petty and arbitrary. Spies lurked in and out of the workplace to report on employee behavior. Supervisors treated subordinates with disrespect and outright cruelty. Pullman gave the porters a job and he paid his manufacturing employees a wage, but in neither case did he acknowledge their humanity.

The porters insisted that their jobs required intricate skills, but George Pullman asserted that blacks were "by nature adapted faithfully to perform their duties." Company officials did not see the porters' smiling, ever-attentive demeanor as the well-honed act that it was. They considered it the product of a naturally obsequious nature. Porters had to endure the further indignity of being called by the name George, presumably a reference to George Pullman. Passengers, especially those from the South, sometimes insisted that a porter sing or perform a dance.

The paucity of jobs for blacks during these decades made it more likely that Pullman porters would offer steady and reliable service to the company even as they accepted a starvation wage. Indeed, the position of porter carried great prestige in black communities. Porters had the opportunity, available to few other blacks, to travel around the country, protected from racial violence by their Pullman uniforms. They earned enough to move their families into the lower middle class and to provide a platform for the black professionals of the next generation. Future Supreme Court Justice Thurgood Marshall was the son of a porter and worked at the job himself while attending law school.

❧

During a blistering six-hour debate at the convention, Debs firmly opposed drawing the color line. He did not, however, propose anything as radical as social equality for blacks. "I am not here to advocate association with the negro, but I am ready to stand side by side with him, to take his hand in mine, and help him whenever it is in my power."

Others rose to argue for the formal exclusion of black workers. A Detroit delegate said the ARU "would lose 5,000 members in the West if colored men were allowed to become members." One fireman said he "would not 'brother' the negro under any circumstances."

Debs countered that "if we do not admit the colored man to membership, the fact will be used against us." Unions that had excluded blacks had seen company managers bring in African American workers to take their jobs during strikes. Debs wanted instead to promote his core idea: to make the American Railway Union an organization that was open to all.

He emphasized that in the event that the union was drawn more deeply into the ongoing Pullman strike, barring black porters from membership would mean relinquishing a potentially decisive advantage in the struggle. If the union members invited these workers into the ARU, the porters could shut down Pullman's sleeping-car service more effectively than any other group of employees. Those cars were the most profitable—during the depression, the only profitable—sector of the firm. Without the knowledgeable porters, the car operation would be crippled.

"It is not the colored man's fault that he is black," Debs told the convention. "It is not the fault of six million negroes that they are here. They were brought here by the avarice, cupidity, and inhumanity of the white race." It was a startling sentiment at a time when race relations in America were reaching a nadir.

Debs could argue, but he could not dictate. When the proposal finally came to a vote, his view did not prevail. By 112 to 110, the delegates declared that their union was for whites only. Years later, when

Debs looked back on the events of 1894, he thought that the inclusion of the porters might have resulted in "a different story of the strike, for it would certainly have had a different result."

The anti-union stance of George Pullman and his successors meant that the porters would suffer low pay, long hours, and demeaning working conditions for another two generations. Only in 1937, under the inspired leadership of A. Philip Randolph, who looked on Eugene Debs as one of his heroes, would the Brotherhood of Sleeping Car Porters win recognition from the Pullman Company.

10

Dance of Skeletons

TWENTY THOUSAND SOULS, MEN, WOMEN, AND LITTLE ONES, HAVE their eyes turned toward this convention to-day," the Pullman strikers proclaimed in their appeal to the American Railway Union delegates.

At eleven thirty on the morning of Friday, June 15, delegates disposed of routine business, formed themselves into a committee of the whole, and took up the issue of the Pullman strike. Central to the debate was the message from representatives of the local unions at Pullman, several of whom spoke at Ulrich's Hall.

The strikers went on: "We struck because we were without hope. We joined the American Railway Union because it gave us a glimmer of hope. . . . We will make you proud of us, brothers, if you will give us the hand we need. Help make our country better and more wholesome."

They enumerated the now-familiar list of complaints about intolerable pay cuts, high rents, shop abuses, and the restrictive life in the model town. During the depression, rents had fallen in Chicago, sometimes by half, but they had remained constant in Pullman. For what they were paying, Pullman residents could have moved to nearby communities and lived in homes "compared to which ours are hovels." Instead, they were forced to contribute "to make a millionaire a billionaire." George Pullman sold them water at a 500 percent markup. He forced them to pay $2.25 for gas that neighbors bought for 75 cents. Painters received 35 cents an hour on the open market, Pullman painters only 23 cents. Many employees suffered under supervisors who crushed them in spirit on behalf of a "merciless, soulless, grasping corporation."

Their complaint was personal. "Pullman, both the man and the town, is an ulcer on the body politic," they insisted. No man or woman among them had "felt the gentle pressure of George M. Pullman's hand."

One Pullman employee declared: "We are born in a Pullman house, fed from the Pullman shops, taught in the Pullman school, catechized in the Pullman Church, and when we die we shall go to the Pullman Hell."

Another asserted that he was the father of four children and that "when a man is sober and steady, and has a saving wife, and after working two and a half years for a company he finds himself in debt for a common living, something must be wrong."

Something must be wrong. The strikers tried to express a fundamental issue that lay at the heart of their discontent. Was labor a commodity? Were their lives subject to the laws of supply and demand that applied to commercial transactions? Pullman vice president Wickes had declared, "We go into the market for men just as we go into the market for anything else." Such a notion was commonplace in the industrial era, but the Pullman workers were dismayed to think that an impersonal market could reduce them to starvation.

Something must be wrong. If any employer could cut pay indiscriminately, it must inevitably begin a vicious cycle. Relying on lower unit costs, that company could underbid competitors. Those competitors in turn would be forced to reduce the pay of their own employees in order to compete in the market. Then another round of wage cuts, and another.

"And so the merry war—the dance of skeletons bathed in human tears—goes on, and will go on, brothers, forever," the Pullman employees predicted, "unless you, the American Railway Union, stop it."

Individual Pullman workers explained in detail how this dance of skeletons had impinged on their own lives. The most affecting story was told by Jennie Curtis, the young seamstress who had now become a union activist. When she stood to speak, the audience fell silent to allow her earnest voice to carry.

She was nineteen years old, Curtis said. She had been employed at Pullman for five years. She was a diligent worker.

The young women in her department spent their time sewing the elaborate carpeting, curtains, upholstery, and mattresses that made the

Pullman sleepers so luxurious. The work was demanding. Their reward was to see their wages cut again and again.

Curtis described how her father had worked at the Pullman factory for thirteen years. When he fell ill, he was laid off but continued to occupy a cottage in the model town. The previous September he had died in debt. The company now insisted that his daughter pay the $60 back rent that he had accumulated on his deathbed. Before the strike, she had tried to make good the debt from her paltry wages at a rate of $3 a month.

"Many a time," she explained, "I have drawn nine and ten dollars for two weeks' work, paid seven dollars for my board and given the Company the remaining two or three dollars on the rent." The company was not grateful for her honest effort. "Sometimes when I could not possibly give them anything, I would receive slurs and insults from the clerks in the bank, because Mr. Pullman would not give me enough in return for my hard labor to pay the rent for one of his houses and live."

Curtis finished her speech with a clarion appeal to ARU delegates. "We ask you to come along with us," she told them, "because we are not just fighting for ourselves, but for decent conditions for workers everywhere."

Her words electrified the gathering. They stirred the heart of Eugene Debs, who did not want the union members to plunge into a boycott. The representatives cursed Pullman as a "bloodsucker" for robbing a girl.

Curtis's words and the report from the Pullman committee prompted an immediate proposal that ARU members on the roads refuse to handle Pullman cars. Debs stepped in again to advise caution. He was willing to label George Pullman a "monumental monster, a pirate on the high seas of labor," but the thought of a full-blown boycott gave him a sinking feeling. Instead, he counseled the delegates to form a committee of twelve, six of them Pullman representatives, to meet with Thomas Wickes and propose arbitration. With the muscle of the ARU behind the request, George Pullman would have to see the value of reaching an agreement.

Eleven men plus Jennie Curtis walked into Wickes's office that same afternoon. Their demand was simple and urgent. The members asked Wickes directly, "Will you arbitrate?"

He told them that George Pullman was in New York. The time of his return was not known. He could not respond to anyone who came as a representative of the American Railway Union—the company did not recognize the ARU's existence. He could say no more.

Would he meet with a committee if it were comprised only of Pullman employees? Yes, he said, but he would speak with them only as individuals, not as representatives of any union.

After reporting to the convention, Curtis and five other Pullman employees returned to Wickes's office the next day without the ARU men. Wickes, having conferred with George Pullman, showed no inclination to waver.

"The situation with regard to wages has not changed," he told them. Would the company arbitrate? No. Would he consider restoring the wage scale of 1893? They had no right even to ask such a question, he replied. They had relinquished their employment. As far as the company was concerned, they "stood in the same position as the man on the sidewalk." Even longtime employees were, in George Pullman's view, expendable ciphers.

⚬

Back at the convention, Wickes's response ignited the delegates' fury. Debs continued to maneuver. He convinced the conventioneers to refer the next step to yet another committee. The representatives voted $2,000 for the strikers' relief and put in place a weekly assessment of ten cents on every member to build a strike fund.

The company's hard line put Debs in a corner. It meant that the union would have to either back down or take action. Giving in would make the ARU look weak, deflate members' morale, and hamper organizing efforts. Action meant attacking the company's revenue by asking all union members to cease handling Pullman cars. Such a boycott would steer the group into uncharted waters.

Debs understood that the delegates were eager to flex their muscles. The victory over the Great Northern had inspired them. So had Debs's own words in his opening address: "The forces of labor must unite. The salvation of labor demands it."

Like Debs, ARU vice president George Howard, who had worked most closely with the Pullman employees during the strike, was now eager to avoid a boycott. He thought an effective tactic would be to close down additional Pullman facilities in St. Louis and Ludlow, Kentucky. These shops handled the repair of Pullman cars, and he had helped organize workers in both of them. Strikes against them, he felt, would pressure the company without requiring the thousands of ARU members on the railroads to put their jobs at risk.

On Wednesday, June 20, the convention appointed a committee to recommend "a suitable line of action" regarding Pullman as soon as possible. The delegates heard reports of telegrams coming in from as far west as Sacramento indicating that locals were ready to begin "aggressive action."

That same day, George Pullman stepped down from his private railcar in Chicago, having returned from his stay in the East. The ongoing strike against his works, he found, might be on the verge of becoming a national issue. If the prospect disturbed him, he gave no sign of it.

After two days of deliberation, the ARU action committee reported back to the convention on its last day in session. Its recommendation was succinct: "Unless the Pullman Palace Car Company does adjust the grievances before 12 o'clock on Tuesday, June 26, 1894, the members of the American Railway Union shall refuse to handle Pullman cars and equipment." The delegates approved the ultimatum. They also resolved to send men to lead walkouts at the other two Pullman plants, as Howard had advised.

Three men were assigned to carry the final demand to Wickes. He flatly refused to deal with them. The next day, Saturday, June 23, the first American Railway Union convention adjourned. In his closing speech, Debs told members that the only action he disagreed with was the continued exclusion of Negroes from the union. He sent the convention delegates home, advising them to become "missionaries" for the cause.

❧

On Sunday, June 24, the *Chicago Tribune* predicted "serious complications" and "widespread disorders" if the ARU went ahead with its threatened boycott. The paper had long advocated for the pro-business policies of the Republican Party. The reporter foresaw conflict between the new union and the established railroad brotherhoods, although he judged that many individual firemen and engineers sympathized with the Pullman strikers.

That same day, the highly popular president of France, Sadi Carnot, was stabbed and mortally wounded by an anarchist. The assassination sent a wave of revulsion around the world, raising the specter of new chaos inspired by radicals. The murder also added another dose of apprehension to the tense situation in America, where the Coxey armies, the anger in the coal fields, and the ravages of the depression all kept nerves on edge.

On the surface, Pullman vice president Wickes was sanguine. He said he did not think that railroad workers were "likely to precipitate a disturbance at this time, when so many people are out of employment." In any case, the question of a boycott was "wholly a matter between the railroads and their employees."

In fact, nobody knew what would happen. Debs was frantically planning for contingencies. He understood that the switchmen would be the front line of any boycott. If they disconnected Pullman cars from trains or refused to couple them, they could inspire other railroad men to act. But, as the *Tribune* said, "the measure of success in this is speculative."

The intent of the union's action was to dry up Pullman revenues, which now came entirely from the operation of company-owned sleeping cars. But Debs knew that railroad workers had a long list of complaints against their own employers, including pay cuts, blacklisting, increased hours, arbitrary treatment, disregard of seniority rights, and discrimination against ARU members. These grievances could prompt ARU locals around the country to take actions on their own. Wildcat strikes would quickly wrench the matter out of the control of the directors in Chicago.

Debs wanted to keep the issue as focused as possible. He insisted that the union was not pushing for recognition by the railroads or trying to undo all wrongs. Members would simply refuse to handle Pullman cars in sympathy with the aggrieved strikers in Chicago. Union officials were sure the public would see that this was a selfless action, necessitated by George Pullman's intransigence.

As events approached a climax, Debs swung between reluctance and excitement. He suddenly knew what it felt like to be sitting on the engineer's side of the cab in the locomotive of history, to have a hand on the throttle of power. The entire nation, for better or worse, would feel the impact of what Debs did, how he exercised control, how he inspired and directed his men.

He set up his headquarters at Ulrich's Hall and spent Sunday and Monday communicating with ARU locals around the country. In frantic dots and dashes, his orders went out over the wires. Although the long-distance telephone had been demonstrated at last year's world's fair, its application was still limited. Western Union remained the principal means of communication between cities.

Debs instructed car inspectors to refuse to approve Pullman cars, switchmen not to attach them, engineers and brakemen not to haul trains that included them. It would be up to railroad managers to decide. They could continue to operate without the sleeping cars, putting pressure on George Pullman to arbitrate. Or they could bring on a tie-up of their own lines by dismissing employees who disobeyed orders or by replacing them with non-union men. In that case, Debs directed all members to stop work on that line until their brothers were reinstated.

On the morning of Tuesday, June 26, the nation held its breath. The clock ticked down. Noon came with no word from Pullman. Messengers wore out their legs running from Ulrich's Hall to the telegraph office.

Officials of the Illinois Central Railroad had ordered that the trains for that day be made up before the deadline, with Pullman sleepers included. The cars were padlocked together and guards assigned to each train.

Large crowds gathered near Chicago rail stations hoping to see "sensational developments," a newspaper said. They were disappointed. A limited train to New Orleans, including a Pullman car, was scheduled to leave at 1:35 p.m. Switchmen made up the train. The engineer backed the locomotive down the track to couple with the cars. The passengers stepped aboard. The train pulled out. A Sioux City express with a Pullman car left twenty-five minutes later, also without incident.

In the evening, with the glow of midsummer washing the sky, George Pullman took a short walk from his Prairie Avenue mansion to the Twelfth Street Station on the Illinois Central line. He wanted to watch the Diamond Special depart. The luxury train, made up entirely of Pullman cars, ran from Chicago to St. Louis every evening. Tonight it was crowded with delegates headed to the Democratic state political convention in Springfield.

The scene was tense but orderly. A dozen police officers eyed curious spectators. Pullman and a group of Illinois Central officials waited. At twenty minutes past the train's scheduled 9:00 p.m. departure time, the conductor shouted his signal. The engine released a chuff of steam. The couplings clicked together. The cars lurched gently into motion.

Disappointed spectators turned away. George Pullman, with a taste of victory on his tongue, headed home. As dark settled on the scene, a roughly clad youth shouted, "Look out for tomorrow!"

11

The Crisis Has Come

ETTLING DOWN IN BED AFTER WATCHING THE DIAMOND
Special chug out of the station on the first evening of the boycott,
George Pullman may have imagined that the whole thing had been
a bluff. His friends among the railroad managers had let him
know they intended to stand firm. Why would their employees risk
their jobs solely for the benefit of a few ungrateful mechanics, carpenters,
and seamstresses in his shops? A sympathy strike, they called it, but how
far could sympathy go? In his experience, not far.

The passengers on that night's Special soon found out differently.
Their trip was interrupted before they cleared the city limits. The train
stopped and started, stopped again. They could hear voices outside in the
dark. The Illinois Central night switchmen were refusing to handle the
all-Pullman train. Supervisors, with much confusion and delay, had to
work the unfamiliar switches to direct the cars onto the proper rails.

By morning, Illinois Central switchmen were refusing all Pullman
cars. The railroad company promptly dismissed any man who refused
to follow orders. By midmorning, thirty-five hundred trainmen and shop
workers had walked off the job, demanding that their brothers' employment be returned and that the company stop running Pullman cars. Debs
quickly offered protection to all categories of Illinois Central workers,
whether ARU members or not. The boycott was taking hold. The entire
line was soon paralyzed.

Illinois Central officials were surprised by the suddenness of the action. Other lines, including the Chicago & North Western, the Burlington, and the Santa Fe, soon began to have trouble moving trains as well. "If the railroad companies insist on handling Pullman cars, they will be tied up," ARU director and secretary Sylvester Keliher announced.

Within three days, the *New York Times* was reporting that "the Illinois Central, Chicago Great Western, Baltimore & Ohio, Chicago and Northern Pacific, and the lines interested in the Western Indiana System are tied up completely. Seventy-five cars of perishable freight tonight lie sidetracked. One hundred carloads of bananas are between New Orleans and Chicago, and it is not thought they can be delivered." It was not long before the heavy sweetness of rotting fruit began to pervade rail yards across the country's midsection.

The Pullman plant in Chicago remained closed. George Howard had organized ARU locals at the Pullman shop in Wilmington, Delaware, but only a minority of the workers there had joined the strike—the rest continued to work on cars. At maintenance and repair shops in St. Louis and Ludlow, Kentucky, most men walked out on the second day of the boycott. Company managers immediately began to recruit replacements. St. Louis reopened after two weeks, Ludlow a short time later. Keeping the lucrative sleepers rolling was far more important to Pullman executives than the shutdown of the company's manufacturing operation.

Recognizing the growing scale of the action, Eugene Debs kept pulling back on the reins. "We do not wish to interfere with trains that are already made up," he said. Nor should members waylay cars containing passengers. "The switchmen are with us and will obey orders." He did not intend to shut down any rail line unless its managers insisted on hauling Pullman cars.

Debs urged railroad employees not to make their own demands an issue. Of course they were eager to regain the wages they had received before recent cuts, but he asked that the matter "be postponed and our whole attention devoted to the Pullman boycott. When it is won, restoration of wages will be an easy matter."

～

To turn water and fire into motion, a locomotive depended on a firebox and smoke box, steam chest and pistons, side rods and main rods and valve rods, brakes and couplings, crosshead, flue tubes, blast pipes, superheater, journal box, and many other pieces of intricate machinery. But another complex technical system was equally critical. A proliferation of roundhouses, train yards, switches, signals, crossings, frogs, points, gates, and interlocking towers enabled men to make up, maneuver, and direct the trains along the vast web of tracks that spanned the country. Dozens of lines crisscrossed, intersected, and merged near stations and terminals. Seeing that each train found its way onto the right set of rails at the right time was a crucial skill.

Switchmen, signalmen, make-up and break-down crews, all worked to shuffle and couple together the cars. Tower men hauled on levers to throw switches to regulate traffic in a station. Shop men cleaned and repaired engines. These men were lower on the labor hierarchy than engineers, firemen, and conductors, but they could add a Pullman car to a train or cut it out. They could pull a switch or close a gate, forcing a train carrying the contraband cars to stop.

The boycott teetered on a fulcrum of action and example. Every switchman looked to his fellow switchmen, every fireman or brakeman cast a glance at what others were doing. If men around them were walking off, they might take heart and join. If not, they were inclined to hesitate. The decision to risk your livelihood and perhaps your career as a railroad man was a weighty one. Often it was the courage of a single man who set the process in motion.

On the Illinois Central, gate tender Frank G. Hackett walked away from his post in a Chicago rail yard. No one at the crossing was authorized to open the gate—a suburban train had to stop. Other trains could not proceed. More men quit.

In St. Louis, John Lally, a boss switchman on the Missouri Pacific, flatly refused to make up trains with Pullman cars. He was dismissed. Sixty switchmen walked out with him. Lally became a strike leader.

Debs encouraged the men. "There will be no settlement on any basis," he assured them, "until each man on every road is reinstated. This is a fight to the finish."

Thousands of individual actions were now taking effect. The vital, intricately organized system of American railroads was slowing down and, in much of the western part of the country, grinding to a halt.

౼

On June 27, the day after the boycott began, congressmen in Washington signaled their regard for the country's workingmen by making Labor

Day a national holiday. The day was already an official end-of-summer tradition in more than half the states. The federal representatives now declared the first Monday in September a federal holiday—Grover Cleveland signed the bill the next day.

The timing of the action led many commentators down the years to cite Labor Day as a direct legacy of the Pullman strike. In fact, the legislation had been reported out of a Senate committee months before the Pullman walkout, and no contemporary observers drew a connection to the strike, which was only beginning to receive national prominence.

~

At the union's headquarters just north of the Chicago River, Debs and the ARU executive committee stayed in session all night. Telegrams arrived almost nonstop. Local unions wanted information and guidance. Should they strike now? Later? What would decide them to act?

If a railroad ran a Pullman car or if managers dismissed a man for refusing to handle such a car, Debs replied, that was cause for the rest of the men to stop work. But he urged the officers of each local to make sure that they had enough support on their line before they declared a strike. If a few men walked out and were quickly replaced, the rest of the employees on the line would be demoralized.

Debs made clear that it was the local union officials who would make the decision. This was a practical necessity—he could not know the conditions faced by hundreds of separate organizations spread across the country. It was also a legal safeguard. The ARU had no official standing in the Pullman dispute, nor was the union recognized by any railroad. Debs wanted to protect the leadership from charges of conspiracy. The entire action, he said, was resulting from the men's initiative, not from his orders. The decisions were made by men "who say they are bound to quit work until the troubles at Pullman are adjusted and ask us to direct them."

In spite of his initial reluctance to commit the ARU to a boycott, Debs embraced his role as a duty and a pleasure. He was a man who liked a fight when he saw it as a struggle for justice. When he knew he was in the right, his moral certainty verged on smugness.

The *Chicago Tribune* labeled the union leader Dictator Debs, a title other newspapers quickly adopted. Editors pictured him as a potentate whose whim was law on the railroads. Yet both his nature and the circumstances made Debs the opposite of a dictator. He was not driving the strike. From the day the boycott began, he was riding a bucking bronco. The actions and aspirations of 150,000 men—their frustration, fear, courage, and rage—were in control.

‫◞‬

Having spent most of his career as an organizer and leader of the Brotherhood of Locomotive Firemen, Debs knew that he could not count on the traditional railroad unions for support. These conservative organizations had fought hard to protect their members—engineers, firemen, brakemen, and others—during a time of layoffs and pay cuts. They were not about to discard their agreements in order to aid the Pullman manufacturing workers. Their leaders viewed the ARU as a potential competitor, but they were well aware that many of their members sympathized with ARU goals and had become members of that union as well.

The railroad companies focused all of their animosity on Debs and the ARU.

"I think there is no necessity for an organization of that kind," judged Everett St. John, manager of the Chicago, Rock Island & Pacific Railroad. "We have gotten along comfortably . . . with the old orders," he asserted, meaning the brotherhoods.

Debs wired all the leaders of the old orders on the first day of the strike. He knew that most of their members would, out of pride and principle, refuse to work alongside non-union men if the railroads brought in scabs. It was in their blood and he counted on it.

The brotherhood leaders were Debs's longtime friends and colleagues. All relayed their reluctance to get involved in the boycott. Some softened their opposition—Frank Sargent, the leader of the BLF, said he respected the strikers for putting up a fight. Others were more blunt—Miles Barrett of the Switchmen's Mutual Aid Society said his group had no argument with the Pullman Company. Thousands of switchmen ignored his directives and joined the boycott.

Officials of the Knights of Labor, on the other hand, backed the ARU enthusiastically. On the second day of the boycott, Debs and Howard met with James Sovereign, the Grand Master Workman of the Knights. The forty-year-old Sovereign, a former marble cutter and experienced labor organizer, had urged all his members to oppose "plutocratic enslavement" and to fight "tyranny and the tyrant." He sent wires to KOL-affiliated freight handlers and stevedores around the country, telling them to be ready to go out at a moment's notice.

"The fight is on," Sovereign declared. "The crisis has come. At no time in the history of the nation was the issue between labor and corporations so sharply drawn and well defined."

⌒

On Friday, June 29, three days into the boycott, George Pullman decided to forgo the social season in Chicago in order to repair to his summer home on the New Jersey seashore. Pullman and his servants rode a Pennsylvania Railroad train out of Chicago. His family followed the next day.

"Strike situation very serious," his wife, Hattie, recorded in her diary. "Did not take our private car." The worry was that the distinctive Pullman "varnish" would attract attention from strikers. Hattie, Florence, Harriett, and George Jr. traveled in a special car hooked to a Pennsylvania Railroad train. The departure was accomplished quietly, with the Pullmans evading the journalists camped outside their mansion. Guards took up posts to police the property.

While the railroad boycott swept over the country, Pullman, ensconced in his seaside mansion, made a show of his nonchalance. He commuted to New York as usual. He kept in close touch with Thomas Wickes and other company executives, but he publicly showed no sign of concern. He followed the course of events through his many contacts among railroad directors.

Wealth often carries with it an underlying dread. Below his placid surface, Pullman was subject to fits of nervousness. During the strikes that had marked the eight-hour movement in the 1880s, he had written to Hattie: "My anxiety is very great although it is said that I appear very cool and unconcerned."

Now he shared the worries of America's propertied class. Like many, he sensed that what the country was facing was not a simple demand for a few dollars more in a paycheck but a concerted effort by workingmen to overturn society and put themselves in the driver's seat. He was determined that it would not happen.

"This trouble has now outgrown our jurisdiction," he observed, insisting that the strike in his shop was merely a "subsidiary feature" of the developing conflict. The ARU boycott, he declared, was "pernicious, destructive to order in society, and in truth anarchistic."

Anarchism, a political philosophy with deep historical roots, was frequently conflated with anarchy, which implied chaos, disorder, and violent action. During the crisis, the editors of hostile newspapers—most of the dailies in Chicago and across the country—hurled the slur of "anarchy" against the railroad workers and their leaders. Soon it would be voiced even by the attorney general of the United States.

12

We Mean Business

ANARCHY WAS ANATHEMA TO GROVER CLEVELAND, AND THE president viewed the developing chaos on the nation's railroads with concern. Like George Pullman, Cleveland had spent his formative years in western New York State. The son of a poor Presbyterian minister, Cleveland had settled in Buffalo in 1852 and become a hardworking lawyer. He traveled rarely, read little, and took no interest in music or culture, relaxing instead with poker games and a bachelor's life.

After a brief stint as Erie County sheriff, eleven months as mayor of Buffalo, and two years as governor of New York, the untested politician won the 1884 Democratic nomination for president. During the election, Cleveland endured references to his illegitimate child and chants of "Ma, ma, where's my Pa?" Yet he managed to win by a hair to become the first Democratic president since the Civil War. For a man conspicuously lacking in charisma, it was a startling political ascent.

Organized labor, responsive to urban Democratic machine politics and repelled by Republicans' obeisance to business interests and high tariffs, backed Cleveland during the election. Yet while the conservative Cleveland mouthed sympathy for the workingman, he had done little to protect employees from the hardball tactics of their bosses.

Cleveland's provincialism limited his understanding of the dynamic changes that the industrial revolution had imposed on the nation. During his first term, he signed a law awarding $26 million in loans to private railroad corporations. With the same pen, he vetoed a $10,000 allocation voted by Congress so that farmers recovering from a Texas drought could buy seeds. "Though the people support the Government," Cleveland had declared, "the Government should not support the people."

In 1888, the people failed to support him, replacing him with Benjamin Harrison. The Republican restored sky-high tariffs to protect American industry. The resulting flow of revenue stimulated a steep rise in government spending. Farmers and ordinary consumers, stung by rising prices, decided that Cleveland was the lesser of two evils after all. In an 1892 election rematch, Cleveland was returned to office, the only president elected to nonconsecutive terms.

Back in the White House at the age of fifty-seven, he governed by rote, promising that "no harm shall come to any business interest as the result of administrative policy so long as I am president."

⁓

Lester F. Ward, a prominent sociologist of the day, concluded that America suffered from "under-government, from the failure of government to keep pace with the change which civilization had wrought." Since the rapid and overwhelming concentration of wealth represented the gravest threat to society, he thought, public officials had a duty to bring it under "judicious regulation."

Cleveland disagreed. He had filled his administration with businessmen, bankers, and Wall Street speculators. In doing so, he had tipped the scales in the great debate that had been raging since the Civil War about the proper balance of power between organized capital and the men and women who toiled.

Prompted by the Supreme Court, the government had ceded more and more power to corporations. These private entities had originally been intended to serve a public function, such as building a canal or running a railroad. Each had to be created by a separate law passed by a state legislature. But with the rapid growth of industrialism, the corporation had shed its public-benefit function and become simply another way of structuring capital. It was a particularly desirable one for businessmen, in that it shielded its owners from personal liability for debts incurred by the company. And unlike most partnerships, it outlived its original organizers.

During Cleveland's first term, the court decided a case known as

Santa Clara County v. Southern Pacific Railroad Company. Its ruling was interpreted to mean that "corporations are persons" in the eyes of the Constitution. The Fourteenth Amendment, intended to endow freed slaves with the rights of citizens, was cited to protect corporations from being deprived of "life, liberty, or property, without due process of law." Later rulings held that the Constitution protected corporations from some government regulatory measures and afforded them a breadth of rights and privileges. Judges and politicians assumed that competition would thwart any effort by corporations to abuse their privileges. The market, not the government, would serve as the regulator.

Railroad managers took advantage of the powers ceded to them by the state, but they preferred to limit competition when it was to their advantage. Railroad corporations had unprecedented amounts of capital at risk, and owners knew that competition could curb revenues. Monopolies, trusts, holding companies, collusion to fix prices, and other methods of avoiding conflict became increasingly common.

If monopoly meant corporations could raise prices, it also allowed them to lower wages. The growing size of railroad companies diminished the bargaining power of workers. This was the imbalance that Eugene Debs hoped to address with his massive industrial union. The ARU, he hoped, would give workers the clout to stand up to the monopolists.

"The corporation plunders by the permission of or through the agency of the state," said populist politician James Baird Weaver in 1892. Corporate law gave George Pullman the right to ignore the requests of the civil authorities even as he called on the government to protect his property. It let railroad corporations soak up subsidies and land grants, then conspire together to raise rates and cut wages.

～

The railroad managers, along with George Pullman and other business leaders, insisted on an axiom of capitalism: workers' wages must be determined by supply and demand. Companies, competing for labor when it was in short supply, would offer higher wages to attract employees. When too many men were looking for work, individuals would compete with each other, causing pay to fall.

In 1886, the railroads formed an organization to short-circuit this dynamic. It was this formal but extralegal body that would become the driving force behind the crisis that was now unfolding across the nation.

The group went by the bland name of General Managers' Association, or GMA. It included the top managers of the twenty-four railroads that were based in or had lines passing through Chicago. They were a formidable bunch, controlling $818 million in capital, 40,000 miles of rail, and 221,000 employees.

Set up to deal in a coordinated way with a potential strike, the GMA was from its beginning an anti-labor organization. To paper over that fact, the managers declared that the purpose of the group was to consider "problems of management arising from the operation of railroads." They claimed to be meeting to sort out issues like the handling of livestock and routines for switching cars. Their goal, they said, was to provide seamless service to shippers as their products traveled the various interconnected lines.

In fact, the managers' principal goal was to hold down wages and to prevent member companies from having to compete against each other for workers. The companies asserted that wage competition on the various lines actually led to worker discontent and that their employees were better off with a single pay rate enforced across the industry. The real goal of a standard wage rate was increased profits for the roads' stockholders.

In 1890, Congress had enacted an antitrust act sponsored by Ohio senator John Sherman, a law outlawing activity that restrained free commerce among states. Although Sherman's law was on the books, Grover Cleveland's pro-business administration had yet to prosecute successfully a single antitrust case. George Pullman took advantage of the lapse to dictate rates on almost all sleeping cars in the country.

Sherman declared, "I regard the Pullman Company and the Sugar Trust as the most outrageous monopolies of the day." The firm made what Sherman considered "enormous and disproportionate profits in the cars." Indeed, profit margins in excess of 50 percent were standard at Pullman.

In 1892, alarmed by workers' growing demands for a bigger slice of the pie, the parent railroad corporations had reshaped the GMA into an even more aggressive anti-labor strike force, but its wage- and price-fixing still brought no government scrutiny. The group established a series of committees to handle labor problems for all railroads. One was responsible for recruiting replacement workers in the event of a strike. Another developed a unified pay scale for each of the jobs on the roads. Yet another kept track of which men should and should not be hired by members—in effect a blacklist committee.

The GMA had become the most coordinated alliance of employers in the country. Its members had watched the strike at the Pullman works carefully. On the Monday before the boycott deadline, they invited Pullman vice president Wickes to a meeting to discuss how they could "act unitedly" to oppose the ARU.

Two days into the boycott, the association appointed John M. Egan as their commanding strategist. Egan set up his headquarters in the elegant Rookery Building in the heart of Chicago's financial district, barely a dozen blocks south of the ARU command post at Ulrich's Hall. He made sure he had enough telephone and telegraph lines, with clerks to man them around the clock.

Egan was a perfect choice for the job. He had lately been general manager of the Chicago Great Western Railway, which stretched from Kansas City to Minneapolis, so he knew the territory and could talk to the other managers as a peer. Having given up the post, he was free to devote all his time to combating the strike.

Now forty-six, Egan had been a railroad man since he started with the Illinois Central as an apprentice machinist at the age of fifteen. A burly, iron-jawed Irishman, he was well known for having overseen the construction of the western portion of the Canadian Pacific during the 1880s, ramming the line through craggy, mountainous terrain.

Egan was determined to play hardball. He instructed member railroads to fire any employee refusing orders. He sent agents out to recruit replacements for the strikers. The East was swarming with unemployed railroaders as a result of the depression, and Egan claimed he could import fifty thousand men if he had to. "We mean business," he told the press.

⌇

Eugene Debs understood that the American Railway Union's primary foe was no longer George Pullman but the General Managers' Association. He had to adroitly direct his own large, untested, and loosely organized union in the fight against this powerful bureaucracy. The task put enormous demands on him.

The handling of the strike depended on a flow of information. Debs faced the considerable challenge of forming a picture of the nationwide situation on the basis of telegrams, occasional firsthand reports, and newspaper accounts. These last were often inaccurate, biased, or confused.

Issues that had not occurred to ARU officers before the strike had to be decided on the fly. Should workers walk out at another car company if managers brought Pullman cars in for repair? Should they strike a Brooklyn streetcar line because the cars had been manufactured at the Pullman plant? Should the union attack a company that made switches if it sent experts to operate signals and gates on railroads that had been struck?

From the beginning, the hand that Debs was dealt had included a wild card: a growing cast of sympathizers, unemployed men, teenagers, hoodlums, and the merely curious who congregated at rail yards and crossings. The second day of the boycott, two thousand people gathered at Grand Crossing. The South Side neighborhood, barely a mile from the site of last year's Columbian Exposition, encompassed a major rail intersection where the Illinois Central converged with the Lake Shore & Michigan Southern line.

Along with Pullman strikers from the nearby model town and idle switchmen, these crowds moved onto the tracks. They blocked suburban trains as well as freight and passenger traffic, turning the morning commute into an unexpected ordeal for passengers.

As one historian pointed out, "Portly officials who had not handled a throttle in twenty years climbed into cabs" to drive trains. Railroad detectives and supervisors roamed the yards to throw switches and direct trains, occasionally getting one through the maze of tracks. With police officers looking on, crowd members were content to watch and jeer—they damaged no railroad property.

Debs said he was ready to send members out to guard railroad property if any rioting broke out. He instructed his men not to interfere with trains except by quitting work. If replacements showed up, "we will coax them not to work" but not prevent them from going about their jobs.

⌇

The goal of the managers, on the other hand, was not just to support George Pullman in his dispute with his employees. The American Railway Union posed a threat to the railroads that the individual brotherhoods never had. Alarmed by the ARU victory over the Great Northern, the managers saw the boycott as an opportunity to crush the union before it gained any more strength.

Egan vehemently denied a rumor that the GMA was pressuring George Pullman to compromise. Just the opposite. "We have organized to resist this strike to the bitter end," he said. The GMA policy was to ignore all communication from the ARU. There would be no negotiations.

In spite of the railroads' combined financial might, Egan and the managers knew they were taking a risk. The depression had already pushed numerous rail lines into bankruptcy. The others were vulnerable to any cutoff of revenues.

Nor could they count on public support. For years, railroad executives had been in wide disfavor for their arrogant and high-handed ways. Citizens in the West, who were particularly dependent on the companies, hated them. The corporations had gobbled up public land and financial subsidies while the directors cavalierly lined their own pockets. They then turned around and charged what farmers and shippers considered inordinate rates to carry goods.

On the other hand, Americans sympathized with the Pullman workers, who had become emblems of the anguish so many were enduring during this disastrous downturn. Even newspapers that raged against the boycott and "Dictator Debs" criticized George Pullman for his frustrating intransigence.

Once the boycott began, the railroads did not want Pullman to arbitrate. Any compromise would be seen as a victory for the ARU and would add to the union's strength. After the initial meeting with Wickes, the managers no longer included Pullman Company executives in their strategy sessions. Whatever its cause, the conflict was now an industrial war between two determined antagonists.

Egan assigned thirty railroad detectives to begin amassing information about ARU leaders. On June 29, he announced that any railroad employee who was discharged or quit work would be blacklisted for life, raising the stakes for the men. Replacement workers, on the other hand, would be guaranteed permanent positions.

The animosity toward the ARU extended beyond the Chicago railroads. Collis Huntington, one of the backers of the first transcontinental line and now the proprietor of the Southern Pacific, wrote privately to his nephew Henry: "I think we should get men on our own line who do not belong to any union." Henry agreed: "We are going to break this strike . . . we are making history."

Everyone from the striking switchman to the president of the United States now saw that the scope of the crisis had widened. Although the boycott was ostensibly a show of sympathy for the Pullman strikers, a *New York Times* reporter wrote, "in reality it will be a struggle between the greatest and most powerful railroad labor organization and the entire railroad capital."

13

Not a Wheel Moving

SATISFACTORY." THAT WAS EUGENE DEBS'S MODEST APPRAISAL of the boycott's progress on Saturday morning, June 30, four days into the struggle. In fact, he was thrilled at the response of the men and at the widespread tie-up of the railroads. The union he had spent the last year building was rising and flexing its muscles. LABOR LEADERS ARE JUBILANT, the *Chicago Tribune* reported.

Not just labor leaders. Philosopher and education reformer John Dewey, who had recently assumed a professorship at the University of Chicago, was also enchanted to watch history unfolding before him. After speaking to a strike organizer in Michigan, he reported to his sister that "my nerves were more thrilled than they had been for years." He was impressed by the man's "absolute fanatic sincerity." Dewey was sure that this "widespread union of men about a common interest" was "a great thing & the beginning of a greater."

The American Railway Union had developed largely as an underground organization. Because so many members were workers in the railroad shops and yards—not engineers, firemen, or conductors—industry observers underestimated the group's power to hobble the railroads. Now the ARU was emerging into the open and its impact startled the nation. The boycott was bringing rail traffic to a standstill in large parts of the country and drawing more than two hundred thousand workers into the conflict, the most widespread coordinated work stoppage in American history.

Almost every western railroad reported at least a thousand men on strike. Both railroad managers and union leaders were surprised at the eagerness of the men to quit work in support of the Pullman employees. One railroad after another had to curtail service. Passengers were stranded, commuters could not get to work, freight shipments ground to a halt.

Messengers delivered a stream of telegrams to Debs, more than two hundred in a single day. He would consider for a moment what each added to the jigsaw puzzle of the boycott, then dictate a reply to go back over the wire.

Two hundred brakemen and the same number of firemen and engineers on the Chicago Great Western had defied their traditional brotherhoods, joined the ARU, and walked off the job. In St. Paul, "the community was startled" by the suddenness of the strike.

Strikers had brought to a halt the entire Northern Pacific system where Hogan's men had hijacked a train in April. No engines were passing Livingston, Montana, in either direction. The action was being felt in Missoula—tourists on their way to visit Yellowstone National Park were stranded.

On the Santa Fe line, "not a wheel is moving on the entire New Mexico Division." Twelve hundred cars were sitting idle. Passenger service from Sacramento to San Francisco had ceased. In Oakland, Southern Pacific officials were said to be offering a $1,000 bonus and lifetime employment to engineers who remained loyal. There were no takers.

The contest in St. Louis, a newspaper reported, was "in a delightful state of uncertainty." No one knew when or if the boycott would start there. Uncertainty was the norm. The strike had failed to take hold in Cincinnati and all trains were on schedule. No, another wire read, the situation was serious in Ohio. No trains with Pullman cars were moving.

By Friday of that first week, the General Managers' Association had reported that the situation was deteriorating and the effect of the boycott "growing more serious daily." GMA strike captain John Egan admitted that the railroads were losing $250,000 a day and had already taken a hit of $1 million. The strikers, he pointed out, had themselves lost many tens of thousands in wages.

In a bad sign for the railroads, men brought in as substitutes at the beginning of the boycott were losing heart. Scabs on the Pittsburgh,

Cincinnati, Chicago & St. Louis Railroad, known as the Pan Handle Route, had been induced to quit work. In one group of thirty-two substitutes, five had joined the union and promised to convince their fellows if given protection.

❧

Not all the wires brought Debs good news. Local ARU men in Omaha refused to strike—Debs threatened to cancel their charter. Engineers on the Denver & Rio Grande Railroad had managed to get trains through Pueblo and Salida by convincing the porters who had been denied ARU membership to couple Pullman cars.

As Debs had warned at the convention, the ARU members had weakened their cause by barring African Americans. "I can see no good reason why the colored people should be concerned in this struggle at all," wrote A. E. Wilson, publisher of the *Chicago Bugle and Africo-American Patriot*. He pointed out that "last week the A.R.U. snubbed us by refusing to admit colored men as members." He advised black workers to "hold themselves aloof" from the strike.

Other black journalists labeled the strike a "white man's war." They accused the ARU of fighting for the "dignity of labor while excluding the downtrodden Negro." In Chicago, African American workers formed an Anti-Strikers Railroad Union to fill the positions of white strikers with unemployed blacks. The secretary of the African-American League of East St. Louis wrote to the General Managers' Association to offer two hundred black workers to replace striking freight handlers in that city.

Railroad managers had assumed that the hordes of unemployed workers in the eastern states would make union inroads there difficult. In rail hubs like Baltimore, Boston, and New York, Pullman cars were running without trouble.

But Debs had sent a dozen organizers eastward two days after the boycott began to try to infect men along the seaboard with strike fever. The union announced a plan to tie up eastern roads as soon as sufficient members were recruited. The Baltimore & Ohio, which already had ARU men aboard, was the first target. ARU representatives went to Jersey City to persuade switchmen and trainmen of the huge Pennsylvania Railroad system to join the boycott. When Monday came, the union, said to have five thousand sympathizers in western Pennsylvania, would ask railroad men in Pittsburgh to stop handling Pullman cars.

༄

Federal circuit court judge William Howard Taft of Ohio had made deputies of trainmen to help managers operate trains on the Queen & Crescent Route out of Cincinnati. "The starvation of a nation," the future president stated, "cannot be a lawful purpose of a combination." He said that the "gigantic character of the conspiracy of the American Railway Union staggers the imagination."

The affair had grown far beyond the Pullman works. "Mr. Pullman is not being considered in the controversy nor will he be," John Egan said. He told the press that he thought the strikers capable of anything. "The situation is becoming critical and in a few hours we will be in the midst of a reign of physical violence."

The *New York Times* declared that the strike had "assumed the proportions of the greatest battle between labor and capital that has ever been inaugurated in the United States."

༄

In Chicago, the first days of the strike had brought the prospect of trouble to the Union Stock Yard. A cutoff of rail service to "Packingtown" would throw twenty thousand butchers and meatpackers out of work. The nation's largest source of meat would be shut down. A union official was reported to have said that the plan was "to starve the people of the East and bring 'em in line."

The *Chicago Tribune* had called the Union Stock Yard the "eighth wonder of the world." This enormous reeking warren of pens, chutes, and slaughterhouses in the center of Chicago's South Side had opened just after the Civil War. Meatpackers like Philip Armour and Gustavus Swift now used assembly-line logistics and cheap labor to kill as many as twenty-five hundred steers and seven thousand hogs every day. The operation, which processed three-quarters of the nation's meat, was America's first big step toward the industrialization of food.

The yard was a city in itself. Twenty separate rail lines ran through and around the great complex to bring livestock in and haul dressed beef and pork out in cars packed with blocks of ice. "We have in our power to cut off all food supplies from Chicago," the chairman of the stockyard strike committee said, "and we will do it, if necessary, to win this contest."

Packingtown was both a boon and a bane to Chicago. An engine of prosperity, it also contributed an effluvium of rancid smells that wafted over whole neighborhoods. The continual bellowing, bleating, and squealing of doomed animals added to the city's discordant music. The tenements around the yards were among the worst in the city, filled with slaughterhouse workers and poor immigrants. Many of the butchers employed by the meat companies had complaints of their own about pay, hours, and working conditions.

By Saturday, the disruption of rail traffic had virtually shut down the vast abattoir, throwing many hog stickers and meat cutters out of work. Supervisors stored as much meat as possible in ice houses, but without deliveries of coal to run the engines that manufactured the ice, the carcasses of steers and hogs would soon begin to stink. The Illinois Humane Society sent inspectors to examine the trainloads of cattle sitting motionless on Illinois Central tracks near Forty-Third Street. The beeves were packed into cars without food or water under a relentless sun. The Society reported great suffering.

⌒

It was not just animals that were suffering. Across the country, the effects of the boycott were beginning to be felt, and citizens' fascination was turning to distress. Particularly in the West, many communities were utterly dependent on the railroads. Horses and wagons could not begin to fill the void. As Jacob Coxey had pointed out, most of the nation's roads were rutted dirt tracks.

Food, fuel, and friends arrived by rail. Milk that was not quickly loaded onto refrigerated cars spoiled. Vegetables rotted. During the first days of the boycott, the Illinois Central began refusing perishable loads. By the end of the week, the line was no longer taking freight of any kind. The Baltimore & Ohio also stopped accepting perishables.

The price of provisions across the country quickly jumped to "astonishing figures," a newspaper reported. The price of meat and vegetables doubled. It was predicted that the price of all foodstuffs would skyrocket the following week. This during a withering depression when many families were struggling to afford a meal. With Chicago baking in eighty-degree heat, the price of ice jumped from $2.50 to $10.00 a ton.

The strike locked up the Chicago and Calumet Terminal, cutting off fuel oil to the Standard Oil plant and the Chicago Sugar Refinery. Two thousand men lost their jobs when the sugar plant curtailed operations.

In northern California, fruit growers and canners were worried. Without a rapid restoration of rail transport, the ripening crop would become worthless. In West Superior, Wisconsin, two flour mills, dependent on the Northern Pacific and the Wisconsin Central, had to close. Three coal docks could no longer operate.

In Milwaukee, brewers could send out only half their usual daily production. Pabst planned to charter a steamboat to take beer to Chicago if the tie-up continued.

♾

None of this had been the intended result of the boycott. Debs and the other ARU leaders had envisioned a struggle over the inclusion or cutting out of Pullman cars. They had not expected the railroad managers to declare all-out war or to risk bringing about such a profound impact on the nation's population.

The effect on passengers in particular preyed on Debs's mind. The traveling public was growing fearful. In Chicago, a Baltimore & Ohio train had been pelted with rocks. The missiles smashed windows and injured several passengers. Police could not cope with the situation. Many patrons began to avoid trains—the Pennsylvania Limited train pulled out of Chicago twenty minutes late with only thirty Pullman passengers aboard.

On that first Saturday of the boycott, a Pan Handle train from New York was halted by a crowd of more than a thousand strikers in Hammond, Indiana, an industrial and residential city that abutted Chicago's South Side. While the crew argued with the rioters, many of the passengers climbed down from the Pullman cars and made their way to Chicago as best they could.

Debs was concerned that public support for the strikers might give way to sympathy for passengers. On some stopped trains, women and children were left for up to twenty hours with no water or food. He gave orders to union men not to interfere with passenger trains already on the road. But the dark green Pullman cars were a tempting target for strikers' anger.

The tie-up of travel produced serious inconveniences. A man trying to reach his desperately ill child in Chicago found himself stranded in Decatur, Illinois. ARU members manned a handcar to help a woman and child from Ellensburg, Washington, travel four hundred miles to reach the bedside of her dying husband in Idaho.

Jane Addams was one of many citizens whose life the strike disrupted. Her sister Mary, who had helped raise her after their mother's death, was gravely ill in a Kenosha, Wisconsin, sanitarium. Jane, occupied with her duties at Hull House and her attempts to mediate the strike, could only get away briefly for visits. When Mary's condition worsened, she rushed to Kenosha, using her connections with the strikers to be allowed passage on a mail train. Mary's husband, hampered by the strike, was not able to reach Kenosha for another day. By then, his wife was unconscious from a brain hemorrhage. She died the next day.

At 10:00 a.m. on Saturday, June 30, strikers in southern Illinois stopped a train carrying a troop of militiamen. It turned out that the passengers were thirty members of a volunteer Zouave unit, decked out in colorful pantaloons and fezzes. They were already late for a drill contest in Memphis and would now have to search out alternative transportation.

Later that day, the Hammond strikers stopped an express train from Louisville. They uncoupled the Pullman sleeper and dining car and pushed them by hand onto a side track. Passengers protested but had no choice but to climb into the remaining day coaches and find standing room. Strikers boarded the disabled dining car and availed themselves of a banquet, a newspaper reported, consisting of "Mr. Pullman's bouillon, porterhouse steaks, ice cream, Apollinaris water, champagne and other good things."

More than anything else, Debs was worried that the strike would descend into violence. He understood that it was the peaceful nature of the Great Northern action that had given the union its opportunity for a victory there.

"I appeal to the striking men everywhere to refrain from any act of violence," he pleaded. "Let there be no interference with the affairs of the several companies involved, and above all, let there be no act of depredation. A man who will destroy property or violate law is an enemy and not a friend to the cause of labor."

Up to that point, the strike had been remarkably peaceful. There had been some minor sabotage—switches jammed open, padlocks on car couplings forced, stones hurled by vandals—but no widespread disorder. The crowds of strikers and sympathizers had been vociferous but not unruly. For the most part, strikers had tried to talk replacements over to their side rather than intimidate or assault them. All of this was gratifying to Debs.

John Egan of the GMA, on the other hand, seemed to relish the possibility of disorder. "I do not see how the police will be able to battle such an extended evil," he said. He too knew that Americans' nightmares included keen memories of the labor unrest of the past. The violence of the 1877 rail strike was still vivid to many. The bombing at Haymarket Square in 1886 had been stamped into the consciousness of Chicagoans. And echoes of the gunfight that accompanied the 1892 Homestead steel strike had barely died away.

The railroad managers pointed to the dangerous potential of the crowds that were gathering at various rail yards and switching points in Chicago and elsewhere. They demanded that the authorities act. Neither Chicago mayor Hopkins nor police superintendent Michael Brennan thought there was cause for alarm. Cook County sheriff James H. Gilbert recruited some extra deputies but reported no violence in his jurisdiction around Chicago's outskirts.

⁂

With summer, the marching drums of Coxey's industrial armies had become muted. The Pullman strike was now the big news. The traveling bands of the unemployed elicited only a paragraph or two on the inside pages.

Yet the murmur of their protest kept the nation on edge. The men would not give up. Coxeyites had gained free passage on more than fifty trains across the West, sometimes simply riding boxcars en masse, sometimes commandeering a whole train. Where one newspaper said it came down to "law or anarchism," another pointed a finger at corporate directors, asserting that stealing trains was insignificant when "so-called railroad kings steal entire railroads."

A manager of the Rock Island Railroad described Charles Kelley as "a man of brains and character and great determination." He said it was sad to find so many "respectable, well-meaning men reduced to such desperate straits in this country."

The men of Kelley's contingent had walked 130 miles from Council Bluffs eastward to Des Moines. One of the recruits who had joined them looking for adventure was an eighteen-year-old Californian named Jack London. The author was impressed by the warm welcome that awaited the bedraggled men at each town.

"Deputations of little girls and maidens came out to meet us," he wrote. "And the good citizens turned out by hundreds, locked arms, and marched with us down their main streets. It was circus day when we came to town."

But having reached the Iowa state capital, they were not about to march anymore. Kelley saw that if they took boats down the Des Moines River they could reach the Mississippi, then the Ohio. Navigating eastward to Wheeling they would find themselves only three hundred miles from Washington, D.C.

Des Moines citizens donated money, lumber, rope, and caulking. Kelley's men built more than a hundred eighteen-foot-long flat-bottom boats. On Wednesday, May 9, 1894, a good part of Des Moines's population came out to watch nine hundred men embark on what London called "our colossal picnic." Kelley's army had become a navy. Twelve days later, they were on the banks of the mighty Mississippi.

They continued to struggle eastward, determined to bring their message to Washington. Along the way, thousands of citizens cheered them on. They landed north of Cairo and prepared to head up the Ohio River. Relying on donations, they hired a tug and two barges. They reached Cincinnati. Labor unions there helped them continue on another hundred miles to Portsmouth, Ohio. By this time Kelley had taken ill. He sent his men on to reach Washington any way they could, promising to join them there later.

The men of the industrial armies accomplished something by standing for something. Critics questioned how these jobless crusaders, a portion of them inveterate hoboes, could represent respectable workers. But they did. They personified the underlying feeling of dread that afflicted so many industrial wage earners. Every workingman in the country knew that a shift in the market or the whim of a supervisor could leave him unemployed and destitute. The Coxeyites were a living demand that something had to change.

"These men," a reporter for the *Seattle Press-Times* wrote, "after their own fashion are building more wisely than they know." They were pressuring a reluctant, laissez-faire government to take more responsibility for the nation's economy and for the well-being of its citizens. It could be called paternalism, or it could be called simple decency, but many Americans were inspired to give it consideration.

"This movement," Jacob Coxey said, "has attracted the attention of the country as nothing else in the way of labor agitation has ever done, and nothing else without violence ever could have done."

In the process, his followers established the march on Washington as a typically American form of protest. It would become with time a venerable tradition. Citizens would march for women's suffrage in 1913, for relief from hard times in 1932, for civil rights in 1963, and for other causes down the years.

Editors of the *Tacoma Daily News* told readers that they had reason to be proud of Coxey's Army, whose members upheld American values. "These men who feel themselves wronged do not propose to kill and overthrow—they do not march with guns—they do not threaten—they appeal—they petition—they protest—they reason."

14

Disaster Threatens

Although Debs had started that Saturday, June 30, feeling events were proceeding satisfactorily, by midday he sensed a change in the tone of the action. Maybe it was the accumulated impatience of the strikers. Maybe it was the weather—temperatures in Chicago pushed into the high eighties that day, with occasional rumbles of thunder. Whatever the cause, the mood—not just in Chicago—grew darker and more ominous all day.

For Debs, the main business of the morning was a meeting with officials of Chicago's Trades and Labor Assembly. They gathered in Ulrich's Hall to show support for the ARU and to discuss the potential for coordinated action. Enthusiasm for the boycott verged on euphoria as hundreds of union representatives expressed their elation at its progress.

Although the gathering had the flavor of a pep rally, the boycott's success raised a question. Was this the time for more unions to join in? Did the boycott represent the great crisis of industrialism that some had long predicted? Should working people across the city and the nation unite to tear down, once and for all, the plutocratic capitalist system?

Speakers followed each other on the platform. They raged against the hiring of private armed forces by the railroads. A representative of the American Federation of Labor called George Pullman a czar more vile than any in Russia. Another orator said this was the greatest battle for human rights in history. The announcement that the Rock Island line was entirely tied up brought an eruption of cheers.

George Howard took the stage to declare that the railroads could not stand the losses they were enduring. Five lines were close to negotiating peace. The companies were clearly violating their franchises by refusing to supply transportation to the public as required by their charters. Their insistence that Pullman cars be attached even to trains that did not normally include them violated the law.

Fanny Kavanaugh, an ally of Jane Addams and a prime mover of the Illinois Women's Alliance, took an important role in shaping the resolutions that the labor representatives passed. She proposed they call on Governor Altgeld to demand that railroad officials run their trains without Pullman cars within twenty-four hours or have their charters forfeited and the lines taken over by the state.

The representatives demanded to hear from Debs. He mounted the podium, sweating in the sultry heat. In the days before microphone amplification, the ability to project speech was important. Debs, an inveterate self-improver, had applied himself to the techniques of elocution and the principles of oratory. He talked in pictures and parables, offered visions rather than statistics. He had learned to enunciate, to explode his vowels and control his pitch. His speaking style was gymnastic—he threw out his rangy arms, pointed with his bony finger, pounded home his message.

It was absolutely certain, he said, that labor would prevail. This was not a fight of the American Railway Union alone, but of all the men on the roads. The railroad directors "for once will feel the full power of organized labor." The strike was a first step toward government ownership of the railroads, the telegraph companies, and any other monopolies that scorned the public good.

"It no longer turns on the question of Pullman cars." The struggle had gone beyond the point of any armistice. "They are going to import scabs," he predicted. "They will employ some miserable persons to set fire to a few old box cars as a pretense for calling out the militia."

But workers would remain united. They would bring to bear their mighty weapon, the withholding of labor. "There will not be a man left to sweep the streets of Chicago." He was sure that the General Managers' Association would fall within a fortnight. A soldier of the Coxeyite armies rose to nominate Debs for president of the United States in the next election.

The participants resolved that the unions of the assembly be prepared to call out their members in the coming week if such an action was deemed necessary to support the railroad men. Debs accepted the potent threat with the provision that they not strike until called upon.

Union men, a newspaper said, "have caught strike fever." It was widely feared that the trade union members would not wait for ARU approval but would soon initiate a general strike in Chicago. "The ultimate disaster which is bound to follow," a *New York Times* reporter declared, "is sufficient in appearance to cause the most courageous to shudder."

～

That weekend, journalists were estimating that railroads covering two-thirds of the nation had been completely tied up or seriously impaired. Tens of thousands of men were continuing to walk out.

The struggle had so far been a contest between the American Railway Union and the nation's railroad corporations as represented by the General Managers' Association. If that had remained the contest, the outcome was uncertain, although the union was thought by many to have the edge. But on that muggy Saturday, a new element entered the equation.

Many assumed that in a controversy between two private entities—the railroads and the union, both acting within their rights under the law—the government would serve as a neutral umpire, maintaining order and enforcing statutes but otherwise staying out of the matter. Grover Cleveland had other ideas.

When forming his cabinet, Cleveland had asked Richard Olney, a railroad attorney with no political experience, to become his attorney general. Olney agreed on the condition that he be allowed to continue representing his clients while in office. He had served as corporate counsel for the Boston & Maine Railroad for the past ten years and, along with George Pullman, was still a director of that company. He continued to supplement his $8,000 government salary with the $10,000 he received as counsel to the Chicago, Burlington & Quincy Railroad. He also sat on the boards of directors of the Vanderbilts' New York Central system and the Santa Fe line.

Cleveland saw no conflict of interest in the arrangement, but the *San Francisco Call* noted that the attorney general had "not shown any disposition to quarrel with the corporations he formerly served and which, so far as the public knows, he still continues to serve."

Olney was the son of an upper-class Boston family and had been a brilliant student at Brown and Harvard Law. He was said never to have had direct contact with any member of the working class except his own servants. He had disowned his daughter for marrying a lowly dentist.

A cold, gruff individual of fifty-eight, he sported a walrus mustache similar to Cleveland's. His official portrait showed a pudgy, neckless man with arms crossed in a defiant, protective gesture—a historian wrote that he "raised truculence to an art form." His thirty-five years of practicing law had left him devoted to property rights and to the worthiness of corporations.

Although he had only met Cleveland once before joining the cabinet, Olney became his trusted adviser. His stubborn inflexibility lent him an aura of authority.

Viewing the Pullman strike and boycott through his railroad-colored spectacles, Olney saw no merit whatever in the position of the American Railway Union. Rather than seek a negotiated solution, he was determined to throw the weight of the government on the side of the GMA and break the strike, by force if necessary. In the ARU he saw a more dangerous version of the fractious marchers of Coxey's Army, whose shenanigans continued to keep him awake nights. His experience that spring had taught him that a muscular response, in the form of court orders and troops, was the best antidote to disorder. He viewed the ARU boycott as an attack on the way of life of the responsible, well-to-do people of the country—his people. He made it his personal mission to bring the union to its knees.

Olney's man on the scene in Chicago was U.S. Attorney Thomas Milchrist. Two days earlier, on Thursday, June 28, Milchrist had sat in on a GMA meeting and assured the managers of Olney's support. He had asked them to provide the names of any strikers guilty of interfering with the mails, promising to expedite warrants for their arrest. The direct collusion between the government and the managers had begun.

Having served almost two decades as a state prosecutor in a remote western Illinois prairie town, Milchrist was suspected by his superiors of having hayseeds in his cuffs. As the scope and intensity of the boycott increased during the week, Olney wanted a more forceful leader for the government's anti-strike effort. On Saturday, without consulting Milchrist, he appointed Edwin Walker to be the special U.S. attorney in

Chicago. Although ostensibly Milchrist's assistant, Walker was to take over command of the federal response to the boycott.

With Walker's appointment, Olney dropped all pretense of impartiality. The attorney had spent the past twenty-four years as counsel for the Chicago, Milwaukee & St. Paul Railroad. His law partner was a member of the General Managers' Association's legal committee. The sixty-one-year-old Walker was well connected in Chicago political circles and had served as counsel for the Columbian Exposition.

Walker immediately began to work closely with the GMA to cripple the strike, communicating directly with Olney, sometimes by coded telegram. Lawyer Clarence Darrow said of this blatant partisanship: "The government might with as good grace have appointed the attorney for the American Railway Union to represent the United States."

Walker's appointment offered evidence that the government was going beyond a simple bias toward one party in the great upheaval. The railroads, through their agents Olney and Walker, were now calling the shots. The corporations had been handed the power to prosecute American citizens with the goal of putting down the strike.

In his letter of instructions to Walker, Olney was blunt. He focused not on restoring law and order, not on compromise, but on stopping the lawful effort of the railroad workers to pressure their employers. "It has seemed to me that if the rights of the United States were vigorously asserted in Chicago, the origin and center of the demonstration," he wrote, "the result would be to make it a failure everywhere else." "It" meant the ARU boycott. Privately, he spoke of crushing the strike.

Olney wrote that it was "advisable not merely to rely on warrants against persons actually guilty of the offense of obstructing United States mails, but to go to a court of equity and secure restraining orders which shall have the effect of preventing any attempt to commit the offense." He was warming to the idea of using federal courts as an ally in the war against the union.

❧

Olney understood that he could employ the government's duty to safeguard the mail as an effective tool against any railroad strike. Because mail cars were normally hauled by passenger trains, the issue was sure to become entangled with the boycott of Pullman cars.

The rapid delivery of letters and parcels held an importance then that is hard to appreciate in an age of electronic communication. Almost all business communication, as well as private correspondence, relied on the postal system. One of the important effects of the spread of railroads had been to speed and extend the delivery of mail. Clerks on special cars picked up letters from small towns by hooking bags on the fly. They sorted mail while speeding down the tracks.

The U.S. postal system was seen as sacrosanct. Obstruction of mail was a federal crime. Debs had given specific instructions that all mail trains were to be allowed to move without delay. In the first days of the boycott, some mail was held up in the chaos. Twenty-six mail trains were delayed in Cairo, Illinois. Others were stopped in Indiana, Idaho, and San Francisco.

Postal authorities complained to the union. Debs responded that the men were not obstructing anything. They had simply withdrawn their labor, as was their right. He pointed out that most mail was getting through and that only a few mail cars had been rerouted. A postal supervisor confirmed that there was no buildup of undelivered mail in Chicago.

Nevertheless, both the railroad managers and the government saw the issue of obstruction as a fruitful pretext for attacking the ARU. The union's position was that no train carrying mail would be molested, as long as it was free of Pullman cars. The railroads complained that leaving the sleepers off scheduled trains would violate their contracts with George Pullman. They had to attach them. The fact was that those contracts in no way obligated the railroads to haul Pullman cars. Legally, their inclusion was entirely at the discretion of the roads' managers.

That was not all. The railroads normally attached mail cars directly behind the tender. Supervisors began to couple them to the backs of trains so that if Pullman cars were detached, the mail car would be as well. They began including mail cars on all suburban passenger trains as well, a move that brought those trains under federal protection.

Even government attorney Milchrist was admitting on Saturday that "all regular mail trains, except those on the Great Western, have gone out to-day about on regular time." Debs hoped he could keep the mails moving and thus deny his opponents a weapon to use against the strike.

Olney could easily have arranged to run a mail train free of Pullman cars down every line daily to assure the timely delivery of letters and parcels. That was not his goal. Like the railroad managers, he wanted the mail to be held up. He had discarded any idea of mediation. "I feel that the true way of dealing with the matter is by a force which is overwhelming and prevents any attempt at resistance." He directed the chief U.S. Marshal in Chicago, John W. Arnold, to begin amassing an armed federal force. Arnold swore in four hundred deputies.

Sparkling with names like Wyatt Earp, Bill Hickok, and Bat Masterson, the myth of the U.S. Marshals Service was already the stuff of dime novels. Those men, who sometimes straddled the line between peace officer and outlaw, had been the guardians of order in the western territories yet to achieve statehood. Most new deputies in Chicago were drawn from the hordes of unemployed men in the city, chosen more for their brawn than for their understanding of federal law.

Arnold would ultimately recruit five thousand marshals in Chicago. He sent them out in groups, mostly by stagecoach, to suburban railroad facilities in Blue Island, Riverdale, and Hammond to guard mail cars. Many more would be deployed in other jurisdictions across the country.

The marshals were, in effect, strikebreakers. At first, Arnold signed up what the railroad managers called "idlers." Then they convinced him to select deputies from the ranks of their own men. Railroad supervisors would select their strongest and most dependable employees, swear them in, give them a revolver, and pin on their chests the stars issued by the U.S. Marshal's office. The men, who made up a majority of the federal force in Chicago, continued to be paid by the companies. They constituted a private army authorized to make arrests and use deadly force.

During the strike, these marshals, aided by police, arrested about eight hundred men in Chicago. In some cases, strikers were arrested "because they refused to turn switches when told to" or "refused to get on an engine and fire an engine."

The idea of turning over the authority of the government to a police force whose clear purpose was to serve a private interest veered far from American ideals and legal traditions. On several occasions, Chicago police officers had to arrest deputy federal marshals for "indiscriminate shooting."

In Colorado, the deputies were instructed to ignore local law officers and arrest strikers without warrant. Governor Davis H. Waite protested that this amounted to "a private army" intent on "waging an active war in Colorado without any declaration thereof by the United States." The Justice Department ignored him.

Attorney General Olney, hardly given to Wild West romanticism, was skeptical of the effectiveness of these amateur lawmen. The *Chicago Herald* described them as "a low, contemptible set of men." A reporter for the *Record* said he saw more deputy marshals than strikers drunk in the streets. Even Edwin Walker would later admit to Olney the men were "worse than useless." For the time being, they were the face of the federal government confronting the strikers.

∽

Eugene Debs had yet to appreciate the new role the government was assuming, but he was becoming more and more aware of the depth of anger prevalent among his own men. He gazed out on a hot, dry emotional landscape ready to burst into flame, and he knew it was up to him to arrest any spark that might ignite a conflagration.

Men of the Chicago, Rock Island & Pacific line, the first road to bridge the Mississippi River forty years earlier, struck at seven that Saturday morning. The railroad managers, not expecting the stoppage, were taken by surprise. The road had extensive tracks through Chicago and soon found its switches spiked and some of its coaches being struck by stones as they moved along the rails.

Early on Saturday, trouble also began to brew in the vast network of rail yards and intersecting tracks south of Chicago. Lines from the east making the turn around the bottom of Lake Michigan met there with other roads from Springfield, St. Louis, and Kansas City. The area had become increasingly urban and industrial since George Pullman built his model town fourteen years earlier. In industrial communities like Riverdale and Blue Island, just south and west of the Pullman factory, great stretches of parallel tracks filling hundreds of acres were used for making up trains and for switching and storing cars. Hammond, across the Indiana border to the east, was dense with more tracks and rail facilities.

In Riverdale, a Pan Handle freight train was taken over by strikers and the cars removed. The crew and engineer were told to man what was left—an engine and caboose—and get out. The strikers said that they would kill anyone who tried to run a Pullman car down the line.

Evidence of frayed tempers began to reach Debs. In Blue Island, just south of Chicago, a mob grew enraged when two men operated a switch engine to move freight cars. Members of the crowd attacked James Stewart, who had recently arrived from Nebraska to take the place of a striking worker. They pulled him down from the locomotive and tried to drag him to a nearby saloon. He broke free and returned to the engine, bleeding and limping on a bruised foot. His companion fled and relayed his resignation by telephone.

A telegram from downstate said that in Cairo, a railroad division superintendent had argued with the switchmen's union president, who accused him of breaking his word by running a New Orleans train with six Pullman cars attached when the union had agreed to only two. They came to blows. The union man knocked the superintendent down and he had to be taken to a nearby hotel in a carriage to be treated by a physician.

A report from St. Paul detailed another tense situation. A switchman making up a train was hit by a rock, then beaten. At one in the afternoon, strikers tried to induce flagman Thomas Cole to quit. He refused. They told him that if he did not clear out he would be killed. Cole drew a revolver and said if they tried violence they were the ones who would die. Strikers jumped him from behind and knocked him down while others kicked him in the face. A policeman ran down the tracks and drove off the assailants. Cole was carried to the roundhouse and then to a hospital.

As the hot day progressed, violence continued to bubble up. Late in the afternoon, a train made up of three coaches, two Pullman sleepers, and a mail car approached Blue Island from the north. The yardmaster was guarding the switch that would allow the train to proceed. A switchman named James Murvin pushed him aside and threw the switch in the opposite direction. The massive engine, traveling slowly, left the tracks, careened down a small embankment, and came to rest at a forty-five-degree angle. Deputy sheriffs arrested Murvin. Although no injuries resulted, the derailment tore up the tracks and the disabled cars blocked the main line.

❦

That evening, the tension even got the best of George Howard. Addressing a gathering of Chicago & North Western Railway men, he told them that the general managers, those "bladder-belly bosses," were on the verge of breaking. "They can't find 'scabs' enough to take your places."

He referred to George Pullman as "a hypocrite and the rottenest-hearted individual who ever stood on American soil." Responding to raucous cheers, he shouted, "I'd like to see him hung!" Shouts of "Let's hang him!" echoed in the hall.

༄

With the arrival of darkness, the engine man who operated the electric plant at Blue Island shut off the power and joined the strike. The arc lights that glared across the yard went dark. Strikers moved through the shadows. The occasional flash of lightning from a summer thunderstorm scalded the scene.

A few minutes later, the Diamond Special, the luxury train to St. Louis, was just approaching Grand Crossing. The all-Pullman train had managed to leave Chicago and was close to clearing the environs. The engineer had made his way carefully through the city and suburbs. He eyed each crossing and switch and watched for debris on the rails. An armed special officer named McConfey was riding in the cab with him in case of trouble.

The engineer suddenly felt the sickening sensation of the engine slipping off the rails. Someone had removed the spikes from a long section of the line. The weight of the engine pushed the steel rails apart. For a moment, the massive machine continued to bump along the ties. The engineer heaved on the brake.

Passengers lurched in their seats. Place settings crashed to the floor in the elegant dining car. Muffled screams could be heard. The engine's momentum kept it moving another hundred yards, but the driver's quick action prevented the train from veering into the ditch. The tender crashed into the engine from behind, pinning McConfey's ankle. The special officer was trapped until the crew finally freed him and rushed him to St. Luke's Hospital. His foot was nearly severed.

༄

Across the country, Americans awoke on Sunday morning, July 1, to the news of the strike's ominous turn.

"LAW IS TRAMPLED ON," the *Chicago Tribune* declared. "With the coming of darkness last night," it went on, "Dictator Debs' strikers threw off the mask of law and order and began the commission of acts of lawlessness and violence."

The meeting of the trade unions was seen as especially ominous. The ARU had shown how a concerted effort could tie up one mighty railroad after another. If other workers joined in, the prospect was utter chaos.

New York Times editors declared it the "GREATEST STRIKE IN HISTORY."

15

To a Standstill

ON SUNDAY, JULY 1, EUGENE DEBS RESTED. HE WAS STAYING at Chicago's Leland Hotel on the downtown waterfront barely a block from the Pullman Building. He shared a room with his devoted younger brother, Theodore, then twenty-nine. After the tense and frantic pace of the boycott's early days, he needed time to regain his wind.

As he relaxed, events buoyed his natural cheerfulness. Momentum is everything in a strike. The boycott had begun on the previous Tuesday, June 26. In the five days since it had gained in extent and velocity. Tens of thousands of men had relinquished their livelihoods in order to stand up for the Pullman car builders. They had shocked the railroad managers with their unity and their determination.

To Debs, the boycott's success validated his idea that workers organized across an entire industry could confront the consolidated interests of even the largest corporations. It had taken him years to see beyond his affection for the insular railroad brotherhoods and to embrace this far-reaching view. Now all the work he had put into his grand concept was paying off.

Samuel Gompers, the American Federation of Labor leader, would later say that he considered Debs an "emotional intellectual." It was an apt description. Debs was incisive, informed, and able to grapple with complex, nuanced arguments. At the same time, he had a sentimental side that was typical of many in the Victorian era.

Debs later said, "I have always been partial to poets." He admired and became friends with the young Carl Sandburg, whom he considered "one of the really great poets of our day." Sandburg returned the compliment, declaring Debs "an artist, adventurer and sun-treader."

Debs was also fond of cornball versification and included regular samples of doggerel in the *Firemen's Magazine*. He loved the work of the "Hoosier poet" James Whitcomb Riley, famous for his children's verse and dialect poems.

Riley and Debs had become close friends, and the poet often stayed with Debs and his wife when he visited Terre Haute. His work evoked the nostalgia and homely values that Debs found comforting. In addition to publishing the most popular books of verse of the nineteenth century, Riley regularly gave readings of his poems to large audiences. A consummate performer, he offered Debs advice on sizing up an audience and improving his oratorical skills.

"There's nothing 'at's patheticker than jes' a' bein' rich," Riley wrote in a line Debs especially loved. Riley praised the labor leader in a poem about "Terry Hut":

> And there's 'Gene Debs—a man 'at stands
> And jest holds out in his two hands
> As warm a heart as ever beat
> Betwixt here and the Jedgement Seat.

༄

Debs's warm heart was encouraged by the progress of the great boycott. He felt that the nation was now coming to see that none of this contention was necessary. Strikes and lockouts and boycotts were futile and old-fashioned. Arbitration had to become the modern way to settle disagreements. Harmony between labor and capital was near if only he could hold fast to the tiller, steer the ARU through this stormy sea, and navigate to a port where such matters could be settled by negotiation.

The prospects were bright. The vehemently anti-Debs *Chicago Tribune* admitted that "the strikers have shown an astonishing degree of strength." The paper's editors detailed what was to them a gloomy outlook. "There is always the cry that 'something must be done' to stop them," they noted. "The trouble is that no one has been able to define the 'something.'" The editors recognized that the breadth of the disturbance made it difficult to contain. The government could not simply lock up the striking railroad men. "You don't want men in jail, you want them at work."

⸝

As he left his hotel on Monday morning, July 2, Debs felt a cool breeze blowing in off Lake Michigan. The heat of the previous week had broken and the fresh air carried with it the tang of hope. He returned to work at Ulrich's Hall with a bounce in his stride. He was unaware that the great strike was about to take a critical turn.

The ARU headquarters swarmed with activity. One telegram after another arrived, each reporting new union members and new actions. But the derailment of the Diamond Special on Saturday night worried him. Controlling the actions of tens of thousands of strikers in cities and towns across the country was difficult. Dampening the tendency of bystanders to use the strike as an excuse to riot was even more problematic.

"We want to win as becomes men," Debs declared in a statement. "We have got the right to quit in a body, and our rights end there." The railroad companies, he went on, had the right to hire replacement workers. Union members could not interfere with that right.

He recognized that the acts of violence and sabotage that had already occurred had begun to sour the public's view of the union. Major rioting would inevitably lead to defeat. He asked ARU men to help identify troublemakers and see that they were arrested.

Debs was gratified that his members had, for the most part, acted in the same disciplined manner that had brought victory over the Great Northern Railway. Although they had now lost a week's pay, they were bearing up with determination and enthusiasm. The railroads had incurred an enormous price for supporting George Pullman's wrongheaded intransigence.

Pressure was growing on all sides. The simplest course of action was to select impartial arbitrators and let them devise an equitable solution to the issues roiling the Pullman works. How much longer could such logic be denied? On that Monday, the GMA's John Egan admitted that railroads had been "fought to a standstill."

⸝

Maintaining peace just in Chicago was a challenge. The city was "practically a network of railways," the city's police commissioner, Michael Brennan, said. Its neighborhoods were filled with "railway tracks, yards, towers, switch houses and freight houses." Each of these facilities was a potential target for saboteurs and mobs. Rail lines snaked down streets adjacent to crowded tenements. The summer weather, which brought crowds of slum dwellers out of doors, added another element of volatility. Any rumor could flare into a spasm of violence.

The mobs that congregated in the suburban rail yards at Blue Island and other suburban facilities also worried Debs. Participants had taken to uncoupling cars, spiking switches to prevent their operation, and damaging railroad property.

The day after the boycott began, the railroad managers met with Mayor Hopkins and Superintendent Brennan to discuss the situation in Chicago. John Egan found Brennan cooperative. He reported back to his colleagues at the General Managers' Association that the superintendent had promised to remove any officer who was negligent in his duty and to arrest strikers causing trouble along the rail lines. Hopkins was determined to resist lawlessness, but he emphasized that the police were there only to suppress disorder and protect property, not to turn switches or make up trains.

During the early days of the strike, Brennan had rushed squads around the city to extinguish outbreaks of disorder. Sometimes they found that the reports submitted by Egan were exaggerated or based only on rumor. Police officers, who were generally sympathetic to the strikers, found little to do. But as the days passed, crowds in the train yards grew more raucous and Brennan's men were kept busy. Sheriff Gilbert, who had sworn in 250 special deputies to patrol Cook County beyond the city limits, also found his force taxed. Still, on that Monday Brennan said he was aware of no riots and that his men were equal to any emergency.

The course of the strike was prompting more and more railroad workers to join the American Railway Union. New locals were forming across the country. Each was told to set up a strike committee and forward the name of the chairman to headquarters so that ARU directors would have a point of contact. Debs sent one telegram after another assuring the men that the strike would soon be won if they stood together.

Rumors that militia or even federal troops would bring the heavy hand of the government against the strikers were worrisome, he admitted. But soldiers, although they might intimidate crowds, could not move trains. "Pay no attention to rumors," he wired a union local in Clinton, Iowa. "We are gaining ground everywhere. Don't get scared by troops or otherwise. Stand pat. None will return to work until all return."

൵

In California, the pervasive hatred of the railroads provided the tinder-dry landscape through which the flame of the strike spread. Frank Norris, a Chicago native who had settled on the West Coast, later wrote a novel called *The Octopus*. He called the railroad corporation a "leviathan, with tentacles of steel." He cataloged the many sins of the Southern Pacific Railroad, whose trunk line ran from New Orleans, through the Southwest, and up the Pacific coast. Its owners had solidified their monopoly by absorbing the Central Pacific, the western portion of the original transcontinental line.

Norris's novel reflected more than two decades of suspicion and animosity that diverse segments of the American public felt toward the railroads. The hatred had begun with the financial flimflams that accompanied the building of the first transcontinental line in the 1860s. The railroads received land grants, loans, and subsidies from the public purse. The owners formed construction companies that overcharged for work done, funneling government money back to the railroads, their promoters, and pliable politicians. When one of these companies, known as Crédit Mobilier, was exposed in 1872 as the "King of Frauds," the resulting scandal besmirched the vice president of the United States, the speaker of the House, and numerous senators and congressmen.

The railroad corporations had used their dominance to wrest special privileges from the government with no corresponding public control. They distorted competition, not only by merging with competing railroads and forming pools with potential rivals, but also by fixing rates to favor one shipper, one product, or one area of the country over another.

Public resentment of the railroads translated into support for the Pullman boycott. By one account, nine of ten businessmen in California were in sympathy with the strikers. An opponent had labeled the Southern Pacific Railroad the most "stupidly managed, the greediest, in the whole union."

Debs was encouraged by the news from Sacramento, a major rail hub and the state's capital. Almost all the city's railroad men had joined the strike and residents were overwhelmingly in sympathy. That Monday,

Southern Pacific division superintendent J. B. Wright informed Sacramento's mayor that "the passenger depot, depot grounds, yards and other property of this company are and have been for the past two days crowded with strikers and idlers," preventing the company from moving any trains. He demanded protection from the city authorities. The mayor, sensitive to the mood in town, said he would not act unless the strikers resorted to violence.

When U.S. Marshal Barry Baldwin arrived, the city was baking under blistering summer heat. He noted more than three thousand men, women, and children milling around the rail station. "This looks more like a fair," he observed, "than a desperate strike." The marshal was known for his opposition to railroad monopolies, but he had a job to do.

To test the strikers' seriousness, Baldwin ordered a mail train made up. Acting according to Debs's general order not to interfere with the mails, ARU members helped to clear the yards of bystanders and coupled together the cars required for the train. But when supervisors defied them by attaching a Pullman sleeper, the angry strikers rushed the station, uncoupled the cars, and pushed them back into the yard.

Baldwin ordered the crowd to disperse. Instead, the men pressed against him, knocked him down several times, and gave him what a newspaper called "a pretty severe handling." Regaining his feet, he came up with a revolver in each hand. For a moment the incident teetered on the edge of a bloody battle. Then a striker grabbed Baldwin from behind. The marshal wrestled free and was joined by several deputies, who were able to hold off the crowd. Baldwin hurried to Superintendent Wright's office, where he immediately wired Governor Henry Markham, demanding he send state troops to restore order. Markham was himself marooned in Los Angeles because of the tie-up.

"Peace officers here are in thorough sympathy with strikers," Baldwin noted. A newspaper reported, "Never in the history of the capital city of California has there been so exciting a day."

Elsewhere in the state, the situation was nearly as tense. In Oakland, where half the population was employed by the Southern Pacific, a large group of strikers and sympathizers took possession of the rail yards. They shut down engines by raking fires and blowing the steam from the locomotives.

That same day, Jane Lathrop Stanford became stranded in the northern California town of Dunsmuir. She was the sixty-five-year-old widow of the railroad tycoon and former California governor Leland Stanford. The union men said they could not let her private car proceed unless she received permission from ARU directors. She wired Debs in Chicago and he graciously offered her safe passage to her home in San Francisco. She was to show his telegram to any striker who questioned her right to break the boycott. A squad of strikers accompanied her as guards. By the time she reached Oakland, her train was festooned with bunting and the letters A-R-U were spelled out in flowers on the side of the engine. Strikers cheered and Mrs. Stanford bowed to them from her car's rear platform.

༄

In Washington, Attorney General Olney had already thought out his next move. On Sunday, he had wired U.S. Attorney Milchrist in Chicago and told him to begin a concerted legal attack against the strikers. Milchrist had stayed up until the wee hours writing out the language of a petition for an injunction.

Injunctions, which superseded ordinary laws, were a potent weapon that had been used only sparingly in labor disputes. Olney had tried them out while combating the battalions of Coxey's Army. Now he saw the legal remedy as a way to both end the boycott and bludgeon the upstart American Railway Union to death.

An injunction gave a court the power to forbid actions that were not illegal under penal law. The rationale was that if the activity of one party unfairly damaged the interests of another, it could be enjoined by the court. To Olney, the attraction of the injunction was that it put the power of enforcement in the hands of a judge, not a jury. Anyone deemed to be defying the order could be jailed for contempt without trial.

Milchrist received plenty of suggestions from railroad lawyers, who wanted a court order that was as comprehensive as possible. He cobbled together a justification for the order from concerns about interference with commerce and obstruction of mail. He added a controversial reference to the Sherman Antitrust Act. The law had been applied to labor only twice before, including a case in which Olney himself had declared its use a "perversion" of the intent of Congress, which had designed the law to be used against corporate trusts, not unions.

In his private practice, Olney had defended the Whiskey Trust, one of the few businesses prosecuted under the Sherman Act. He would later pronounce its reasoning "no good." While attorney general, he consistently refused to enforce its provisions against corporations' monopolistic practices, its intended target.

Now he saw that its ban on any "combination" that restrained trade among the states could be applied to a labor union. Leaving no base uncovered, he allowed Milchrist to employ it as one more weapon against the union.

To make sure the net was fine enough, two federal judges, William A. Woods of the circuit court and Peter S. Grosscup of the district court, relinquished their judicial objectivity and helped Milchrist polish his petition. Both judges were known for pro-business bias from the bench. Grosscup had been labeled "an earnest individualist" opposed to any regulation that impinged on property rights.

Having ascertained the thoroughness of the government petition, they mounted the bench that Monday and granted the injunction they had helped to write. The edict, which forbade "any act whatever" that might hamper a railroad, would initially apply in Indiana, Illinois, and Wisconsin, but its language was quickly picked up by other federal judges who fashioned similar injunctions for their own districts.

The judges' order was known as an omnibus injunction, a set of restrictions that in effect required all ARU members to cease all activity connected with the boycott. Legal experts were amazed at its scope. Eugene Debs and ARU directors were forbidden from "ordering, directing, aiding, assisting, or abetting" any act in furtherance of the boycott. They could not communicate with members or with each other on any matter related to the strike. They could not send telegrams or otherwise contact workers to encourage them to forsake their duties on the railroad.

All railroad men had to cease coercion or interference with the trains—the definition of interference was left to railroad officials. Strikers could not block replacement workers or induce "by threats, intimidation, persuasion, force, or violence any of the employees of said railroads not to perform any of their duties." For union men to try to talk scabs out of taking their jobs was henceforth illegal.

The writ put no restrictions whatever on the railroads. They could confer together to set strategy all they wanted, could refuse to run trains that did not include Pullman cars. The court might have deemed the General Managers' Association an illegal combination that was actively restraining trade. Instead, the group went unscathed by the order.

The idea that an attempt to persuade a fellow citizen could be a crime struck many as un-American. The judges declared that the injunction was justified by the fact that the men were creating a public nuisance, which the government had a duty to remove. They were also obstructing the mails, contrary to law. For good measure, they were breaking the Sherman Antitrust Act by restraining interstate commerce.

The *New York Times* reported that the judges who had written the injunction had proudly referred to it as a "Gatling gun on paper." Even the anti-strike *Times* was taken aback by this "extraordinary injunction," which editors called a "a veritable dragnet in the matter of legal verbiage."

The order made it punishable for men to do things that were, in ordinary circumstances, perfectly legal. No one needed to be served personally with the order. It would be promulgated by being published in newspapers and read in public. Once any man committed a forbidden act—suggested to a friend that he stay home from work, for example—he could be arrested and locked up for contempt.

The *Chicago Tribune* crowed that the injunction was "so broad and sweeping that interference with the railroads, even of the remotest kind, will be made practically impossible." So far, the Gatling gun was only on paper, but Richard Olney saw the injunction as groundwork for an even more dramatic attack on the alarmingly successful strike.

16

Ragged Edge

WITH THE RISK OF ARREST AND IMPRISONMENT HANGING over their heads, Eugene Debs and the other ARU leaders continued to act in defiance of the omnibus injunction. Their first reaction was that the order was so egregious that it would guarantee their victory by prompting many more outraged railroad men to join the boycott. On Monday, July 2, Debs sent out a telegram stating that "if strike not settled in forty-eight hours, complete paralysis will follow. Potatoes and ice out of sight."

The railroad managers, caught in an unexpected stalemate and concerned about the strike's increasingly painful impact on their operations, applauded the injunction. John Egan declared that the roads were being held up by "conspirators and lawless men." He recommended that regular army soldiers stationed in Fort Sheridan be sent to Chicago without delay. On their arrival, he predicted, "the strike would collapse like a punctured balloon."

The fort, twenty-five miles up the coast of Lake Michigan, had been the pet project of George Pullman, Marshall Field, and other Chicago businessmen. Alarmed by the Haymarket bombing, they felt that the federal troops five hundred miles away in Fort Leavenworth, Kansas, were too distant to respond quickly to a disturbance in Chicago. They sent their neighbor, Civil War hero Philip H. Sheridan, to Washington to lobby for the post that would be named for him.

Egan glossed over the fact that the main reason trains were not running was because they lacked crews. The GMA members' idea that they could fill empty positions with strikebreakers had yet to bear much fruit because of the vast extent of the boycott. Privately, the managers recognized that replacing an entire labor force overnight was a huge logistical undertaking.

But instead of admitting a draw and suing for peace, the managers complained about the crowds swarming rail yards and the occasional acts of sabotage against railroad property. Raising the specter of anarchy, they insisted that legal maneuvering had to be backed up with military action. After all, Olney had promised "force which is overwhelming" to suppress all resistance.

Grover Cleveland was circumspect about calling out the military. He understood that the deployment of federal troops against American citizens was a momentous and politically perilous course of action. If he was going to do it, he wanted to be sure he had the solid support of the public. In this, he was encouraged by the newspaper coverage of the boycott.

During the first days of July, many of the editors of the thousands of papers around the country gave over their entire front pages to strike coverage. The stories were inevitably contradictory, distorted, and deeply colored by the papers' editorial philosophy. In Chicago, all the dailies except the *Times* took positions against the union. The *Inter Ocean* declared that "the belligerent invasion of the country by a foreign foe could not be more injurious" to the nation than the boycott.

Some papers printed outright falsifications, including fake interviews with Eugene Debs. Several reported that a New York City doctor had labeled Debs non compos mentis because of his drunkenness. Two years earlier, the physician said, he had treated Debs for "neurasthenia and dipsomania." The labor leader was no longer responsible for his own actions and should give up his position.

Another widely reported story said that Debs had luxuriated on a Pullman car while traveling during the strike and was therefore a hypocritical humbug. Debs vehemently denied the truth of these accounts. He also scoffed at the tale that a railroad worker in Danville, Illinois, had struck him because the man had lost his job. That fiction had gone out on the Associated Press wire and been picked up by papers around the nation.

The press was quick to link the murder of French president Carnot by an anarchist with the unsettled conditions in America. Covering a July 1 memorial service for the assassinated leader, the *Inter Ocean* had labeled labor agitators "another form of anarchy."

Newspapers of the day relied on drawings and cartoons for illustrations. Sketches left everything to the artist's imagination, and illustrations of stories about the strike showed disorder, vandalism, buildings in flames, and crowds rampaging along rail lines. The artist Frederic Remington was among those who sketched the action near the Chicago stockyards. He saw the rioters as "a seething mass of smells, stale beer, and bad language." One soldier, he wrote, surveyed the crowd and remarked: "Them things ain't human."

Although the ARU took the brunt of the press's scorn, George Pullman was also vilified, even by dailies like the *Tribune*. His refusal to arbitrate had come to seem churlish and petty. The *Chicago Times* printed a drawing on July 2 of Pullman as a malevolent Richard III, obese and glowering. He was, the paper declared, a "cold-hearted, cold-blooded autocrat."

Joseph Pulitzer's *New York World* regarded the government's bias with skepticism. "More dangerous and menacing than any strike," an editor wrote, "is the carefully laid plan for bringing about the intervention of the Federal Government on the side of the railroads."

The *New York Herald* printed a cartoon labeled "The Dictator of Dreams." It showed Eugene Debs seated on a throne with his feet propped on a cushion identified as "Labor Rank and File." Uncle Sam, hat in hand, paid homage to the dictator.

Debs struck back on July 2, urging ARU members and sympathizers to boycott anti-union publications. He asked merchants to stop advertising in them and newsboys to stop selling them. If advertisers persisted in supporting the papers, union proponents should take their trade elsewhere.

That same day, Debs requested all who supported the strike to wear a white lapel ribbon, the device the ARU had picked up from the Pullman strikers. Within days, Jane Addams reported she saw "almost everyone on Halsted Street wearing a white ribbon, the emblem of the strikers' side." Even policemen were wearing them. Debs's wife, Kate, helped by fashioning white rosettes, which were distributed to women who supported the union.

∽

While the decision to send federal troops against the strikers hung in the balance, state military forces were already active in suppressing outbreaks of rioting around the country. The militias had traditionally served as the guardians of order when local law officers were unable to cope with a situation. The men could be called up quickly and were familiar with the local terrain. Since before the Civil War, they had included both state-sponsored troops and volunteer corps. During the 1890s, the units were being modernized into a more professional but still part-time National Guard.

From the beginning of the boycott, Illinois governor John Peter Altgeld had been keeping a close watch on the drama unfolding in his state. For the time being, the decision to militarize the dispute there rested entirely with him.

During his short tenure, Altgeld had experienced both the glory of the world's fair and the dire consequences of the depression. His physical appearance, *New York World* reporter Nellie Bly observed, "marks him peculiarly as a caricaturist's prey." Sporting short-cropped hair and beard, along with a lean and hungry-looking countenance, the forty-six-year-old Altgeld could have played Cassius in a production of *Julius Caesar*. Like the Roman senator, he thought too much and was considered, by some, to be dangerous because of his reformist and pro-labor views.

Altgeld's family had emigrated from Germany in 1848, when he was six months old, and settled on a farm in Ohio. Following a hardscrabble childhood and a brief stint in the Union Army, he had pieced together an education while working as a teacher and a railroad laborer. He became a lawyer, settled in Chicago, made money in real estate, entered politics as a Democrat, and served for a number of years as a state superior court judge before winning the governorship in 1892.

Because of his background, Altgeld possessed an instinctive sympathy for laborers and immigrants. Working-class voters formed his political base. He was one of the most forward-looking politicians in the country and an early prophet of the coming Progressive Era. Having been taunted during his youth as a "little Dutchman," he had published a fierce defense of the rights of immigrants and their value to society. His 1884 essay entitled "Our Penal Machinery and Its Victims" brought a remarkably modern perspective to reform of the prison system, putting the emphasis on rehabilitation. The criminal justice system, he noted, seemed to recruit its victims "from among those that are fighting an unequal battle in the struggle for existence."

As governor, he had faced a political dilemma. Like many, he felt that the anarchists who had been tried for the Haymarket bombing had been convicted entirely for their beliefs rather than for their involvement in the crime. They had been prosecuted, he thought, with "malicious ferocity," and he saw the judicial wrongdoing as a greater threat to society than any anarchist bomb. As he contemplated pardoning the three convicted men still alive, Altgeld told his protégé Clarence Darrow that if he did so, "I will be a dead man, politically."

In June 1893, Altgeld announced the pardon. The reaction was what he had predicted. In spite of the abundant evidence of the men's innocence and the jury's bias, newspaper editors across the country had heaped contumely onto Altgeld. The *New York Times* had accused him of doing everything in his power "to encourage again the spirit of lawless resistance and of wanton assault upon the agents of authority."

The opposition to Altgeld's action, like the frenzy surrounding the bombing itself, was rooted in a surging nativism. The fact that most of the accused were immigrants fed Americans' xenophobia. The *Chicago Tribune* said Altgeld was motivated by his "alien temperament." Even his appearance suggested perfidy—a college professor decided that Altgeld looked like "a typical German anarchist, fanatical and intense." The *New York Times* questioned his citizenship and suggested a search for his "papers." Angry crowds burned him in effigy.

For now, he was the man in charge of Illinois. He felt that his duty was to maintain order but not to break the strike. The distinction was not always clear. "I have reason to fear," Altgeld wrote, "that these troops were wanted at that place only to help the railroad defeat the demands of their men for higher wages, but I cannot refuse to send them, in the face of allegations of public danger."

Four days into the boycott, on Saturday, June 30, events outside Chicago forced Altgeld's hand. Illinois Central officials asked the governor to dispatch state militia troops to Cairo, at the southern tip of the state, where strikers and sympathizers were choking off the line. The governor asked a militia colonel to investigate and readied several companies of soldiers. He soon dispatched three hundred state militiamen.

The next day, Sunday, July 1, a telegram arrived reporting passenger trains detained in Decatur, not far from Springfield. The local sheriff was unable to handle the situation. Altgeld immediately sent 265 soldiers. That same day, the sheriff in Danville, on Illinois's eastern border, asked for a supply of rifles to use for confronting strikers. The governor sent 220 soldiers instead. Shifting militia forces as needed, he followed the action on a map dotted with colored pins.

༄

The dispatch of state troops was not unusual and was covered by existing laws. A call for intervention by the federal army raised two thorny issues. The first was practical. The regular army numbered barely 28,000 soldiers stationed in forts across the country. Could this force effectively control railroad workers, whose numbers topped 750,000? Could it deal even with the riotous mobs in Chicago? Could it patrol the vast reaches of the rail lines? Any military force directed at a large group of civilians had to have enough mass to intimidate rioters and quell the disturbance by its presence. The danger of sending too few troops into a riotous situation was that it would provoke rather than subdue violence.

The second issue was a matter of principle. The idea of a permanent army whose purpose was to restrict the rights of citizens had been detested since colonial times. Jefferson had complained of such armies in the Declaration of Independence. "A standing military force, with an overgrown Executive will not long be safe companions to liberty," James Madison had written in *The Federalist Papers*. Politicians were always wary of using federal forces for domestic duty.

Under the Posse Comitatus Act of 1878, Congress had explicitly prohibited the army from taking a role in domestic law enforcement. That law had been aimed at ending Reconstruction, during which federal troops had occupied territory of the former Confederacy. Any use of the army on U.S. soil required a strict constitutional justification, such as protection of federal property or support of specific U.S. government functions.

As to whether the army was up to the job of suppressing the boycott, Olney had been assured by military men that civilians, even if many were armed with pistols and rifles, could not stand up to disciplined squadrons of infantry and cavalry, no matter what the disparity of the numbers. Army officers pointed out that state militiamen, with far less training, might give in to personal sympathies. Hardened soldiers were far less likely to flinch when called upon to apply the bayonet, the saber, or the bullet.

When it came to justifying the extraordinary use of federal troops in the current crisis, Olney was careful to build a legal foundation on which the action could stand. Before he had the blanket excuse of the omnibus injunction at his disposal, he had fallen back on the same rationale that he had used to justify calling out federal forces against the western factions of Coxey's Army—interference with federally controlled property.

During their boycott, ARU members had disrupted insolvent railroads that had been placed under the control of government-appointed receivers. The lines were, in effect, government operations, and the attorney general construed any interference with them as a direct challenge to federal authority.

The bankrupt Santa Fe line, which ran south through Colorado and into New Mexico, was one of these federally controlled railroads. Managers had neglected to pay workers their wages for the past four months, and the men were in an ugly mood even before the boycott. Trouble broke out along a dry, sparsely populated stretch of line south of Denver. The men sidetracked Pullman cars and brought traffic to a halt, isolating towns like Trinidad, Colorado, and Raton, New Mexico. Both mail and passengers were stranded along the line.

On Saturday, June 30, Olney had asked the federal attorney for the district, J. B. H. Hemingway, to request a writ from a judge to suppress the strike. Hemingway said he knew of no mail obstruction in the Territory of New Mexico, only a refusal of employees to do their jobs. "I do not understand that the mere refusal to work is obstruction of the mail," he said.

Olney told him that the Cleveland administration did indeed consider such a refusal obstruction. And since the road was in the hands of federal receivers, authorities could do as they pleased. Hemingway quickly realized the error of his ways and asked for a restraining order. He sent U.S. Marshals to protect the Santa Fe trains.

These federal officers had no effect. A crowd disarmed fifty-two deputies as they approached the town of Trinidad and tore up the restraining order. On Monday, July 2, President Cleveland ordered five companies of army troops to proceed to the scene from Fort Logan near Denver. Along the way, they found the telegraph wires cut in Pueblo and trains unable to move. The soldiers repaired the damage and pushed on to Trinidad. They managed to partially restore rail service at bayonet point while marshals arrested forty-eight ringleaders supposed to have made "incendiary speeches." The men were charged with contempt of court for disobeying the restraining order.

Down the line in Raton, five hundred ARU members were backed up by three hundred striking miners from the local coal fields. The sheriff was sympathetic to labor and warned the U.S. Marshal to stay out. Not to be defied, the marshal and eighty-five deputies marched into Raton. The employees of the hotel where they planned to stay quit rather than wait on them—the law officers had to serve themselves. They found that they could do nothing to get trains moving. The marshal wired Olney for federal troops. Men of the Tenth Infantry would arrive two days later, on Wednesday, Independence Day.

༉

Olney saw that the omnibus injunctions against the strike offered the clearest path to military intervention. On Monday, the day the judges issued the first writ, Chief U.S. Marshal Arnold and Sheriff Gilbert took 135 deputized men to the Blue Island yards just outside Chicago where the train had been derailed on Saturday night. A sentinel began clanging the bell on the overturned engine as soon as the marshals' train approached. A crowd of more than two thousand gathered within minutes.

Numerous trains had been stranded at Blue Island, and Arnold announced to the bystanders that he was determined to move them. They included five passenger trains that had been immobilized for a day and a half. Their passengers had found themselves stuck on an isolated stretch of prairie twenty miles from downtown Chicago. They had suffered from the heat, from lack of food and water, and from the stress of the uncertain situation.

After Arnold ordered the onlookers to keep off the right-of-way, leaders of the mob told him that only mail trains could move. They had the numbers to enforce their will—strike sympathizers were now standing a hundred deep across the track. A standoff followed, while both sides eyed each other warily and negotiations proved fruitless.

Arnold ordered his men, who included deputized railroad officials, to form up in front of the first train he planned to move. Even a reporter from the *Chicago Tribune* was drafted and handed a star. All the deputies were armed with revolvers.

The train's engineer eased open the throttle and the locomotive began to creep toward the crowd at a "very slow walk." The deputies marched forward in front of the cowcatcher. The protesters did not give way. A shoving match began. A barrage of stones and coupling pins flew toward the deputies. Shouts and abuse turned to blows. One man cut Arnold's deputy John Logan in the back with a knife. The lawmen drew their pistols, but, as the *Tribune* reporter noted, "nobody wanted to be the first to shoot."

Now a general melee broke out. Arnold "in all his dignity was rolled in the dirt." The marshals and sheriff deputies swung clubs freely. Dozens of rioters were dragged from the crowd and arrested, but most of these prisoners quickly broke free with the aid of their fellows. The train's engineer was hit in the head by a stone. Men pulled coupling pins to break the train into its separate cars. After dozens of deputies "literally fell over one another in their rush to the rear," Arnold gave up the attempt.

Calm returned until about 4:00 p.m. By then, the excitement had drawn even more of the curious to the scene. A passenger train from Chicago appeared and began to crawl slowly through the yards. The crowds moved in to block it.

By this time, the omnibus injunction had been issued and ten thousand copies printed. Marshal Arnold climbed into the doorway of a mail car and told the mob that he was going to read an order from the federal government. At first, the reading was met with quiet attention. As soon as the gist of the injunction began to register, the onlookers erupted.

"I command you in the name of the President of the United States to disperse and go to your homes," Arnold shouted. The people cursed and laughed. Screams of "To hell with the courts!" and "We are the government!" rang out.

Mob leaders offered to let the passenger train go on its way as soon as the Pullman cars were detached. Arnold would not allow the train to be altered. His remaining men managed to clear a way through. The train finally navigated the crossing and proceeded on its way.

At 6:15 p.m., Arnold wired Olney directly. "I am here at Blue Island. Have read the order of the court to the rioters and they simply hoot at it. . . . We have had a desperate time here all day and our forces are inadequate . . . impossible to move trains without having the Fifteenth Infantry. . . . Mail trains are in great danger."

༤

That was Monday, July 2. Olney did not act immediately on Arnold's request. Instead, he wired U.S. Attorney Milchrist about the injunction: "Congratulate you upon the legal situation, which is all that could be desired. Trust use of United States troops will not be necessary. If it becomes necessary, they will be used promptly and decisively." He added that Milchrist should make sure that, if the time came, Arnold, Edwin Walker, and Judges Grosscup and Woods should all join in the request for troops. The hint was taken.

On Tuesday, July 3, the pieces of Olney's plan fell into place. He brought the president alarming telegrams from federal officials in Illinois, New Mexico, Colorado, and California. Together, they painted a landscape aflame with lawlessness. The report angered the one-time sheriff who now occupied the White House.

In recent weeks, Grover Cleveland had been struggling to get a bill through Congress to achieve his longtime goal of dramatically lowering tariffs. Only in the past few days had he turned his full attention to events on the railroads. Now he called an emergency meeting of his cabinet. After a general discussion of the situation, he huddled with his inner circle to settle on a course of action. Besides Olney, they included Secretary of State Walter Gresham, Secretary of War Daniel Lamont, and two chief military advisers. Army commander John Schofield, who had shared a lunch with the president following the opening of the Columbian Exposition, was a career soldier. At sixty-two he was marked by florid muttonchop whiskers and a brusque manner. General Nelson Miles, whose territory as head of the Department of the Missouri included Chicago, had been on leave in the East and had to be summoned urgently to the White House.

At first, Miles, Schofield, and Gresham were reluctant to dispatch troops. Although Miles expressed the view that the strike was "more threatening and far reaching than anything that had occurred before" and might "paralyze if not overthrow the civil government," he hesitated at the thought of ordering his men to fire on fellow citizens.

While the discussion was under way, Olney played his trump card. He announced that he had received a telegram from Marshal Arnold.

The marshal said that the defiant crowd at Blue Island had thrown "a number of baggage cars across the track, since when no mail trains have been able to move." Arnold could not disperse the mob or clear the tracks.

"Believe that no force less than the regular troops of the United States," he wrote, "can procure the passage of the mail trains or enforce the orders of the court." For good measure, Arnold amplified rumors circulating in Chicago that a wider strike was imminent. The Chicago trade unions "are quitting employment today, and in my opinion will be joining the mob tonight, and especially tomorrow." The troops should be dispatched "at the earliest possible moment." As Olney had suggested, Arnold's message came with the endorsement of Milchrist, Walker, and Judge Grosscup.

Olney ignored the fact that Monday's disturbance at Blue Island had largely dissipated by Tuesday. Nor did he bother explaining why a combination of police and state troops could not at least try to handle the situation first. Lacking the president's political instincts, he looked only to his own constituency, the directors of the nation's railroad corporations.

It was a consequential decision. President Rutherford B. Hayes had reluctantly called out federal troops during the spontaneous labor upheaval of 1877, but that had been at the request of state officials. Governor Altgeld had not asked for help and was not about to. The president, who had run on a states' rights platform in 1884, would have to take action while ignoring local authorities, a politically risky and legally dubious course.

But John Arnold's description of the disorder in Chicago brought all participants of the meeting on board. Olney made his case that only bullets and bayonets aimed at American citizens could keep the country from plunging into chaos or worse. The president was convinced. At 4:00 p.m., Grover Cleveland made the fateful decision.

Only General Miles, whose roots were in the working class, still harbored qualms. He worried about giving orders that might lead to a massacre. He asked the president point-blank if he should order his men to fire on the rioting strikers.

The short-tempered Cleveland snapped that it was Miles, the man in command, who would "be the judge on questions of that kind."

Miles left to book passage to Chicago. Secretary Lamont returned to the War Department and sent orders to officers at Fort Sheridan that their units should begin moving immediately. A locomotive had been waiting under steam to speed the transport. Troops gripped their Springfield rifles and clattered aboard the train. Wranglers loaded cavalry horses. Artillerymen wheeled cannon onto flatcars. The U.S. Army was on the move.

The next day, Richard Olney declared: "We have been brought to the ragged edge of anarchy."

PART III

July 4–July 12, 1894

17

We Shall Have Debs

Independence Day. A cloudless sky stretched over Chicago and temperatures were expected to top out in the seventies. Perfect weather for picnics.

Eugene Debs awoke early. From his hotel window, he saw the morning star wink out over the lake and heard the distant bang of torpedoes and firecrackers set off by young patriots eager to commence the holiday celebration. And something else: a commotion in the hotel's courtyard. He glanced down. Soldiers. Men in khaki were stacking their rifles. He called excitedly to his brother. These were not militiamen. "They're regulars, Theodore, they're regulars. Do you get that? Cleveland has sent the troops in."

Debs had known that the deployment was a possibility, but the sight of the soldiers struck him with a jolt. Excited, anxious, and confused, he instinctively reached for a hopeful slant on the development. Federal troops, he imagined, would tamp down the growing disorder. They were not a threat to the ARU. They could not operate trains and would not molest lawful strikers. They would prevent rioters from "destroying property, the stigma of which is placed by capital on labor," he said.

In his heart, he knew he was wrong. The appearance of federal soldiers marching through an American city was not a good omen for the outcome of the strike.

That Wednesday, July 4, marked a change in the trajectory of the crisis, but at first no one knew the direction events would take. Workers accustomed to long hours and six-day weeks relished the luxury of a day off. All citizens welcomed the brief pause from the tension of the nation-wide boycott.

Chicago's business district was deserted. Even the bustling ARU headquarters at Ulrich's Hall was quiet that day. Debs had directed union members to stay away from rail depots and yards. All day, he and the other officers roamed the city addressing public meetings, encouraging the strikers, warning against violence.

Paraders strutted through Chicago's streets to the robust beat of John Philip Sousa tunes. Politicians and clergymen intoned patriotic plati-tudes. Picnickers thronged the city's parks. At night, bonfires blazed in residential neighborhoods, accompanied by the bang and sparkle of fire-works. Intoxicated crowds made merry in saloons until closing time. Cit-izens across the city wore the white ribbons that showed their support of the strikers.

The nation had stopped to acknowledge the 118th anniversary of the Declaration of Independence. Men and women were still alive whose grandfathers had fought alongside George Washington. Many were prompted to reflect on the questions the current impasse between labor and capital had raised about the country's founding principles.

Eugene Debs and George Pullman personified two views as to the proper course for the Republic. Citizens revered the sanctity of property, but Debs would wrench control of the railroads from private investors if they did not bend to the needs of employees. Americans also clung to the notion that a workingman should receive fair pay for a day's labor, but Pullman would run his business as he saw fit, even if his men were forced to work for starvation wages.

The son of immigrants, Debs revered American ideals. His notions were rooted in the era of the country's founding, when citizens had to join together or perish. He looked to America's spirit of volunteerism and its history of cooperative enterprises as models for a new society. He be-lieved in a sense of common interest that could balance the dominant ethos of individualism. He was sure that there was more to life than ran-cor and competition, more than what Walt Whitman called "the mania of owning things."

The George Pullmans of the nineteenth century had amassed re-sources and applied their imaginations to creating the fantastic para-phernalia of the modern age. They had convinced Americans of the value of enjoying all the wonderful things they had seen in the White City. Pullman put his faith in bold self-assertion, personal responsibility, and material gain.

Both Debs and Pullman were fighting for deeply held principles: community versus self-interest, cooperation versus competition, equality versus liberty. On this anniversary of independence, each felt that he was a patriot upholding the best of the American tradition.

But for today, citizens were occupied with relaxation rather than rancor. One reminder of the simmering conflict was the absence of excursions to lakes and parks outside the city. Normally, the days leading to the Fourth were busy ones for the railroads. Dispatchers added extra coaches to scheduled runs; political, fraternal, and church groups chartered whole trains so that city folk could spend the day among the trees and flowers. This year, not a single group in Chicago applied for a special train.

"No one cared to take the risk of leaving the city," a newspaper reported. Rail travel had grown hazardous. At any moment, a tie-up along the line could leave revelers stranded. The railroads reportedly lost $500,000 in revenues on the Fourth alone.

~

The troops that Eugene Debs had seen outside his hotel that morning had come down by train from Fort Sheridan the night before. They had marched through the streets to Lake Front Park. Along the way, bystanders in middle-class neighborhoods had cheered; working-class spectators had met the soldiers with icy silence. In a few instances, city police had to intervene to protect the infantrymen from abuse.

Now the troops were setting up their camp in the park facing the hotels and office buildings of Michigan Avenue. In the absence of General Miles, who was boarding a train in Washington as the men entered the city, the regulars were commanded by Colonel Robert E. A. Crofton, who had arrived with eight companies of the Fifteenth Infantry. He had also brought two troops of the Seventh Cavalry, a reconstituted version of the famed unit that General George Armstrong Custer had led at the Battle of the Little Bighorn eighteen years earlier.

Crofton conferred with U.S. Marshal John Arnold, with Special U.S. Attorney Edwin Walker, and with GMA strike czar John Egan on what they thought was the best way to get the mail moving and to enforce federal laws and court edicts. He conspicuously avoided any conversation with police officials or with state or city authorities.

Earlier that year, General Schofield had told department commanders that in the event of domestic disturbances, regulars were to operate only as cohesive tactical units under direct orders from their military superiors. Troops, he ordered, "should not be scattered or divided into small detachments." The commander recognized that the ability of a corps of soldiers to intimidate a crowd was dangerously diluted when they were broken into small groups, each of which could be overwhelmed by a mob.

Nor were U.S. troops to serve as reinforcements for law enforcement agencies. Their only duty was "to protect federal property and prevent obstruction of the mails—not to restore order." Schofield, who recognized that the antagonists the troops faced would likely contain innocent observers as well as lawbreakers, cautioned against firing into groups of citizens without specific orders from commanding officers. Bayonets should be the weapon of choice when facing mixed crowds.

Nevertheless, Arnold and the railroad men convinced Crofton to ignore the directive and to disperse his men to the various railroad hot spots around town. Crofton sent four companies, about 250 men, to Blue Island, two companies to the Union Stock Yard, and two companies to Grand Crossing. Arnold would persuade the infantry commander to break up his force further, assigning squads of as few as ten soldiers to help arrest strikers. During such operations, the men necessarily received their orders from the marshals.

The soldiers had expected to arrive in a city on the edge of anarchy. But when they boarded local trains at four thirty in the morning and rode through the streets before dawn, they found no signs of disturbance. The strikers had heeded Debs's call to stay away, and the rail yards were "quieter than a blue law Sunday."

Grand Crossing was placid. The engineer kept up steam in case the soldiers needed to move to where the trouble was. After a breakfast of coffee, bread, and beans with bacon, the troops were able to move two freight trains through the rail yard without incident. One held meat from the Swift plant; the other was loaded with fruit. Otherwise, the soldiers had little to do. They even had time for a game of baseball. Just after dark, they watched the Diamond Special roll by, protected by a carload of police.

Only in the maze of rails that adjoined the Union Stock Yard was there a hint of trouble. The two companies sent there arrived as the sun was coming up. By seven thirty they had their tents pitched in Dexter Park, a horse racing track along Halsted Street adjacent to the yards. Curious onlookers began to gather early, drawn by the novelty of the federal troops themselves. The officers' nerves tightened as they eyed a growing crowd of rough-looking immigrants. They sent a message to Colonel Crofton requesting reinforcements. He dispatched by train a troop of cavalry and a battery of artillery. They would be delayed for hours as they tried to make their way through the awakening city.

﹏

During the holiday respite, reporters questioned both Eugene Debs and George Pullman about their views of the strike. Pullman spent the Fourth at his desk facing the ocean off New Jersey. He kept in touch with events in Chicago and around the country by telephone and wire. A reporter noted that "he preserves his customary calmness and evenness of temper" in spite of the anxiety generated by the strike.

"The story of the origin of this strike has been pretty fully told," Pullman said to the correspondents, but he did not hesitate to tell it again. By his account, workers in his plant were satisfied with their lot until they "were called out by the American Railway Union." The union had inaugurated the strike at Pullman "as a pretext to spread their influence." Although it was not true, the story helped him justify his obstinate stance.

The sole demand of the ARU was that Pullman submit his differences with workers to arbitration, but the sleeping-car magnate concluded that "the Pullman Company could not settle the strike now if it would. It is now in other hands."

He applied to the situation a simplistic logic. There was nothing to arbitrate. No outsider could dictate the market price of his cars. If he were to let others determine what he charged for housing in the model town, then all landlords would have to set rents by arbitration. That was absurd. As for the sympathy strike, "the question, to my mind, has resolved itself into this: Shall the railroads be permitted to manage their own business, or shall they turn it over into the hands of Debs, Howard, and the American Railway Union?"

When it was pointed out that neither the model town nor the Pullman works had been subject to rioting, he insisted that "credit be given to the administration of the company which prohibits drinking saloons and provides various sources for the elevation of character."

He said that he had received a telephone message from Chicago saying that companies of cavalry and artillery were just then marching by the company offices. "We think that the presence of the troops on the ground is having a very good effect."

He ended by expressing his feeling "that the employees will, on sober second thought, conclude that the owners and managers of railroads are the proper parties to control the policy and operation of the roads." But he modestly added that "one citizen's opinion on such a question is as good as another's."

For his part, Eugene Debs did not see matters with George Pullman's cool composure. He predicted dire consequences if Pullman and the railroad managers continued their obstinacy. He momentarily broke his rule of tamping down talk of violence. He predicted: "The first shot fired by the regular soldiers at the mobs here will be the signal for a civil war."

The sudden appearance of the military may have pushed Debs toward apocalyptic utterances as dire as those of Richard Olney. "Bloodshed will follow," he declared. He envisioned 90 percent of the country's population warring with the privileged 10 percent. "And I would not care to be arrayed against the laboring people in the contest." He was not an alarmist, he said, but speaking "calmly and thoughtfully."

"It is corporation greed and avarice alone," he judged, "that have brought us to the verge of a revolution." Retreat from the struggle would mean enslavement and the workingman's "complete and utter degradation for all time to come. And I would rather be dead."

Almost all the parties to the strike had come to see themselves as bystanders. Pullman had shifted responsibility to the railroads. Debs insisted that matters were beyond his control as well. "I have ordered no boycott or strikes personally, and have acted as a servant of my organization."

In Washington, Richard Olney declared, "The subject has now passed out of my hands." This was not true, as he continued to monitor every detail. But the effort would now be spearheaded by "other branches," namely the U.S. Army.

John Egan, the strike leader for the railroads, insisted that his group had also become mere spectators. "It has now become a fight between the United States Government and the American Railway Union," he noted. "And we shall leave them to fight it out." At the same time, he could assure the public that the railroad managers were not about to break ranks—they were determined "to fight this strike shoulder to shoulder to the finish."

Edwin Walker, erstwhile railroad lawyer and now an agent for the government, took the most pugnacious stance. "Every man who has trampled on the law will be punished," he declared. "It is the instigator of the lawlessness that the government wants to punish. That is Debs. We shall have Debs. We have the evidence against him now and he will be punished."

⌇

General Miles arrived in Chicago just past noon to take command of the federal troops. He was known by all as a competent, ambitious officer. Coming up from poverty in New England, he had advanced his career with conspicuous heroism during the Civil War. Miles had served in the army through the decades-long wars against the Plains Indians. He had taken Geronimo into custody and had helped subdue the Apache, the Cheyenne, and the Sioux.

Three and a half years earlier, in December 1890, he had ordered a band of Lakota braves to give up their rifles and move back to their reservation in the Dakotas. According to a regimental adjutant, they responded "with the sullen defiance so often displayed by strikers during labor troubles." Miles wired to a subordinate: "Use force necessary." Seventh Cavalry troopers surrounded the Indians and began to disarm them. Gunfire broke out. More than 150 Lakota, including many women and children, died in the fusillade. "I have never heard of a more brutal, cold-blooded massacre," a furious Miles wrote, "than that at Wounded Knee."

Miles was now in line to take over the leadership of the entire U.S. Army. Many said that his sights were fixed even higher, that he saw himself occupying the White House. During October 1892, he had served as grand marshal of the spectacular Chicago parade that celebrated the four hundredth anniversary of Columbus's arrival in the New World and heralded the coming Exposition.

Arriving back in Chicago on the Fourth, Miles did not seem inclined to defuse the situation. He made a statement from his headquarters in the Pullman Building, pointing out that his men were not deployed "for display or for picnic purposes." He discussed the lethal nature of modern rifles and said the soldiers would not "stand too much nonsense." If his men were to open fire "they will take aim and will shoot to kill, and will keep on shooting as long as is necessary."

✐

No one had been shot yet, but the holiday atmosphere that prevailed in the morning became increasingly strained as the Fourth of July progressed. An excited crowd grew hour by hour around the stockyards. By afternoon, twenty-five thousand strikers, sympathizers, and thrill seekers were challenging the 150 soldiers of Companies C and D. The police handled crowd control as railroad supervisors and loyal employees tried to move stalled trainloads of chilled meat.

When the crowd grew too rowdy, the federal soldiers advanced on them with bayonets, quickly dampening the bystanders' enthusiasm. The anti-union newspapers, which had castigated the strikers for their audacity, now mocked them for falling back "like a flock of frightened sheep." The troops, divided into small squads, marched through the maze of cattle pens and rail lines to support police and defend engineers and firemen who were trying to move trains. General Miles had not, after his arrival on the scene, countermanded the orders of Colonel Crofton. His command remained fragmented.

The men soon found themselves lining up beside a locomotive, loading their guns, and moving along the tracks at double time, scattering the jeering onlookers as they went. A police officer rode on each car. The troops kept pace for a half mile, ending at a brisk run, before the trainload of meat, which had been stalled in refrigerated cars for two days, was deemed safe. The winded and sweating soldiers halted and watched the train depart on its way east. Similar duties filled the rest of the day.

Mayor Hazen S. Pingree of Detroit said that the federal troops had been sent to Chicago "not so much to quell a riot as to crush labor unions." Adding to the problem was the continued presence of several thousand deputy marshals, consisting mainly of railroad detectives and what Chicago police superintendent Michael Brennan called "thugs, thieves, and ex-convicts." Although they were brawny men, they tended to panic and retreat when confronted by a crowd. Their effect was to goad and anger the rioters rather than establish order.

The harried infantrymen at the stockyards kept looking up the line for the arrival of the cavalry troops coming to reinforce them. Unfortunately, this force was stranded on the train bringing them south from their waterfront camp. Railroad rights-of-way ran down the middle of city streets and were vulnerable to interference by residents darting out from tenements. More than twenty times, bystanders were able to pull coupling pins, breaking the train into pieces that had to be laboriously recoupled. By late afternoon, the troopers had still not covered the six miles to the stockyards. Officers decided to leave the train, unload the horses, baggage, and artillery pieces, and walk the rest of the way.

Drinking was a time-honored tradition on the Fourth, and as the sun relaxed into the West, alcohol was having an effect on the mood of the populace. False courage induced rowdy onlookers to taunt the troops. The civilians sensed correctly that the men had orders from superiors to fire their rifles only to ward off a direct assault. After dark, crowds roamed from one train yard to another. Vandals tied up the lines by overturning boxcars and a few passenger cars. Rioters set fire to some old cattle cars they found on a siding.

"It was hoped the presence of the troops would have a quieting effect," a reporter noted, but it "only inflamed the mob."

∽

Nationwide, the effects of the strike were becoming more worrisome as the second week of the tie-up began. Drug wholesalers were complaining that they were not receiving shipments. The price of quinine had soared. Much less milk than usual was arriving in Chicago and shortages were being felt. The price of meat was up across the country—it was feared that soon only the well-to-do would be able to afford it. Shortages of coal and ice affected a wide range of businesses.

Some saw signs of the strike losing momentum. The *Chicago Tribune* was sure that the government had "Mr. Debs where the hair is short, and that it will yank him from his throne with a shock that will jar his entire system." Illinois Central officials declared that they would move local trains the next day if possible. The news "created joy in the hearts of the tens of thousands of suburbanites" who depended on trains to get to work.

But when a marshal in Ogden, Utah, read publicly a copy of the omnibus injunction, strikers laughed him off. He did not dare arrest anyone. In Mattoon, Illinois, a supervisor had climbed aboard a New York–bound train and told the engineer to go ahead.

"Where's my fireman?" the man asked.

"I am going to fire for you."

"Then I'll not go." The engineer turned and climbed down from the cab.

A nervous General Miles ordered four companies of regulars from Fort Leavenworth to hurry to Chicago. Traveling by train at breakneck speed, they would arrive in Chicago during the night. Three more companies were on their way from Fort Brady in Michigan. The new men would double his force. They would also bring a battery of Hotchkiss revolving cannon whose five barrels could spit out sixty-eight lethal rounds in a minute.

Contention did not reign everywhere. Passengers who had been stranded on trains tied up in Grand Junction, Colorado, celebrated the holiday by joining with local residents for a game of baseball against the striking railroad men. U.S. Marshals joined the audience to watch the travelers and townsmen beat the strikers by 29 to 19.

‿

Violence was spreading in the West. Oakland newspaperman Frank A. Leach remembered in his memoir: "No act of violence or mob action took place prior to July 4, but on that day the West Oakland men gathered for desperate work, which had evidently been carefully pre-arranged. The railroad yards were rushed by mobs of strikers, engines were stopped and killed, and engineers and firemen were lucky if they escaped a beating. The mechanics in the shops were made to quit work."

Sacramento remained one of the most volatile spots in the country. After U.S. Marshal Barry Baldwin had lost control of the situation there the day before, Governor Markham ordered out several regiments of state troops from San Francisco to support the militia already on the scene. Their commander, General William H. Dimond, issued his soldiers twenty rounds of ammunition each and told them: "You will fire low, and fire to kill." An artillery unit with a brass Gatling gun accompanied them. They had marched down Market Street in San Francisco to both cheers and jeers before riding a ferry to Oakland and boarding a train to Sacramento.

Taking a roundabout route to dodge obstructions or sabotage, the men arrived in the state capital at midmorning on the Fourth. They ate a quick breakfast and marched to the Sacramento armory, where local troops were already waiting. Officers questioned the men and found all ready to do their duty except one company of Sacramento militia, who said they would not fire on friends and family. Those men were disarmed and left at the armory.

The remaining soldiers demonstrated their inexperience by twice accidentally discharging rifles, killing one bystander. At 1:00 p.m. the battalion marched to the train station. A large crowd of spectators, including many children, had turned out to watch what they thought would be a parade and drill to commemorate the holiday. When it became clear that the troops would not be putting on a demonstration, they decided "to go over to the scene of the strife," a reporter wrote, "and witness a 'sure-enough' riot drill."

The strikers who occupied the depot and the surrounding area alerted the town by setting off a nearby factory whistle. A mass of citizens rushed to block the east entrance to the depot. The first two units of soldiers in the line of march were both from Sacramento. They fixed bayonets and came face-to-face with their neighbors. Their commander, Sacramento newspaperman Timothy Sheehan, fearful that a celebratory firecracker could incite a massacre, pleaded with the ARU leaders to allow a mail train to leave the station. The strikers, who felt they had been deceived by a similar request the day before, said they would rather die on the spot than give in.

With temperatures climbing over a hundred degrees, the sweating soldiers could do nothing but stand in ranks under the sun and await orders. Their officers conferred among themselves and tried to conciliate the strike leaders. A number of soldiers collapsed from the heat and had to be carried into the shade.

Marshal Baldwin, who had been roughed up by strikers the day before, announced that trains would now commence running. ARU strike committee chairman Frank Knox urged his men not to molest the militiamen, but the strikers were adamant that no Pullman cars would move.

As the sweltering afternoon progressed, strike sympathizers mixed with the troops, urging them not to fire on workers who were only trying to achieve justice. "Don't you know that we were raised with you," one striker pleaded, "that we are your brothers and that the fight you are making on us is only to enable a hungry corporation to grind its employees down."

Another said, "Frank, if you kill me you make your sister a widow."

In spite of their officers' efforts, discipline among the troops began to slacken. Some soldiers unloaded their rifles. Some lowered their guns and left the scene, the union men cheering them on. A few handed over weapons to the strikers. The Stockton contingent walked off in a group to sit in the shade. Soon, according to a *San Francisco Examiner* reporter, "soldiers and strikers were wandering off arm in arm, drinking together, laughing together."

General Dimond ordered militia commander Sheehan to clear the tracks and depot. Sheehan refused to act without a written order from Baldwin to open fire. Baldwin did not want the responsibility. He mounted the top of a locomotive and exhorted the strikers to relent. No one budged.

Negotiations lasted until 6:00 p.m. Militia officers then ordered all their men to march back to the armory. Strikers cheered their victory in what was called the Bloodless Battle of the Depot.

Even a hint of insubordination from a military force was unsettling. The *New York Times* noted that this was the "first instance of this sort of lawlessness on the part of the militia." It was well understood that both militiamen and private soldiers of the regular army were drawn from the same class as the railroad workers. The idea that they would support rather than crush the strike was terrifying to the country's elite. At Sacramento, the soldiers had not switched sides, but they had disobeyed orders and turned away from their duty. The *Times* called the incident "disgraceful and dangerous."

Equally ominous was the arrival at Sacramento of another contingent of railroad men. They had commandeered a train at Dunsmuir two hundred miles to the north and run it down to the scene of the action at the state capital. Having collected rifles and ammunition at towns along the way, they appeared ready for open rebellion. The prospect of an armed revolt rattled nerves across the state.

᠅

Two glimmers of hope glowed, however dimly, on the evening of the Fourth. Peter Studebaker, one of five brothers who ran the nation's premier carriage manufacturing works in South Bend, Indiana, was said to have inserted himself into the controversy. He lived in Chicago, was a friend of George Pullman, and owned a significant chunk of stock in the Pullman's Palace Car Company. He also knew Eugene Debs, who called him "a true friend of the working men."

A rumor reached reporters that he had met with Debs as well as with Pullman vice president Thomas Wickes. Studebaker's interest in resolving the matter was blown up into an effort authorized by George Pullman himself to seek a compromise. Others said he was acting on behalf of stockholders fed up with Pullman's intransigence. The news cheered all those who simply wanted the boycott to be over.

Studebaker's efforts were shrouded in mystery. Chicago mayor John Patrick Hopkins acted publicly in his attempt to resolve the dispute, which was increasingly threatening his city with chaos. Joined by an arbitration committee of his city council, he attempted to arrange a negotiated settlement. He called in ARU secretary Sylvester Keliher on the Fourth and set up a meeting for eleven the next morning.

Representatives of the General Managers' Association were also invited. The usual posturing—the union making no promises, the managers denying they would meet with the archfiend Debs—did not completely quell the hope among ordinary citizens that reason would now prevail. Those of an optimistic bent breathed more easily as they went to bed that night.

18

Strike Fever

N o Americans had more vivid nightmares of fire than the citizens of Chicago. The 1893 world's fair had been the crown on the city's miraculous, generation-long rebirth after the devastating conflagration of 1871. The Great Chicago Fire had killed three hundred citizens and left ninety thousand, a third of the city's population, homeless. The building boom that followed had given the city the reputation of a phoenix. On Thursday, July 5, the element of fire entered the Pullman boycott and set nerves on edge across the city.

Just before noon on a track outside the stockyards, rioters torched a string of freight cars. Firefighters were on the scene quickly and were able to extinguish the flames, but it was an ominous sign. A block away, rioters overturned a dozen freight cars and set one of them on fire. Around the city, firemen found switch towers and railroad tool sheds burning as well.

General Miles seemed intent on exacerbating rather than calming tensions. "A grave crisis is before Chicago," he said. He was afraid the crowd of rioters, "worked up to a fever," would desert the rail yards and bring their wrath into the city's residential and business districts.

Throughout the disturbance, Miles often seemed more concerned about revolutionary and anarchist conspiracies than about performing his assignment of protecting federal property and getting mail trains moving. He even assigned a Polish private to infiltrate union ranks to gather intelligence.

After praising the "extraordinary coolness of the men," he added the unsettling observation that "fifty of those soldiers could mow down two thousand people in a few minutes." Asked if the government might soon put the city under martial law, he conceded that it was a good possibility.

Attorney General Olney, irritable in the best of times, said "if Miles would do less talking to newspapers and more shooting at strikers he'd come nearer fulfilling his mission on earth and earning his pay."

Even with the additional soldiers who were on their way, Miles thought his force inadequate. He sent General Schofield a request for even more troops. The army commander mobilized more men at forts around the country. In the end, sixteen thousand federal soldiers would take part in actions against the strike, including almost two thousand in Chicago.

～

That Thursday began with a dispute on paper that put a spotlight on the collusion between the government and the railroads. When Grover Cleveland sent federal troops to Chicago to act within Governor Altgeld's jurisdiction, he did not wait for the customary request from local authorities. He did not even notify the governor of his intention. Altgeld wired a protest to Washington.

Cleveland did not know what was going on, he wrote, "or you would not have taken this step." The State of Illinois was "able to take care of itself." State troops, he said, "have been ordered promptly whenever and wherever they were needed." He had stationed three regiments of infantry and a troop of cavalry in Chicago, but the local officials had not yet requested their aid. He thought the federal government had been manipulated "by men who had political and selfish motives."

While it was true that some railroads were paralyzed, Altgeld contended, it was "not by reason of obstruction, but because they cannot get men to operate their trains." The railroads were "anxious to keep this fact from the public." There was no anarchy in the city or state. Any disturbances could easily be handled by local officials.

Perhaps, he suggested, the president had been influenced by newspaper accounts, many of them wild exaggerations. "You have been imposed upon in this matter," he wrote, and went on to lecture Cleveland that "local self-government is a fundamental principle of our Constitution." He asked for the immediate withdrawal of federal troops.

Grover Cleveland replied that "Federal troops were sent to Chicago in strict accordance with the Constitution." He briefly listed his reasons, including the need to execute the court order and to maintain interstate commerce.

Altgeld fired off another vitriolic wire, asserting that Cleveland's curt message "involves some startling conclusions and ignores and evades the question at issue," which to Altgeld was the principle of self-government. The president was putting forth his right to send federal troops into any community "at his pleasure."

Caught up in his own indignation, the governor declared that "the autocrat of Russia could certainly not possess or claim to possess greater power than is possessed by the Executive of the United States if your assumption is correct." Only at the end of his telegram did he tack on his most cogent objection: Far from tamping down violence, the very presence of the troops "proved to be an irritant, because it aroused the indignation of a large class of people."

No doubt grinding his teeth as he dictated his message, Cleveland replied: "I neither transcended my authority or duty in the emergency that confronts us." He thought that "in this hour of danger and public distress," they should all be working to restore order.

Altgeld told reporters that Attorney General Olney had given many the impression that he was "the especial representative of the great trusts and monopolies of the country that have been plundering the public and are trying to use the government as a convenience."

The reaction to the public exchange was predictable. Newspaper editors fell over each other to castigate the impudent governor. The *Philadelphia Evening Telegraph* called him "a sausage-maker from Wurttemberg," who had offered "a gross and outrageous affront to the President of the United States."

Altgeld had touched on a crucial issue. Before his first term, Cleveland had run on a typically Democratic states' rights platform. Ten years later he was, at the behest of railroad corporations, trampling state prerogatives and assuming police powers usually exercised by local officials. Rejecting any attempt to settle the dispute peacefully, he was expanding federal executive authority in ways that troubled even those who had little sympathy with striking workers.

Altgeld was an immigrant who had risen to high office. It was testimony to the robustness of the country's political system that he would feel comfortable lecturing the president in such scathing language. He may have been a dead man politically—indeed, he would not be reelected—but his attack on Cleveland was consistent with a lifelong devotion to justice.

❧

The morning of Thursday, July 5, the crowds around the rail yards were sparse. Many Chicagoans were at home nursing hangovers from the previous day's celebration. Then just before noon, a thousand people gathered spontaneously along the Rock Island line near the stockyards. The crowd attracted a crowd—within minutes the single policeman on the scene was facing three thousand unruly citizens. He ran to a call box and begged for reinforcements. Before additional officers arrived, the mob began tipping over cars.

The boxcars of the day had two main parts: an upper body that was essentially a large wooden box and two trucks below, each consisting of four iron wheels, axles, springs, brakes, and coupling mechanism. The box and the trucks were attached at swivel points, allowing the wheels to follow the curves of the track as the train moved. A hard shove by a group of men could get the car swaying on those pivots. Eventually the momentum of the upper part carried it beyond the car's center of gravity. It overcame the weight of the trucks and carried the whole thing over onto its side.

In less than half an hour, the rioters were moving on, leaving scores of overturned cars scattered along the tracks. These hit-and-run tactics made life difficult for the authorities trying to guard the lines. During the day, the scene took on an antic quality as the police and troops rushed from one point to another in pursuit of crowds that could easily melt away into alleys and tenements.

Shortly after noon in the stockyards, authorities attempted to use federal troops to move a train of cattle along the Baltimore & Ohio line. A hundred police officers were on hand to protect the cars, but within minutes they were surrounded by an angry mob. While rioters screamed curses and the steers bellowed their laments, the police swung their clubs with little effect. Eighty cavalrymen and two companies of infantry rushed to the scene. Having forced the crowd back, the horsemen preceded the train while soldiers took up positions on top of the cattle cars, rifles at the ready. They moved only a few blocks before they encountered overturned cars obstructing the tracks. Judging it unlikely that a wreck-ing train could reach the scene, the rail officials conceded defeat. Late in the afternoon they returned the train and put the cattle back in their pens "amid the wildest enthusiasm on the part of the strikers," a reporter ob-served.

The day continued in a series of clashes and obstructions. General Miles dispatched small bands of troops to trouble spots around the city. The soldiers might quell the disturbance around them only to have it break out a hundred yards farther up the line. Rioters stopped trains. They stoned cars. Strikers halted a passenger train and induced its engi-neer and fireman to quit. Stranded passengers were called fools for rid-ing trains during the strike. They had to walk or take streetcars to reach their destinations.

Hope of conciliation dimmed as GMA representatives insisted that their demand was for unconditional surrender. Their stance "acted as a kind of wet blanket on the good intentions of the would-be mediators of the Studebaker stripe," a New York Times reporter noted.

Hopes were also dashed that the conference proposed the day be-fore by Mayor Hopkins would lead to a settlement. The arbitration com-mittee of the Chicago City Council found that the railroad managers would not sit down with union representatives under any circumstances.

Hopkins sent a message to George Pullman in the name of the City of Chicago requesting that he return to the city, meet with his employ-ees, and arbitrate their differences. Such an action, the mayor felt, would speedily settle the crisis. Pullman refused.

Hopkins would later testify that railroad officials had assured him their property had been afforded "the most efficient protection they had ever received during similar troubles; that condition of things lasted until July 5." But as the level of rioting accelerated on that same Thursday, July 5, Hopkins's concern about the city overcame his sympathy for the strik-ers. Seeing the federal troops as both inadequate and counterproductive, he asked Governor Altgeld to assign an Illinois National Guard force to the city.

The federal government had initially sent five companies of soldiers to Chicago. Altgeld mobilized a much larger force, five regiments of the state militia totaling three thousand men. At noon they began to take up positions in the city. Altgeld urged caution. "There is no glory shooting at a ragged and hungry man." The soldiers were to keep their rifles unloaded and strictly obey the orders of their officers.

Hopkins sent men to fifty train stations and crossings around the city and assigned other units to switching areas and to the stockyards. He would eventually deploy almost six thousand soldiers—Altgeld told him that fifty thousand could be raised if needed. But the governor also warned that the troops were not the "guards or custodians of private property." Their duty was only to "keep the peace, quell riots and enforce the law."

Chicago citizens were seeing more and more soldiers patrolling their streets and rail facilities. With his reinforcements, General Miles commanded a thousand men. Several thousand deputy marshals were operating, in addition to five hundred sheriff deputies and more than three thousand police officers. The arrival of the state troops brought the total to more than ten thousand armed men on patrol in a city of 1 million.

❧

By early evening, the soldiers were worn out and discouraged. Their officers acknowledged that they were "utterly unable to cope with the mob that now holds sway in the district." It would require "nine miles of soldiers strung out along the tracks," a lieutenant observed. U.S. Chief Deputy Marshal J. C. Donnelly said nothing short of placing Chicago under martial law would improve the situation. "No ordinary force can handle these men."

"The police and the soldiers were as helpless to preserve the peace," a *New York Times* reporter wrote, "as a regiment of two-year-old children."

The only bullets that flew that day were not fired by troops. A detective on the Western Indiana line was accompanying a locomotive and tender southward when an overturned railcar forced the train to stop. A crowd surrounded the locomotive and threatened to take it over. The detective fired his revolver from the window of the cab, killing striking switchman Edward O'Neill and wounding another man. Under a hail of rocks, the desperate engineer threw open the throttle and pushed the obstruction aside. The engine surged forward, outdistancing the furious mob.

❧

Around the country, the boycott continued to generate anxiety. In New York, papers reported that the meat shortages were driving up the cost of fish. "California fruits are now so scarce," the *New York Times* declared, that by Monday they would be unavailable. There were poultry famines, milk famines, even a lemon famine. It turned out that the lemons for most of the country were normally shipped through New York on trains affected by the strike. Meanwhile, carloads of peaches, strawberries, and cherries were rotting on sidings. The shortages were a sign of how in a single generation the railroads had woven the U.S. economy into a vast, interconnected network.

California remained in turmoil. Large mobs roamed the rail yards of Oakland. After the state militia's failure to restore order, officials at Sacramento admitted they were unable to cope. Strikers had secured all the rifles in the area of the state capital and enough blasting powder to wreck any bridge or tunnel. Southern Pacific Railroad officials were shipping supplies of Winchester rifles to their loyal employees to help protect property. In San Francisco, waterfront stevedores, who loaded and unloaded ships, walked off the job because of earlier wage cuts. "Strike fever" was spreading.

Some federal troops went about their duties reluctantly. One soldier in Los Angeles told a reporter he did not like "this idea of shooting down American citizens simply because they are on a strike for what they consider to be their rights."

Milwaukee unions representing a wide swath of workers were threatening a general strike. The Federated Trades Council in that city had called an open meeting to discuss the matter. The brewers and streetcar men declared themselves ready to go out at a moment's notice.

Colorado's Populist governor Davis Waite said that "Deputy United States Marshals have no right whatever to be employed by any individual or corporation." A conservative newspaper blasted back with the headline: GOV. WAITE ON ANARCHY'S SIDE.

Eugene Debs issued a statement to clarify the position of the American Railway Union. He reiterated the fact that the Pullman employees had struck "entirely of their own accord" and against union advice. "Patience deserted them," he said, because their "souls rebelled." One reason for this insistence was the injunction that had been issued on Monday, July 2, and had now been hanging over the ARU leaders' heads for three days. Advised by his lawyers, Debs felt he had not violated the edict. But rumors that he would be arrested for contempt of court continued to circulate.

Debs responded to George Pullman's contention that there was nothing to arbitrate by asking, Why not allow a fair and impartial board to determine that it was so? Pullman's employees, he guaranteed, would accept any reasonable proposition. He put his faith in the American people, who "believe in fair play."

That day, the *Chicago Tribune* carried a notice of a coming theatrical entertainment to raise money for the women and children of Pullman, who were suffering "want of the actual necessaries of life." The sponsors appealed to all, no matter their position on the boycott. Debs raised "the spectacle of Mr. Pullman fanned by the breezes of the Atlantic while his employees are starving." The image would rouse workers across the country, he asserted. "Labor will stand by labor."

ᘓ

Labor would stand by labor. The government had raised the stakes, first by issuing the omnibus injunction, then by inserting federal troops into the dispute. Debs conceded that the situation had become "alarming" and a subject of "grave concern" to every citizen. He was increasingly contemplating a contingency that had arisen in the Trades and Labor Assembly on Saturday.

"A million of men stand ready to quit work and unite in the struggle for justice and liberty whenever called upon to do so," Debs declared. He raised the prospect that the boycott would swell into a general strike, a rebellion of workers in all fields, the apocalyptic struggle of labor against capital that some had long been predicting. The vast legions of the unemployed with little to lose, of which Coxey's armies had been merely a vanguard, made the prospect all the more frightening.

Samuel Gompers, who stood at the head of the American Federation of Labor, would be a key player if the boycott were to expand its scope. He had expressed his support for the railroad workers and lamented the fact that the interstate commerce law, enacted to protect the people from discrimination and injustice on the part of the railroads, was being used as "an instrument of oppression" to deprive workers of the right to strike. However, his position on a general strike to aid the boycott was unknown.

Trade unions in New York City were actively discussing the possibility of a wider strike. Grand Master Workman James Sovereign of the Knights of Labor wired Debs advising him to "neither make nor accept any compromise. Nothing but complete victory would satisfy our people."

Debs met with members of Chicago Typographical Union on the afternoon of July 5. The typesetters offered to strike if it would help the boycott. That would mean closing down all the newspapers in town.

A general strike was labor's ultimate weapon. When successful, it could paralyze a city. Debs understood the serious and unpredictable ramifications of such a move. His perpetual optimism was buoyed by the ARU's success. The momentum of the boycott was so powerful, the prospects so hopeful that it made sense to consider a final push, an effort that could result in an overthrow of the economic system and the arrival of a new order.

A meeting of all the leaders of the building trades unions had been called for the next night to discuss the crisis. It was widely rumored that if nothing changed, many unions were ready to call their members out. It all foretold to a sudden and alarming escalation of the conflict that had begun in the Pullman factory.

❧

Around 6:00 p.m. on that July 5, the sun was being eclipsed by scudding clouds driven by hot, blustery winds. Angry mobs were roaming up and down Chicago's railroad tracks. In Jackson Park, on the South Side, the buildings of last year's Columbian Exposition stood deserted, a vast, derelict wonderland waiting for the wrecker's ball. Some of the buildings had been damaged by a fire in January. The remaining exhibit halls where the marvels of the coming century had been shown to millions were now used for shelter by unemployed men and women stranded by the sudden collapse of the economy.

A band of the homeless had started a small cooking fire in the Terminal Station, the ornate portal through which so many had stepped into the magic of the fair. The tramps left after consuming a meager meal. Some boys, coming in after them, found the fire still smoldering. And spreading. They tried to stamp out the flames, but fire had already crept into the building's walls. The rail station's interior, which elicited dreams of a vast Roman bath, quickly filled with smoke.

The entire White City, although it appeared to be made of stone, was a pipe dream of wood and iron framing supporting whitewashed plaster mixed with fiber. Exposed to fire, the materials shed their false fronts and burned like kindling. The second floor of the terminal was in flames before the alarm reached Chicago's fire brigades. Burning embers leapt onto gusts of wind and sought new fuel along the splendid Court of Honor. The Administration Building, where President Cleveland had officially opened the fair, was soon ablaze.

Alerted by sirens and smoke, citizens rushed to watch. Tens of thousands of spectators soon roamed the grounds, seeking vantage points from which to take in the blaze that rivaled the Great Chicago Fire itself. In the center of the city, citizens rushed to rooftops to marvel at the smoke billowing over Lake Michigan, the flames dancing a hundred feet in the air, and the great explosions of sparks that surpassed the previous day's fireworks.

The massive dome of the Administration Building came crashing down in less than twenty minutes. Firefighters could do little to abate the destruction. A willful wind whipped the flames. The men of Engine Company 18 had to abandon a pumper as the fire counterattacked. They were unable to rescue one of their draft horses, which suffocated in the smoke. Three men barely escaped death.

The stupendous Manufactures and Liberal Arts Building, the largest structure in the world, fell with a crash that was heard for thirty blocks. The Transportation Building, where George Pullman had proudly displayed his luxury cars, caught fire. It was far enough from the central inferno that firemen were able to save it.

Flames crept into an underground passage that carried electrical lines and burned away the supports. At seven thirty, the ground caved in under two Marshall Field's bookkeepers who had come to behold the spectacle. One man was incinerated. Bystanders managed to pull his badly burned companion from the flames.

Sparks landed on the statue of the Republic. The giant golden effigy was, like the age, merely gilded. The plaster and wood underneath caught, and Big Mary went up in flames.

Most of the buildings of the White City had already been sold to a salvage company, whose owners planned to remove valuable lumber and steel girders. Many citizens thought the fire was a more appropriate and glorious ending. "There was no regret," a reporter wrote, "rather a feeling of pleasure that the elements and not the wrecker should wipe out the spectacle."

The most popular song of the decade, which had been played all through the summer of the Exposition, was "After the Ball." Its lyrics lamented:

> After the stars are gone;
> Many a heart is aching,
> If you could read them all;
> Many the hopes that have vanished
> After the ball.

No evidence ever surfaced to suggest the fire that consumed the White City had anything to do with the railroad boycott. Yet the symbolism was lost on no one. The overflowing promise of the fair had made Chicago an icon of progress. The strike and boycott had turned the city into the focal point of anger and anarchy. The future had disappointed. Instead of wonders, it had delivered unemployment; instead of abundance, soup kitchens; instead of hope, despair. At the fair's opening, General Miles had been hailed by the crowds as their heroic grand marshal. He now threatened to kill citizens wholesale.

Three hours after it began, the fire had scythed the entire White City. In the quiet that followed, the bell-like voice of girl was heard to exclaim, "O, it's all over."

The next day, all hell broke loose.

19

Pandemonium

ALARM BECOMING GENERAL AMONG THOUGHTFUL CITIZENS," U.S.
Attorney Thomas Milchrist wired to his superiors in Washington
on Friday, July 6.

Although the thoughtful citizens of Chicago liked to imagine
themselves living in a modern metropolis, the city still had the heart of
a raw western town. The combination of crowded slums, widespread poverty, and rampant vice made for a coarse and unruly atmosphere. An
Italian visitor during the 1890s observed that "the dominant characteristic of the exterior life of Chicago is violence."

Chicago led the nation in its rate of criminal arrests. Almost two
thousand citizens died violent deaths each year, a fifth of them run down
by trains at grade crossings. Men routinely carried pistols when they went
abroad. A stretch of Randolph Street that accommodated gamblers was
known as the Hairtrigger Block. The infamous Levee vice district adjacent to downtown had scandalized out-of-towners for a decade. "All
America," a tourist wrote, "looks with fear at this city."

City residents were not easily intimidated, even by armed soldiers.
Aware that the troops had been sent into the city in spite of Governor
Altgeld's protest, working-class Chicagoans were angered by the pre-
sumption of the federal authorities. They took the troops' presence as a
personal insult. ARU vice president George Howard, himself a veteran
of the Union Army, noted that "the very sight of a bluecoat arouses their
anger. They feel it is another instrument of oppression."

That Friday, citizens awoke to a cascade of alarming headlines:

MOB WILL IS LAW

GUNS AWE THEM NOT

RIOTERS DEFY UNCLE SAM'S TROOPS

REGULARS POWERLESS BEFORE CHICAGO'S RIOTOUS ARMY

Residents anxious to keep up on events paid premium prices for extra editions. The *Tribune* judged that the strike had become an "insurrection." Editors hoped Dictator Debs and his drunken followers "will be fired upon, they will be bayoneted, will be trampled under foot by cavalry, and mowed down by artillery." The *Washington Post* predicted "war of the bloodiest kind in Chicago."

It was clear that most of the rioters were, as a police inspector affirmed, "not railroad men." A *Chicago Herald* reporter recognized them as "rough, vicious and lawless elements" from local neighborhoods. Another witness said that those engaged in destruction "are not strikers, most of them are not even grown men."

Whoever they were, they held the city under siege on Friday. For Eugene Debs, the developments were ominous. There was no question that the mobs in the Chicago rail yards were running riot. They attacked any train that the railroad supervisors had the audacity to operate. With the help of marshals and police, Baltimore & Ohio officials tried to bring four passenger trains through during the morning. By the time the trains reached the station, all the windows on each of them had been smashed.

Police began to respond with pistol fire. A lieutenant fired once in the air to disperse a crowd, then directly into a mass of people. A "young Pole" was seen to drop—his friends helped him limp away.

By afternoon, pitched battles were breaking out around the stockyards, with "heads cracked by the score." Police made no attempt to arrest rioters, a reporter observed, but those who could not run fast enough "felt the hickory." A squad of army regulars made three charges on gangs of rioters who were overturning cars, driving the culprits out of the yards and returning with blood on their bayonets.

〜

As the day went on, fire became a dominant theme of the disturbances. It was as if the immolation of the White City the night before had touched an incendiary nerve. Crowds overturned more than 150 empty boxcars on a mile-long stretch of tracks near the stockyards. Starting in the morning, they also set fire to isolated switching towers and other railroad property. The arson spread during the afternoon and by nightfall a "roaring wall of fire" had formed along the tracks from Fifty-Fifth to Sixty-First Street, a few blocks west of the site of the fair.

Along the Pan Handle road outside the stockyards, as many as seven hundred freight cars burned. Arsonists removed oil-soaked rags packed into the axle bearings of the cars and fashioned them into torches. Local residents roamed the yards, looting loaded boxcars before dispatching them in flame. Twenty meat cars went up, lacing the air with the prehistoric aroma of roasting flesh. Two hundred open-topped gondola cars filled with anthracite coal were lit. When their wood frames burned through, the glowing coal spilled onto the right-of-way. Ties burned. Iron rails warped in the intense heat.

Another fire tore through more than 250 boxcars on sidings. It was reported that two of them contained loads of provisions gathered by a relief committee to aid the Pullman strikers.

Exhausted firemen struggled to keep the blazes from spreading. Many of the fires were located far from any hydrant. Crowds actively interfered with their efforts to save railroad property. They jammed the fireboxes used to send alarms, threw stones at fire trucks, and in some cases slashed hoses. The frenzy at the stockyards culminated in the burning of a huge barn holding almost seven hundred tons of hay. Overtaxed fire brigades could only watch the inferno vomit its dense gray-white smoke as tongues of orange flame licked up its sides.

❧

More than one observer noted that the freight cars seemed to be set on fire systematically. The perpetrators showed "none of the wild howlings and ravings that marked their work of the night before." The accusation would be floated, although never proven, that railroad managers had hired provocateurs to ramp up the riots and add to the arson. "We have it upon reliable authority," Debs said, "that thugs and toughs have been employed to create trouble so as to prejudice the public against our cause."

Many of the targets of arson were worn-out and surplus freight cars. Few Pullman cars were attacked. The cars that burned were packed very close together, beyond the reach of fire hoses. The announcement by the corporations that they intended to sue the city for damages because police had failed to protect their property—losses were estimated at as much as $1 million—added to the suspicion.

Others pointed to the role of the detectives and other employees of the railroad corporations who were serving as deputies. These marshals "were armed and paid by the railroads and acted in the double capacity of railroad employees and United States officers." A report by fire department officials, who kept track of all damage, said that when firefighters extinguished blazes on the night of July 6, "they caught men in the act of cutting the hose and that these men wore the badges of deputy marshals."

City officials put the total railroad losses for that Friday at $340,000. On no other day of the strike had the damage reached more than $4,000.

✧

As turmoil engulfed the stockyards, violence also flared ten miles away in the rail yards of the southern suburbs. At daybreak on Friday, a mob gathered in Kensington along the Illinois Central tracks just opposite the Pullman works. At 9:00 a.m., a Michigan Central train approached and was surrounded by a mass of humanity. Gerald Stark, chief detective for the road and now a deputized marshal, stood on the platform of a car. The crowd surged around him. He pulled his revolver, pointed it at the crowd, and fired. Its sharp report sounded above the clamor. Again. One shot wounded spectator Frank Udess over his right eye. Another caught William Anslyn in the forehead. According to witnesses, Anslyn tried to rise, but Stark fired a third bullet into his back. He died of his wounds.

The mob erupted. Police managed to get Stark off the train as a woman cried, "Lynch him!" The officers pulled the detective to a police station and disguised him as one of the wounded men. They spirited him away in a patrol wagon.

Soon afterward, a milk train passed through the station on the way to Chicago. The rioters forced the engineer to stop. They chased him and his fireman out of the cab, uncoupled the cars, opened the engine's throttle, and jumped off. The empty locomotive went careening wildly up the tracks until it collided with an overturned boxcar and derailed.

This was the closest the rioting had come to the model town. Strike leader Thomas Heathcoate had worked hard to keep the wave of vandalism and arson from spreading to the shops and to the four hundred idle Pullman cars parked nearby. Union men were still manning a guard force around the plant.

That afternoon, two hundred rioters overpowered several watchmen and entered the Pullman factory. They forced out the skeleton crew still employed in the plant. Panicked office workers locked financial records in safes and fled. The invaders destroyed nothing. More company watchmen, now armed with riot guns, appeared to hasten their departure. A threat by mob leaders to return and burn down the Hotel Florence convinced most of the guests there to depart before evening.

Pullman vice president Thomas Wickes, along with plant manager Harvey Middleton, had been inspecting the shops three times a day since the strike began back in May. Wickes had asked Mayor Hopkins to station more police around the facility. Hopkins said he did not think the beefed-up security was warranted. But with a mob now burning cars just across the tracks, Hopkins sent to Pullman 240 men of the First Regiment of the Illinois National Guard. They brought along a Gatling gun, a weapon considered superior for crowd control.

Although Heathcoate criticized the deployment of the troops as inflammatory, the soldiers set up their bivouac on the lawn of the hotel and their officers commandeered rooms inside the building. Sentries were ordered to admit no civilian to the factory without a pass. Additional state troops took up positions in surrounding towns.

It was not only in Chicago where the strike was entering a crisis. Montana had been caught up in the action from the beginning. The state's agriculture, lumber, and mining depended on rail transport. In the first days of the boycott, switching crews on the Northern Pacific Railway had refused to handle Pullman cars. They were discharged by railroad managers, touching off a strike up and down the line. Engineers, conductors, and firemen soon joined the boycott. The state's far-flung towns were isolated from each other and dependent on rail lines. By early July, the stores in many of them were barren. Tons of strawberries rotted in Missoula. In Billings, with poultry, vegetables, and other foodstuffs on the verge of going bad, officials sponsored a "feast of famine," serving hearty meals to two thousand citizens at nominal prices in order to use up the perishables.

Support for the strike in the state was widespread. A minister in Billings said the corporations were "the pliant tools of the codfish monied aristocracy who seek to dominate this country." In the south-central railroad town of Livingston, which huddled along the Yellowstone River where it dropped out of the mountains, nine of every ten residents supported the strikers. Valley farmers with deep grievances against the railroads provided the men with donations of food and provisions.

On Tuesday, July 3, Northern Pacific managers had demanded relief from the federal courts, and Judge Hiram Knowles, who in April had authorized troops to arrest William Hogan and the train-stealers of Coxey's Army, issued an injunction against the strike. Like other federal magistrates, he was guided by a legal theory that sacrificed government neutrality to a sanctified view of property rights.

That same day, Brigadier General Wesley Merritt, commander of the Department of Dakota, wired Washington to say that mail was being obstructed along the Nothern Pacific. Nor was he able to send a paymaster or supplies along the line. He recommended to Secretary of War Lamont that he be allowed to "remove the obstruction." Railroad managers concurred, insisting that troops be sent.

President Cleveland asserted that he had a duty to keep open any railroad over which military supply trains or the U.S. mail ran. "If it takes the entire army and navy of the United States to deliver a postal card in Chicago," Cleveland was reported to have said, "that card will be delivered."

On Friday, July 6, the president ordered General Schofield to open the Northern Pacific. In dispatching troops to Chicago three days earlier, Cleveland could cite reports, however inaccurate, of rioting and violence. The strike in Montana had been entirely peaceful. Without any pretense of restoring order, Cleveland was choosing to occupy the state with federal forces. His goal was clear—to break the strike.

General Merritt headed west from St. Paul and ordered another force to set out from Seattle in a pincer operation. A third battalion, fifty Tenth Cavalry troopers, African American enlistees known as Buffalo Soldiers, rode on horseback the forty-five miles from Fort Custer to Billings.

A speaker at a rally in Helena insisted that discontent could not be conquered by force. Another orator called it "a battle for supremacy between dollars and cents on one side and humanity on the other." A Livingston newspaper warned of "military despotism."

While the military maneuver was getting under way, officers of the ARU local at Butte sent a crew to rescue a circus train stranded in the mountains near Lima. In gratitude, the Great Syndicate Shows and Paris Hippodrome put on a free performance that night in Butte. More than twelve hundred spectators from all over the region welcomed the break from strike-induced anxiety and hard times. They filled the bleachers to watch the clowns, the equestriennes, and Rialto, a strong man who could lift the soldiers of an entire army platoon with his teeth.

On Tuesday, July 10, the first regular train, complete with Pullman cars, reached Livingston under military guard. The officer in charge, Captain B. C. Lockwood, feared a violent reception. He ordered his soldiers to walk in front of the train with loaded carbines and fixed bayonets. Seven hundred residents turned out to hurl insults and threats at the invaders.

Soldiers hammered with rifle butts any citizen who did not move out of the way fast enough. Captain Lockwood whacked the flat of his sword against the head of I. F. Toland, a Northern Pacific foreman who backed the ARU. He wildly drew back the blade, accidentally striking a small boy. Approaching hysteria, the captain screamed at Livingston's mayor: "I am running this town!"

⁓

On that same busy Friday, July 6, the U.S. attorney in Chicago, Thomas Milchrist, wired Olney for permission to draw up a request for an order of contempt against Debs for violating the injunction, which had been in effect since Monday. The attorney general gave the go-ahead. Lawyers working for the railroads offered to help Milchrist with the wording of the charge. He wrote the document on his own but thought it wise to submit it to the railroad managers for their approval before filing it with the court.

The next step was to indict union officials for conspiracy. Edwin Walker, who was putting together that case, told Olney the same day that he had enough evidence and planned to present it to a federal grand jury the following Tuesday, July 10. Olney was sure Debs and the ARU officers could not escape this finely woven net.

John Egan, representing the General Managers' Association, felt that since the contempt charge was ready to go and would require only a judge's order to enforce, the government should make that their first line of attack. Walker thought that if Debs were to make bail on the contempt charge, it would add impetus to the general strike rumored to be in the works. He wanted to wait and file his criminal charge first. Bail on that could be set so high that the "dictator" would have to remain in jail. He predicted that as a result, a "strike upon any railroad will not again occur for a series of years."

〜

As he dealt with the tactics of the boycott, Debs was also thinking strategically. On the one hand, he felt the need to prevent retaliation against the scabs who were filling ARU members' jobs. On the other hand, if the corporations were free to bring in replacements and operate trains, the strike would be lost. Increasingly, he was coming to think that the solution to the dilemma was to broaden the attack, to throw his support behind a general strike. The prospect of all workers joining in solidarity spoke to his deepest principles.

Debs knew the history of the labor movement. The few general strikes in the United States up to that point had been limited to single cities. A strike of all workers in Philadelphia back in 1832 had won a ten-hour day. A nationwide strike for shorter hours had been tried in 1886, but it ended in the disastrous bombing in Chicago's Haymarket Square.

More recently, in 1892, the American Federation of Labor had helped organize a successful general strike in New Orleans. A labor alliance representing both white packers and black teamsters there struck for shorter hours and better pay. The employers' Board of Trade offered to settle only with the white workers. The alliance members refused to be divided. They were joined by forty-nine other AFL trade unions in a general strike. More than twenty-five thousand workers, half the city's workforce and almost all its union men, walked off the job. The Board of Trade agreed to arbitration, which won the employees many of their demands.

Debs had already begun reaching out to his many contacts in labor unions around the country. "We have assurance," he declared to reporters, "that within forty-eight hours every labor organization in the country will come to our rescue." The prediction heartened workers and shocked the public.

On that Friday evening, workingmen and their representatives from around Chicago poured into Ulrich's Hall. The Building Trades Council represented twenty-five thousand organized workingmen including architectural ironworkers, cement finishers, plumbers, and gas fitters. The overflow conference met behind closed doors until two in the morning to discuss a strategy to meet this unprecedented attack by the government on working people. Talk of a general strike buzzed through the hall.

Although excited by the prospect, Debs continued to hope for conciliation. Labor, he said, was willing to meet "any gentlemen of standing" who could effect an honorable settlement. "Let Mr. Pullman agree to the appointment of arbitrators," he declared. "And if they agree there is nothing to arbitrate, Mr. Pullman's position will be sustained."

If arbitration was the carrot, the men of the Building Trades Council hefted a stick to back up the offer. It would be good for all if George Pullman would accept arbitration. If he refused, they agreed to promote "a general cessation of all industries throughout the country."

The delegates called on the American Federation of Labor to take the lead in organizing the action. They scheduled another conference at Ulrich's Hall on Sunday, with each Chicago trade union to send three delegates. While not agreeing to an immediate strike, they had set the machinery in motion for an action whose consequences could shake the country.

෴

As Debs monitored the wires, the flames of anarchy crackling through Chicago seemed to be dropping embers in distant locations. In Sacramento, two days after the failure of the militia to restore order on July 4, the standoff continued. "Not a wheel is turning," a newspaper reported. Strikers there upped the ante and now said they would not return to work until the company restored the wages of the railroad men to the 1893 scale.

Tie-ups in Detroit and Cleveland were strangling lines from the East. Switchmen, trainmen, and firemen were ready to strike in Buffalo. Fire had erupted during the night in Cairo, Illinois. The Cudahy Packing plant in Omaha had laid off three hundred hog killers. The nearby Omaha Smelter was nearly out of ore and would soon be shut.

In Pittsburgh, ARU organizers spoke to a standing-room-only mass meeting and employees there were ready to strike. "You had all better get on the band wagon when it comes along," the union men advised.

That afternoon, Debs sent a telegram to ARU members in Jackson, Michigan. "The fight is on, and our men are acquitting themselves like heroes. Our cause is gaining ground daily." Success, he wrote, "is only a question of a few days."

∽

The federal infantry and cavalry troops in the stockyards had sought greater security by combining their camps. The soldiers removed fences surrounding Dexter Park in case they needed to flee a fire in their midst. The night sky took on a rosy hue. "The whole horizon seemed afire," one man said.

The assistant fire marshal for the area around the stockyards said nearly 150 boxcars had burned there, along with eight switch towers. In the district to the south, more than 750 cars had been ignited.

A reporter for the *Chicago Inter Ocean* that night had observed a "moving mass of shouting rioters" from which squads of a dozen would break away and run into the yards with firebrands. Silhouetted against the flames were "men and women dancing with frenzy." It was, he said, a grand spectacle. "It was pandemonium let loose."

20

Day of Blood

EUGENE DEBS HAD A MIND NOURISHED BY ACTION. THROUGH-
out his life, he was constantly on the move, meeting people, talking,
organizing, delivering speeches. He was rarely contemplative.
Things always needed to be done.

Like a man sprinting on a tightrope, he had traveled the country for
a year preaching the gospel of the American Railway Union, leading the
strike on the Great Northern, and overseeing the ARU convention. He
had taken charge of the greatest labor action in the nation's history, plotted strategy, sent hundreds of telegrams, talked repeatedly to reporters,
and addressed rallies around Chicago and across the Middle West.

Now he sensed that the situation was approaching a turning point
and he struggled to make sense of the mixed messages. In Cleveland,
switchmen were staying out and no trains were moving. In Van Buren,
Arkansas, "not a wheel on the Missouri Pacific" was turning. In Bir-
mingham, telegraph operators had joined the tie-up.

Yet some trains were beginning to roll, guarded by soldiers' guns. The
first mail trains had left Los Angeles. The U.S. Ninth Cavalry Regiment
was riding out to open the Union Pacific from Cheyenne to Ogden.

What to make of it all? The union had set up a bicycle intelligence
service to report on events around Chicago and to carry messages into
the field, a useful innovation with many local trains frozen in place. He
learned that three-quarters of the factories in Chicago would soon close
for lack of fuel, supplies, or business. A hundred thousand in the city

would be thrown out of work. The Illinois Steel Company was banking nineteen furnaces for lack of coke and would be laying off 5,750 men. The Great Western Refining Co. had fuel for only two more days.

In these early years of electric power, towns, factories, and some private homes depended on their own generating facilities. The steam engines that powered them now thirsted for coal. Lack of power knocked out lights, streetcar lines, water plants.

Would the distress translate into public rage against the intransigence of George Pullman and the devious tactics of the rail companies? Or would it swing against the union? Debs could do nothing but urge the men to keep up the pressure as they waited to see.

"Capital has combined to enslave labor," he wrote. "We must all stand together or go down in hopeless defeat."

That Saturday, July 7, George Pullman, also sensing a climax, wired orders that company officials were to remove all servants from his Prairie Avenue mansion and see that they were taken to places of safety. It was whispered that his silver plate had already been transferred to vaults at the Pullman Building downtown. More armed guards were sent to patrol his home.

To some, the violence and disorder suggested divine retribution. Mormon elder John H. Smith, a cousin of the sect's founder, wrote in his diary: "Blood has been spilled at several places and Millions of property has been destroyed at Chicago. Said Joseph the Prophet, you will have mob[b]ings to your hearts content. Are his words being fullfilled?"

လ

The burning, shooting, and widespread chaos that had gripped the city on Friday, July 6, prompted a conference between General Miles and Mayor Hopkins. The general said he had talked to the president over a long-distance telephone line. Cleveland hoped to soothe the hard feelings that his ignoring of local authorities had created. Now he said he wanted "unity of action." The federal soldiers would be deployed to move the mails and facilitate interstate commerce. Miles said they would also be available to charge crowds and restore order, but only at the request of the mayor.

Hopkins still resented the intrusion. He made it clear to Miles that he now had four thousand National Guard militiamen, along with more than three thousand police officers, under his command. Both men agreed that they needed to give their forces more backbone. Orders were changed. Now federal troops would be allowed to shoot at anyone setting fires, destroying property, throwing objects, or attacking marshals or trainmen. State soldiers and police would be issued similar instructions. Crowds would no longer be allowed to jeer and threaten troops with impunity.

After meeting the mayor, Miles sat down with U.S. Attorney Edwin Walker, John Egan of the GMA, and other railroad men. They wanted troops to back up the armed marshals, many of them railroad employees, who were guarding the trains. Miles, still unconvinced of the need to concentrate his forces, sent his men out by companies to depots and key crossings. He ordered each soldier to carry a hundred rounds of ammunition and five days' rations.

❧

The critical action on Saturday was to be undertaken by state, not federal, troops. Before dawn, the forty men of Company C of the Second Illinois National Guard Regiment, under the command of Captain Thomas I. Mair, rose early, ate a quick breakfast, and headed out at 4:00 a.m. The pearly light of a summer dawn was just brightening the sky. Their assignment was to back up a squadron of police and to guard a wrecking train that was clearing an east-west section of rail line that ran the length of Forty-Seventh Street along the southern edge of the Union Stock Yard.

The wrecking train consisted of an engine and a tender pushing a flatcar mounted with a heavy wooden derrick. Maintenance workers used a block and tackle, wedges, jacks, and muscle power to right capsized and burnt boxcars and get them back onto the rails.

It was tedious work, punctuated by catcalls and jeers from the residents of nearby houses, most of them Polish and Bohemian immigrants. Children turned out in numbers to watch the intriguing process. Men and women grumbled in foreign tongues.

Around three in the afternoon, after eleven hours on the job with no break for dinner, the crew was working on an overturned car near Loomis Street. By this time, several thousand spectators had gathered. A publishing company employee named J. R. George had the afternoon off and was watching from the steps of a nearby saloon. He reported that hoodlums, mostly teenage boys, started the trouble. One of them "shied a stone at the soldiers." Half a dozen others followed suit.

The troops and trainmen found themselves under a hail of stones and pieces of iron. An exasperated Captain Mair ordered the onlookers to disperse and told his men to load their rifles. Some spectators, especially the women and children, drifted back toward the stables and alleys that lined the tracks. Others, curious about what was happening, pushed forward. The disturbance attracted more onlookers, swelling the crowd to several thousand.

Tension thickened the air of the overcast afternoon. The barrage of thrown objects increased. A stone ricocheted off the engine and struck a policeman. He fired his revolver into the crowd. The onlookers surged backward. A return shot sounded from one of the sheds. More police officers fired, some into the crowd, some over the heads of the watchers. A great roar of rage poured from the citizenry. More missiles. The electric crackle of gunfire sounded back and forth. A baseball-size stone struck National Guard lieutenant Harry Reed on the temple and knocked him to the ground bleeding and unconscious.

Captain Mair shouted his orders to the militiamen.

"Make ready." A clatter of arms.

"Take aim." A single beat of silence.

"Fire!" The rifles blasted in unison with an intimidating, ear-numbing crash far louder than the snap of the revolvers. It was the first coordinated volley fired during the boycott.

The crowd flinched. Half a dozen men fell. A cloud of white smoke wafted over the onlookers.

A young man standing on the saloon steps beside J. R. George grabbed his arm and announced, "I'm shot!" George panicked and began to run. He saw a woman who was hit by a bullet sink to the ground.

"Then ensued the real rioting," George noted. Joining a stampede up Loomis Street, he darted down an alley, leaped over a fence, tore across a vacant lot, stumbled over a man's body, and came upon a white-faced woman, her leg a mass of blood. He ran on.

Back along the tracks, the enraged members of the crowd were bellowing and pushing forward. More volleys rang out from the militia. Captain Mair ordered his men to deploy bayonets and charge.

The soldiers' Springfield rifles were equipped with an innovation in the form of a built-in, round, spring-loaded bayonet similar to a ramrod. The flick of a catch snapped the weapon into position. The men drove the crowd with these pig stickers, pushing them north along Loomis Street, then east on Forty-Ninth Street. Rioters fought back with stones and clubs. A dozen men in the front lines were stabbed by soldiers.

While this battle was in progress, a separate mob approached the wrecking train from the south. The terrified engineer opened the throttle and the train began a clanking retreat down the right-of-way. The soldiers hurried back to the tracks and marched along behind it. The crowd, sensing a victory, surged toward them. The company of militiamen wheeled and charged again.

By this time, chaos gripped the entire neighborhood, one of the slums that surrounded the Union Stock Yard. The police had called for reinforcements. A patrol wagon filled with officers came stampeding toward the scene. The driver whipped the horses and charged full speed into the menacing crowd. The police began firing point-blank into the mass of people. The rioters wavered, then retreated. A barbed wire fence that ran parallel to the tracks slowed them, giving the officers, who were "not inclined to be merciful," a chance to wade in swinging clubs.

Another militia company, called in as reinforcements, came running up the tracks at a brisk trot. When they were welcomed by a barrage of stones, their captain, too, ordered a bayonet charge. The fight again moved away from the rail line and into the streets and alleys of the neighborhood, a mixture of three-story tenements and small bungalows interspersed with storefronts. Residents fired rifles and pistols from houses. Police and soldiers shot back. A group of men fled up the avenue and took refuge in a saloon. Police officers smashed in the door. They were met by a barrage of billiard balls.

When it was over, the ground "was like a battlefield," with hats knocked off, jackets shed, men lying bleeding. In an alley, a neighborhood ruffian named John "Engine" Burke lay shot through the torso. Police carried him to a nearby drugstore, where he expired. Thomas Jackman had been shot in the stomach—he too would die. At least four persons were killed in the skirmish, probably more. Some of those killed and wounded were spirited away into houses and tenements and never reported by residents of the insular immigrant communities.

News of the shooting began to blare from extra editions of newspapers. IS A DAY OF BLOOD, cried the *Chicago Tribune*.

National anxiety soared. William Steinway, New York City businessman and scion of the piano-making firm, had, like George Pullman, established a company town near his factory to discourage union organizing. On Saturday, July 7, he recorded in his diary: "Terrible scenes at Chicago and the West, murder and destruction of property, RR Cars by the strikers and the mob, adding to the general business depression, and raising prices of meat, also preventing shipment of goods."

Although strikers were enraged by the violence, many of their sympathizers were sobered. The sharp danger made those who were out to have fun or to loot think twice about venturing into the rail yards. The battle at Loomis Street delivered just the type of shock that some had hoped would quell the disorder.

Others had been killed during the day, including Richard Zepp, a detective hired by Baltimore & Ohio officials to protect their property. He was shot through a window of the Union Depot at Adams and Canal Streets in downtown Chicago. He left a widow and nine children. Joseph Warzowski, a Polish laborer, was shot in the back by either a marshal or a federal soldier at Twenty-Second Street just north of the industrial district that lined the South Branch of the Chicago River.

In the opinion of former Union Army general Lew Wallace, "Civil war is imminent if the great strike is not promptly subdued."

⁀

The killing was not over. Hammond, Indiana, was a choke point for trains from the East, and the people there overwhelmingly supported the strike. Adjacent to Chicago's South Side, the town had seen serious disturbances since the beginning of the boycott eleven days earlier. Sheriff deputies, federal marshals, and Indiana militiamen had all tried their hand at keeping trains moving. Eugene Debs and local union officials had cautioned strikers and sympathizers against illegal acts. On that Saturday night, July 7, crowds again invaded the Hammond rail yards.

In the darkness, rioters turned over fifteen freight cars, blocking the Michigan Central and Nickel Plate lines. The rioting went on all night. The protesters, many armed with revolvers, stopped another train and ordered the engineer and fireman out. Indiana National Guard troops returned. Railroad officials wired General Miles for federal military assistance. He ordered Company D of the Fifteenth Infantry to speed south by train from their Lake Front Park camp early on Sunday.

About eleven thirty that morning, the forty-nine men of the company climbed down into Hammond's maze of tracks. Jeering citizens turned the scene into a "veritable bedlam." The crowd quickly swelled to more than two thousand.

Captain Wilson T. Hartz ordered his men to clear the tracks so that a mail train could move through. They walked the onlookers back to the sidewalks at bayonet point. Then Hartz took a squad aboard an engine and headed up the tracks to assure they were clear. After they traveled a short distance, they received word that the rioters were in the process of overturning a Pullman car onto the tracks to block their retreat. Hartz ordered the engineer to reverse and told his men to load their weapons.

The Springfield was a single-shot rifle. After the men slid a cartridge into the chamber, they customarily held a few rounds in their mouths to be ready for additional shots. An observer that day said the men appeared to have "steel tusks."

As the soldiers arrived at the scene, the rioters remained oblivious of the danger. A reporter judged them to be "roughs from Chicago who had been brought there by the excitement." They were intent on using a rope and tackle to upset the heavy Pullman car.

Without warning and without orders, the soldiers began to fire before the locomotive came to a halt. The explosion of the first volley caught the crowd of forty rioters by surprise.

"They were firing directly at us," a witness reported. "Instantly there was a panic, men and women screaming." By the third crash of the rifles, the vandals were in full retreat.

"About thirty shots were fired," Captain Hartz estimated, "before I could get the engine to a standstill and get control."

Half a dozen people were shot. Victor Seitor's knee was shattered; an amputation would be needed to save his life. W. H. Campbell received a fatal bullet wound to his thigh. Annie Flemming was not even a spectator. She had been crossing the tracks four blocks away to visit a neighbor. When a bullet grazed her leg above the knee, she fainted. She was carried bleeding to a nearby house.

Charles Fleischer likewise played no part in the riot. A thirty-five-year-old carpenter, he had come down to the yards to search for his son, who had been attracted by the excitement. Fleischer had climbed onto a freight car to see if he could spot the lad. A bullet tore open his abdomen and killed him outright. His frantic wife, waiting anxiously for her son to return, instead watched as neighbors approached carrying her husband's body.

The shooting inspired many in the crowd to rush home and return with revolvers and shotguns, intent on slaughtering the soldiers. Hammond's mayor, Patrick Reilly, who was already on the scene, climbed onto a boxcar and pleaded for calm. He ordered the people to go home. He encouraged a local priest to intercede with his parishioners. But it was the arrival of three more companies of regulars that finally convinced the rioters to retreat.

Reilly bitterly denounced the shooting. The troops, he said, should have used their bayonets to manage the crowd rather than fire indiscriminately. "I would like to know by what authority United States Troops come in here and shoot our citizens without the slightest warning," he demanded of Indiana governor Claude Matthews. The head of the ARU local in Hammond also contacted the governor. "Federal troops shooting citizens down promiscuously without provocation," he wired. "Act quickly." Governor Matthews said that if authority was resisted and inoffensive citizens suffered as a result, it was a source of "extreme regret."

Hammond residents convinced a justice of the peace to issue murder charges against the troops involved in the shooting. But the soldiers were already on their way back to Chicago and the warrants were never served. Mayor Reilly ordered all saloons in town closed for the duration.

In Ohio, federal judge William Howard Taft wrote to his wife: "It will be necessary for the military to kill some of the mob before the trouble can be stayed." They had only killed six so far, he said, and "this is hardly enough to make an impression."

⁓

The killing was not over. That same Saturday night, July 7, Bohemian and Italian rioters burned cars in the Burlington Railroad yard at Ashland Avenue just north of the port facilities on the Chicago River. A seventeen-year-old girl named Martea Bach went to the roof of her tenement building at Nineteenth Street and Ashland to watch the excitement. Police arrived to break up the mob. They fired over the heads of the crowd. One of the bullets struck Martea in the heart and she fell down dead.

21

I, Grover

FOLKS ON BOTH SIDES OF THE BOYCOTT PLEADED WITH George Pullman to return to Chicago and help resolve the crisis that was now causing Americans to be killed in the streets. Instead, that weekend he traveled from his oceanfront home to his secluded retreat in the Thousand Islands. He told a reporter that he did not feel up to giving an interview. "I am so worn out and tired." In any case, "the strike has gone beyond me, and I could say little of interest."

He denied the rumor that President Cleveland had urged him to arbitrate. Others certainly had. Cook County judge Murray F. Tuley expressed the opinion that "Pullman could have, I am satisfied, prevented it all." Detroit's Republican mayor Hazen Pingree traveled to Chicago with telegrams from the mayors of fifty other cities urging a negotiated settlement. To all came the same answer. Nothing to arbitrate.

Pullman's brother-in-law George West suggested to reporters: "Let [the employees] return to us as they went out, non-union men, and we will then see what amicable arrangements can be made."

Positions showed no sign of softening. The General Managers' Association strike leader, John Egan, noted that in Chicago "only two roads are making any pretense of operating." The situation had reached a point "where none but violent measures can produce a better condition of affairs. This thing must come to an end."

"The railroads," Egan said, "can do no more than they have done." He described Debs as "an egotistical ass" who could be "squelched by a strong hand." He insisted that "quibbling over legal technicalities and hair's breadth definitions of the constitutional rights of the citizens will not ease up matters in the slightest." Saturday's gunfire, he thought, was "a move in the right direction."

Reporters asked Egan's colleague, U.S. Attorney Edwin Walker, whether Debs was about to be arrested. No warrants for ARU officials had yet been issued, he said. "He will not be arrested until after the grand jury meets."

Debs himself was in good humor and standing firm. He told reporters the strike was strengthening hour by hour. "I consider our position impregnable. I am not worrying much about this rumored arrest." He had consulted with his lawyer, a friend from Terre Haute, and was sanguine that the injunction was an absurd overreach by the government.

The South Side of Chicago, where violence had flared the day before, remained calm on Sunday. It was, a reporter noted, the "quietest day that the neighborhood experienced in many years." Most saloons near Loomis and Forty-Ninth Streets were closed. Instead, sightseers came to view the scene of Saturday's violence as if it were a Civil War battlefield. They stared at the bullet holes, which riddled the modest frame cottages near the Grand Trunk tracks. "Relic hunters and camera-snappers were plentiful," a reporter wrote.

The wreckage of hundreds of burned freight cars that filled the Pan Handle yards was also a tourist draw. A pall of smoke still hung over the neighborhood. The air was filled with the acrid smell of the anthracite that continued to smolder on the tracks. All afternoon, a nearby boulevard swarmed with the brougham carriages of the well-to-do and the hired hacks of the middle class. Bicycle riders chose the area for their outings, and the day found the "bloomer girl much in evidence."

⁓

Grover Cleveland had never seen a gun fired in anger. During the Civil War he had hired a Polish immigrant to take his place in the ranks. An isolationist at heart, he had avoided overseas conflicts during his first term. Now he found himself unexpectedly directing a military campaign at home. He had not gotten a good night's sleep since activating the troops on the previous Tuesday, July 3. Emergency meetings with Olney, General Schofield, and Cleveland's old law partner, Postmaster General Wilson S. Bissell, often went on until two or three in the morning.

"The pulse of the great strike was being felt in the White House," a news report said. All day Saturday and Sunday, July 7 and 8, visitors streamed in and out to report and consult. Cleveland handled a deluge of letters and telegrams—he established a direct wire to General Miles's headquarters in Chicago.

The feeling among members of the high command was that more force was needed. All day Sunday, Cleveland consulted with his confidants. After dinner, he called the entire cabinet together.

General Schofield, the army commander, still grumbled about General Miles's tactic of dividing his command. He thought the shooting by militiamen at Loomis Street offered a clear example of how facing crowds with too little force "may have a bad effect on the mob." He convinced Cleveland to send a thousand additional federal troops to Chicago, including more artillery and cavalry. Infantry would be dispatched immediately from as far away as Sackets Harbor, on the eastern end of Lake Ontario. Three thousand more U.S. Marshals would be recruited and sworn in.

The cabinet members perused a long dispatch that Eugene Debs and James Sovereign of the Knights of Labor had sent to the president earlier in the day. The labor leaders once again pleaded their case against George Pullman's stubborn refusal to talk. They blamed the railroads, not the strikers, for any disruption of the mails. They noted that the military, so quickly deployed during the strike, had never been called out to protect working people "from the ravage and persecution of corporate greed."

The message ended with a pledge that they would use the power of both their organizations to maintain peace and good order, even as they struggled on behalf of the "inherent rights of all men." Cleveland ignored the message. He had something else in mind.

✍

In Chicago that Sunday, July 8, delegates from the city's trade unions filed into Ulrich's Hall for a late-afternoon meeting. They represented a wide array of professions: wire workers, horseshoe-nail makers, waiters, iron molders, stationary engineers, carpet salesmen, theatrical stage workers, bakers, stonecutters, harness makers, and cap makers. The great meeting room was filled to suffocation, and the corridors were packed with those who could not get in. Hours were spent sorting through the men's credentials to make sure no railroad detectives were present.

The delegates represented more than a hundred local trade unions. Each had the authority to act for his members. The chiefs of several national unions were also on hand, including John McBride of the mine workers, James J. O'Connell of the machinists, and William B. Prescott of the typographers.

Every day, Eugene Debs had seen the stakes mount. Hundreds of thousands of railroad men were in economic freefall, without income or resources. Great corporations had watched their revenues dry up. Americans were divided and afraid. The U.S. Army was in the streets. Thousands of militiamen were on patrol. Men and women had died. People in towns cut off by the boycott were going hungry. There was only one way to resolve the situation, Debs told the meeting: a general strike.

Faced with a momentous decision, the delegates argued late into the night. The booming contention of the voices at times rattled the windows of the hall. Reporters sat on fences outside, trying to hear. A man shouted: "If you want to save united labor, if you want to save the unions, if you want to save Chicago, you must strike and help us."

Others protested. Now was not the time. Too many unemployed men were desperate for work. The printers of the International Typographical Union were reluctant. The plumbers did not want to strike. The radicals, comprised largely of Germans and other immigrant laborers, wanted to declare a general strike immediately. Many native-born delegates were more cautious.

Leaders of the teamsters shouted their eagerness to strike. Their union had great "fighting ability," allowing them to virtually shut down the transportation of cargo throughout the city. With the workers on Chicago's elevated lines also threatening a strike, they said, "interminable broils" were likely to tie up the town. Members of the National Union of Seamen, sailors on the lake schooners that frequented Chicago's harbor, also planned to walk out, cutting off another mode of transportation.

Many saw in a general strike a benefit beyond helping the Pullman employees. "If this fight is won," one man said, "it will establish a recognition of all labor and not organized labor alone." The president of the

Journeymen Horse Shoers Union called the boycott "a battle between capital and labor in which labor must hold together."

John McBride, president of the United Mine Workers, who had met with Debs for breakfast that morning of July 8, held what some called a trump card. He was prepared to call out forty-five thousand miners. Such an action would quickly starve the railroads of coal and bring trains to a halt in every corner of the nation.

Ballots were taken to judge the mood of the meeting. With a solid majority in favor of striking, the delegates began to shape a plan of action. They would give George Pullman one final chance to agree to arbitration. Some wanted to set the ultimatum for the next afternoon, Monday, July 9. Others insisted they should wait until they could effect a general strike across the whole country.

At midnight, a bombshell erupted. Word of the development spread in a murmur that quickly grew into a howl of anger. President Cleveland, having sent troops into Illinois without even a courtesy call to authorities there, had now issued a proclamation to the state's civilians.

"I, Grover Cleveland, President of the United States," it read, "do hereby admonish all good citizens . . . against aiding, countenancing, encouraging, or taking part in . . . unlawful obstructions, combinations, and assemblages." It ordered anyone already involved in the disturbances to disperse before noon on Monday. "Those who disregard this warning . . . cannot be regarded otherwise than as public enemies." Cleveland made it clear that troops would not discriminate between "guilty participants and those who are mingled with them." The "only safe course" was to stay home.

It was not a declaration of martial law—not exactly. But, General Miles said, it "amounts to the same thing." It gave Miles ample authority to act as he saw fit. "Whoever disobeys it," Miles said, "is a public enemy, and as such is to be destroyed." Now simply talking with a group of friends in the street could get a man shot.

The proclamation was delivered to local authorities and to newspapers late on Sunday night. Mayor Hopkins thought it unnecessary but said he was "not prepared to criticize the President's Proclamation."

To the delegates at Ulrich's the proclamation was an outrage and a bold provocation. It slapped the label "public enemies" on working men and women who were standing up for their rights. Radical union men welcomed the decree, which they assumed would further spur the representatives to action.

The delegates voted to send the Pullman strikers a thousand dollars for their relief fund. They would also forward a wire to Grover Cleveland denouncing corporations drunk "with the wine of special privilege" and asking him to "no longer drink of the poisoned cup that is now being held to your lips."

A committee of union members would approach Mayor Hopkins and ask him to serve as a go-between with Pullman officials to plead once more for arbitration. If the request was denied, a general strike would begin on Wednesday, July 11. They requested American Federation of Labor chief Samuel Gompers to hurry to Chicago as soon as possible to help broaden the impact of the walkout.

Questioned by reporters in New York, Gompers said that yes, certainly he was in sympathy with the Pullman boycott. Would he commit to a general strike? "We have not come to the bridge yet. When we get to it we may cross it."

E. J. Lindholm, the Master Workman of District Council 24 of the Knights of Labor, said, "The Pullman Company has taken away the last hope of an amicable settlement of these labor troubles. Now it must be war to the bitter end. Wednesday morning will witness the biggest strike ever known in this country."

22

Watching a Man Drown

GEORGE PULLMAN PREFERRED THE SIMPLICITY OF BUSINESS arithmetic to the calculus of social reciprocity. "Nothing to arbitrate" was a tool that could hew a path through a jungle of entangling considerations like equality, manhood, dignity, and fairness. To him, the ideas of property, ownership, and control were clear and absolute. He was willing to expend his effort and imagination in measures that he was sure would benefit his employees but would not let his employees tell him what to do.

What many sensed would be the decisive week of the crisis began on Monday, July 9. Pullman was aware that his role in the calamity had been roundly criticized. Secretary of State Walter Gresham bluntly asserted that "a serious mistake has been made by the Pullman people in refusing to meet and counsel with their employees as to real or fancied grievances." Pullman, he said, had made it appear that he was using the power of the federal government "to crush out labor organizations." He called for the sleeping-car magnate's resignation.

Congressmen were also complaining about Pullman's intransigence. Senator John Sherman was one who suggested that the government should begin regulating the fares for sleeping cars, as it already did the rates for freight. This slap at Pullman's monopoly would pay him back for the obstinacy that had proven so costly to the country.

More than one contemporary commentator described Pullman as soulless. Yet Pullman never showed the malicious streak or the disdain for others that were attributed to men like Henry Clay Frick and Jay Gould. The model town was evidence of his idealism. Pullman's paternalism may have been outmoded, but his intentions were at least in part altruistic. He was never effusive or sentimental about his concern for others, but the construction of libraries, progressive schools, parks, and athletic clubs was not the action of a man lacking a soul.

Pullman stood on principles of which he had no doubt. He felt he must adhere to his precepts whether the goal was to make a profit or to benefit humanity. If his company failed, no one would have a job. If his model town did not earn a profit, it would be a meaningless charity.

Pullman was obsessive in his determination to control his own affairs. He knew how to run his business better than his employees, better than government bureaucrats, better than labor leaders, and better than any arbitrator. That fact was so transparently clear that Pullman was willing to allow the whole population of the country to be inconvenienced, willing to watch railroad property burn and men die violent deaths rather than waver.

～

The criticism Eugene Debs faced was far more vociferous than that endured by Pullman. The strike was now a rebellion, a *New York World* reporter wrote. Debs was directing "open war against the state." The *New York Times* decided that Debs was not only a "lawbreaker," he was also "an enemy of the human race." He needed to be locked up. As for the violence, "no friends of the Government of the United States are ever killed by its soldiers—only its enemies."

Although dark clouds of arson and bloodshed had gathered over the boycott, Debs kept insisting that the sun, which he had never lost sight of, was about to break through. "We will win," he told newsmen.

Debs rose early on Monday morning, July 9, in spite of the previous night's prolonged meeting with the trade unions. He was "cheerful and hopeful as ever," a reporter noted, adding, "He is a smiler." His seemingly indestructible optimism had helped sustain the boycott through all the turmoil. An essayist would later write of him: "He has ten hopes to your one hope."

Debs was subject to the whims of hundreds of American Railway Union locals. Some of their members had struck, returned to work, and struck again as hopes and fears sloshed back and forth. Mobs of rioters with no relation to the union had taken up the banner, turning the situation into what the *London Daily News* reported was "a madman's dream."

Debs's fixed idea of the rightness of his cause, like Pullman's bedrock notion of business principles, served as a moral compass. He firmly believed what he had read in Victor Hugo, that the invasion of an army could be resisted, but not the spread of an idea. Debs's idea was solidarity. The labor leader was steeped in and guided by just those ambivalent human qualities that the sleeping-car mogul could not grasp. Although he tossed rhetorical bombs at capitalists, Debs's dream was always a harmony of interests that would allow owners their rewards and workers their dignity.

Like Pullman, Debs was inclined to ignore certain home truths. The first was that solidarity had its limits. Certainly the boycott, waged almost entirely for the benefit of the relatively small group of employees at the Pullman works, was a stunning example of selfless action. Tens of thousands of men had walked away from paying jobs out of sympathy for others. But Debs's idea that the railroads would never be able to replace the strikers was a chimera. Selfishness, animosity toward fellow workers, and pure desperation prompted hundreds of firemen, engineers, switchmen, brakemen, and humble laborers to seek the positions that had been vacated by the strikers.

The sudden loss of labor had crippled the railroads at first. But now the companies were hiring replacements and climbing back to their feet. They did not lack for applicants. The work of skilled railroad men was a commodity that the corporations could purchase on the open market. This was an idea that repelled Debs, for if it was accepted as truth, not only this boycott but any strike was vulnerable.

Nor was it accurate, as Debs consistently asserted, that the tremendous tie-up along the rails was entirely the result of the managers not having the men to run the trains. From the beginning, strikers had done more than walk away from their jobs. Some at least had actively interfered with trains, uncoupled cars, cut brake lines, caused derailments. In spite of Debs's repeated calls to obey the law, the rioting had played a significant role in paralyzing rail traffic. With the deployment of state and federal troops now smothering the mobs' interference, the railroads were beginning to bounce back.

The doubt that occasionally floated to the surface of Debs's sea of confidence was that his great idea, the American Railway Union, might have been ill-timed. He had moved too quickly. He had overreached. If the strike failed, the union itself was in jeopardy.

For Debs, solidarity was the sun and he could not keep himself from staring into its light. Now it had taken the form of a general strike. He was not able to make out clearly what lay beyond its brilliance—the dazzling vision was enough. He was convinced that a wider display of brotherhood would save the situation. All the workingmen of Chicago—all the workingmen across the continent, if it came to it—would rise up and support the railroad men just as the railroad men had supported their brothers and sisters at Pullman. A general strike was the answer.

༄

That Monday, July 9, Chicago was quieter than it had been since the boycott began. The prospect of a general strike convinced many that the calm was a portent of even more serious trouble. If Pullman did not agree to arbitrate, a reporter predicted, "the most tremendous strike known to history will be inaugurated tomorrow when the evening whistles blow."

Perhaps with this great threat hanging over his head, George Pullman would finally agree to a peaceful solution. That morning, a group of union representatives went to see the Chicago City Council's Committee on Arbitration. Their visit prompted committee chairman John McGillen, accompanied by three other aldermen and three union men, to proceed to the Pullman Building to meet with Vice President Wickes.

Ushered into the plush office, the men put forth their proposition. No, they were not asking Wickes to agree to arbitration. Rather, they suggested that a committee be established, with representatives from both sides, to ascertain whether there was a cause for arbitration or not. In other words, they were asking the company to agree to arbitrate the question of arbitration.

Perhaps all involved, if they had reflected on the absurdity of this notion, would have laughed out loud. But the stakes were too high. They all knew what was really being proposed. This was George Pullman's last chance. By the convoluted nature of the arrangement, the aldermen were affording him an opportunity to save face. They appealed to him "in behalf of the community."

The company, Wickes stated, "cannot recede from the position it has already held." McGillen pleaded the enormity of the decision.

Wickes now excused himself. He and a company lawyer left the room. The others assumed that in the ten minutes they were gone, they had communicated by wire with George Pullman at his Thousand Islands retreat. When Wickes came back, his face showed no sign of conciliation. "The Pullman Company," he stated, "has nothing to arbitrate."

McGillen was dazed. "Am I to understand that the Pullman Company refuses this slight request, made at so grave an hour, and upon which so much depends?" When Wickes repeated the mantra once again, the alderman argued that a corporation was a "kind of quasi-public" entity. Pullman had invoked the protection of patents issued by the government. The company had relied on the government to protect its property and business. "Yet you ignore a fair request made by the city?"

"There is a principle involved in this matter, which the Pullman Company will not surrender," Wickes said, echoing his boss. "We must manage our own business. We cannot allow our employees to do it for us."

The meeting was over.

༄

George Pullman had again forced the hand of the organized workingmen. Grand Master Workman James Sovereign, whose Knights of Labor would be a crucial ally in any wider strike, issued a statement that set the tone for the day. "A crisis has been reached in the affairs of the Nation that endangers the peace of the Republic," he proclaimed. Every union man would be "remiss in his duty" if he did not act to help the strike succeed. "Every labor union in the country should go out."

It was not known how many men in Chicago were union members. Some said seventy-five thousand, others a hundred or even two hundred thousand. Most reporters and union leaders alike predicted that a mass walkout would spread to all workers, including non-union men. The city would face unprecedented paralysis.

Enthusiasm for the general strike ran high and citizens across the country worried that the escalating dispute would drive the country over a cliff. A representative of Chicago's Amalgamated Clothing Cutters envisioned the beginning of a revolution. The result would be "a remodeling of the Government."

"The question," Debs told reporters, "is in the hands of the allied trades." He tried his best to ignore a fly in the ointment. At the previous night's meeting, trade union members had made an urgent call for Samuel Gompers, president of the American Federation of Labor, to rush to Chicago. His presence on the scene was "imperative."

The careful and thoughtful Gompers agreed that it was his duty to "make an effort to bring order out of what threatens to become chaos and confusion." Certainly he would come. He hoped, by his presence, advice, and action, "to help in bringing this industrial crisis to a peaceful and honorable ending."

Gompers called for a meeting at Briggs House, an elegant Chicago hotel. The conference would include the AFL's Executive Council and a wide range of other union officers. But the meeting would take place, Debs was disappointed to hear, on Thursday, July 12, the day *after* the general strike was to begin.

Any call by the federation for a nationwide walkout would have to await the judgment of AFL officers. Local trade unions would need to decide on their own whether to lay down their tools as planned on Wednesday.

Perhaps after Gompers's arrival, the giant Federation would endorse and widen the general strike. Perhaps not. Debs harbored deep suspicions that Gompers's expression of sympathy for the strike might not translate into forceful action, that peace rather than honor might be his priority.

❧

On Monday evening, July 9, the idea of the general strike received a boost from an unexpected source. Grover Cleveland decided that his proclamation of the day before, which labeled strikers as "public enemies," was not good enough.

Now he extended the prohibition of "unlawful obstructions, combinations, and assemblages" from Illinois to all the western states where there had been major disturbances, as well as along all rail lines where mail or interstate commerce was carried. Citizens connected with the disturbances in any way were to "disperse and retire peaceably to their respective abodes on or before three o'clock in the afternoon on the tenth day of July, instant." The president was, in effect, putting most of the country under martial law as of Tuesday afternoon. The general strike was now almost certain to begin Wednesday morning.

To back up his order, Cleveland set in motion even more federal troops. Eight infantry companies from New York arrived at the Lake Front Park camp in Chicago. He mobilized a force of U.S. Navy sailors and Marines at Mare Island in San Francisco Bay and gave them orders to proceed against the strikers who were besieging Sacramento.

General Miles was still worried. The next day he wired Washington that in Chicago "rioters or anarchists have 6000 Winchester rifles and bushels of dynamite bombs."

〜

For Debs it was the best of times and the worst. The flow of wires was encouraging and disheartening. Brakemen had joined firemen to tie up Indianapolis, but the Santa Fe line had resumed accepting livestock and perishable freight. Workers in Guthrie, Oklahoma, had struck, but Illinois Central passenger trains were running on schedule. Conductors and brakemen had walked out in St. Louis, but in Sioux City, the strike was reported to be over. A general strike was likely in Cleveland if the railroad brought in non-union men. Five hundred federal infantrymen were moving trains in New Mexico. In Toledo, employees of both the Pennsylvania Railroad and the Ohio Central had walked off "with a final good-bye cheer."

Significantly, the tie-up of traffic around Chicago's Union Stock Yard had fallen apart. Forty-five mounted men of the Chicago Hussars, a volunteer militia, were patrolling there. Illinois National Guardsmen were on the scene with a shiny brass Gatling gun mounted on the roof of a boxcar. At 11:00 a.m. that morning, a shipment of meat had rolled out of the yards. Cavalrymen rode in front and an army sharpshooter sat on the roof of the last car. Tomorrow, butchers would begin killing cattle, sheep, and hogs for the first time in almost two weeks. General Miles, fortified by President Cleveland's proclamation, had declared a literal "dead line" a hundred feet from all railroad tracks. Any unauthorized person crossing it could be shot.

〜

Late Tuesday, July 10, the trade unions' ultimatum for George Pullman to accept arbitration came and went. Around five o'clock that afternoon, Chief U.S. Marshal John Arnold and several deputies knocked at Eugene Debs's room in the Leland Hotel. When Debs opened the door, Arnold did not need to show him his gold star—the labor leader knew him well.

Arnold said he had a warrant for Debs's arrest, charging him with conspiracy to interfere with interstate commerce, obstruct mail, and hinder execution of the laws of the United States. Debs put on his coat. His brother, Theodore, joined him. The men proceeded to the office of U.S. Attorney Thomas Milchrist.

Milchrist, in consultation with John Egan and the general managers, had decided that the eve of the general strike was a strategic time to arrest Debs and ARU officers George Howard, Sylvester Keliher, and Louis Rogers. Fourteen rank-and-file union men who had allegedly participated in acts of sabotage or riot were included in the warrants.

The members of the grand jury had been empaneled before noon that day in the courtroom of federal judge Peter Grosscup. The only glitch was the initial refusal by Western Union manager E. M. Mulford to hand over copies of the hundreds of telegrams Debs had been sending around the country. Mulford, acting on the advice of his company's attorney, asserted the wires were privileged communications. But when threatened with jail for contempt, he sent a clerk to bring in the bundle of papers.

By four that afternoon, the evidence had been laid out and the jurors were listening to Judge Grosscup's charge. He began by saying he recognized that "the opportunities of life under present conditions are not entirely equal, and that changes are needed to forestall some of the dangerous tendencies of industrial life." Nevertheless, the law had to be obeyed. He proceeded to charge the jury in a way that left little doubt there were grounds for them to indict the ARU officers.

The arrests had been anticipated, but the timing was unsettling. As the news spread through the city, it generated outrage in some sectors, glee in others. The accused, insisting on their innocence, took the matter in stride. "The arrest will not deter from our work," Debs insisted. Grosscup set bail at $10,000 for each man. He scheduled a trial for October.

Debs's mood flashed from nonchalance to white anger when deputy marshals appeared with all the records of the ARU, including Debs's personal papers and unopened mail. He protested vehemently at what he considered "an infamous outrage" worthy of the czar of Russia. Milchrist insisted that he had a subpoena that allowed the seizure. "It is no longer a question of right in this country," Debs said, "but a question of force." He sent Theodore running out to secure a bail bondsman.

Debs would later learn that the marshals had thoroughly ransacked union headquarters while gathering the documents. Judge Grosscup realized that the seizure was illegal. He ordered court officers to return Debs's personal papers and mail the next day.

Theodore quickly returned with First Ward gambler Bill Skakel and Black Bill Fitzgerald, a political logroller from the stockyards. They signed bonds for Debs and the other officers—bondsman was a sideline of many of the city's saloon keepers and petty politicos. Union lawyer John F. Geeting said the defense would be handled by an up-and-coming young lawyer named Clarence S. Darrow.

The grand jury was not finished. They continued to hear evidence and finally indicted sixty-nine individuals for conspiracy. Most were men whom detectives had identified as participants in the rioting, either by committing acts of violence or delivering incendiary speeches. The charges were grave and the arrests sent a warning to all involved.

Reporters asked Milchrist if he had any intention of instructing the jury to investigate the railroad managers. By law, the companies had an obligation to deliver the mail under virtually any circumstances. During the boycott they had refused to move mail simply because the trains lacked Pullman cars. "As to whether they will be criminally investigated I do not know," the U.S. attorney said, "but I know of no such intention on the part of the government."

⌇

As the nation held its breath awaiting the onset of the general strike, outbreaks of violence continued to flare across the country. The boycott had exacerbated the bitterness of miners, some of whom had yet to return to work after the recent strike in coal country. In the central Illinois mining town of Spring Valley, a passenger train protected by federal troops pulled into the depot on Tuesday afternoon. It was met with a barrage of stones from protesting miners, recent immigrants from Lithuania, Belgium, and Poland. Soldiers scrambled onto the platform. The crowd refused to disperse. The troops opened fire. One man was shot through the head. Another, hit in the leg, bled to death. Several more were wounded. Angry miners looted two grocery stores in a nearby town.

At Grape Creek, another mining town on the eastern edge of Illinois, miners blocked the line by overturning coal cars and removing rails. State militiamen rushed to the scene and fired indiscriminately. They killed a woman, a sixteen-year-old girl, and one miner.

The situation in California remained critical. The three thousand

American Railway Union supporters in Sacramento were armed with sixteen hundred rifles and shotguns and plenty of ammunition. They had already faced down federal marshals and the state militia. Now two troops of federal cavalry were riding east along the Sacramento River as an advance guard. They were followed by riverboats loaded with infantrymen, marines, five batteries of light artillery, and several Gatling guns. It was feared that the streets of the state capital would soon run ankle-deep in blood.

The steamers landed outside Sacramento at six on the morning of July 11. The regulars and marines marched into town, arriving at the rail depot at seven. The show of force took the wind out of the strikers' resistance. The soldiers' bayonets restored order in the rail yard and the station. Troops arrested four men for complicity and seized a number of rifles and shotguns.

The battalion's colonel recruited Sam Clark, the oldest engineer on the line, who was willing to drive the Overland Express to Oakland. The train had been sitting in the yards since the disturbances began. Now it was made ready: five mail cars, six coaches, three Pullman sleepers, and a dining car. The train carried eight porters but only one passenger, a couple of newspapermen, and twenty-two army guards. Six of the soldiers sat on the coal in the tender, "their Springfields leveled threateningly at the dense crowd." The locomotive chugged out of the station at twelve miles an hour.

Two and a half miles west of Sacramento, the engine approached a wooden bridge over a muddy creek. Someone had removed the spikes and fishplates that held the rail to the ties. As the engine moved onto the trestle, it pushed the loose rail out of alignment. Its momentum carried it partway across the long bridge before it tipped and plunged ten feet into the shallow river. The tender remained upright, but several mail cars also fell.

Four soldiers were killed. Sam Clark was crushed beneath his engine. Several other soldiers were injured, including an artillery private who lost an arm.

The soldiers who rode out to the scene of the disaster returned in an ugly mood, but the only further violence was an exchange of gunfire back and forth across the river. Militiamen accidentally shot and killed a Japanese boy who stood by the bank watching.

❦

Following his arrest, Eugene Debs made a final appeal to all working-men who had offered to help. It was essential, he said, that they be "orderly and law-abiding" in this supreme hour. "Our position is correct, our grievances are just." They must work patiently toward the time when "right will be enthroned."

A man in a Hammond saloon said, "I for one will die rather than submit. I say let every workingman turn out and fight to the death."

Tuesday night, the White House experienced its quietest evening since the boycott had begun two weeks earlier. Having nailed the principal culprits, Secretaries Lamont and Gresham, Postmaster Bissell, Attorney General Olney, and General Schofield all puffed on celebratory cigars with President Cleveland and talked over the mostly favorable news coming over the wires.

It was apparent to everyone that night that cracks were opening in labor's united front. John McBride had not, as he had promised, ordered out forty-five thousand coal miners. Because of dissension in their ranks, the Building Trades Council in Chicago had put off their strike until Saturday. Forty trade unions in Milwaukee had expressed their sympathy with the ARU but delayed taking action.

The government men smiled at a statement from a leader of the Chicago musicians' union. "To strike now," he said, "would be like standing on the shore watching a man drown and saying to him, 'never mind, another man is coming out there to drown with you.'"

23

Last Resort

ON WEDNESDAY, JULY 11, THE GENERAL STRIKE IN CHICAGO failed.

Plenty of workmen made good on their promise to walk out. Teamsters. Foundry workers. Boilermakers. But the city's lumber shovers reported to work. Longshoremen fought each other for scarce jobs on the docks. German waiters and bartenders decided to hold on to their positions rather than participate. Cigar makers postponed their strike until Thursday afternoon. Carpenters resolved to strike later but fixed no date. Bakers, who knew there were plenty of men to fill their jobs if they struck, continued to work. Plumbers, who had fought a tough strike three months earlier, did not want to jeopardize their gains. They subscribed $1,200 for the relief of the Pullman strikers but remained on the job.

The teamsters' places were filled by new men in less than six hours. Commerce in the city went on with barely a hitch.

The great walkout that would paralyze the city and serve as the nucleus of a nationwide shutdown had attracted twenty-five thousand strikers. In other circumstances, it could have been viewed as a potent showing. But expectations and momentum demanded a far larger result.

In the model town, George Pullman's employees stood in groups discussing the glum news. Their relief fund had shrunk to $1,500. Providing a single meal a day to all the families cost $500. In the ARU paper *Railway Times*, editor Louis Rogers wrote that "it was not expected that all the trades unions of this city would promptly stop work this morning." Workers needed time to prepare. "It is thought that by Saturday everybody will be out." The claim rang hollow.

That evening, Kensington bars were crowded with angry, disappointed Pullman men who drank and talked in dark terms. Tomorrow's meeting of the American Federation of Labor became their last best hope. Members of many Chicago trade unions were waiting for the decision of that gathering before acting. All eyes turned to Samuel Gompers.

᪗

Although he had gone to work when he was ten, Gompers had continued his education at night. He had learned Hebrew and studied the Talmud, the ancient record of Jewish civil and ceremonial law. Such study, he later wrote, "develops the more subtle qualities of mind." He had learned "to make careful discriminations."

Like Eugene Debs, Gompers possessed an enormous reservoir of sympathy for working people, a hatred of injustice, and a desire to purge the world of some of its pervasive cruelty. But where Debs was a dreamer, Gompers was a realist. Where Debs saw his American Railway Union confronting and defeating the growing power of the monopolies, Gompers shaped the American Federation of Labor to defend limited gains. Where Debs saw a new, cooperative society, Gompers saw a larger paycheck for his members.

On the surface, Debs and Gompers were cordial and supportive, yet their different perspectives contributed to a complex relationship. Before the strike, Debs had praised his colleague as "one of the most brainy men now connected with the great labor movement." But Gompers bluntly rejected the idea of industrial unions like the one Debs had created. In his view, workers' power was in their skills. Merging their interests with those of unskilled laborers dangerously diluted that power.

The differences between the two men were apparent in their approach to the railroad brotherhoods. Debs, after long and intimate involvement with them, had come to see the brotherhoods as disunited, overly conservative, and weak. Gompers saw in them the most effective way to pressure the railroad companies on pay and working conditions. Gompers was not about to support Debs's radical new approach. He would later judge the ARU a "disruptive movement."

Gompers also felt that workers needed to accommodate the corporate reality, not harken back to an earlier age of artisans and yeomen. He disagreed with Debs that strikes would ever become obsolete. The best chance for working people to advance was by incremental steps and by leveraging their advantages. That meant organizing around skills that employers depended on. It meant withdrawing those skills when a strike offered a tactical advantage.

To Debs, a union was more than a business arrangement intended to secure higher wages. Solidarity was more than a tactic. "I would make an injury to one in the cause of labor the concern of all," he insisted.

Before Gompers left New York, his friend and fellow organizer Peter McGuire wired him to "go slow on Chicago meeting of Council." McGuire was afraid Gompers might catch the "strike fever" that seemed to be infecting so many of the labor leaders in the West. He had no reason to worry.

❧

The forty-four-year-old Gompers stepped down from the New York train late on Wednesday evening, July 11, and ate dinner at a Chicago hotel. Short and solidly built, he had a large head and broad face. His dashing handlebar mustache, curly dark hair, and suave manner gave him the aura of a stage actor. When he finished his midnight meal, he agreed to talk to reporters. Yes, he said, he would meet at Briggs House with the AFL Executive Council and with the leaders of Chicago's trade unions. Yes, he had invited the railroad brotherhoods to attend. About the current strike, he could say nothing. For George Pullman, he had utter contempt.

Summer heat returned to the city the next morning, with temperatures headed toward the nineties. The morning sun was already glancing from the awnings that shaded the windows of the banquet room where the men were to meet. As they filed in, they traded rumors and opinions. All knew that their decisions that day would, one way or another, have a mighty influence on the course of the greatest labor uprising any of them had known.

Fanny Kavanaugh, an important figure in the Chicago labor movement, was told she could attend as a delegate of the Ladies' Federal Labor Union but could not participate in the deliberations. Offended by the treatment, she walked out.

In addition to the AFL officials, the attendees included representatives from two dozen Chicago trade unions. Gompers's invitation to the officers of the railroad brotherhoods, which were not affiliated with the AFL, put him at odds with Eugene Debs. While many brotherhood members had supported the boycott, their leaders had either actively opposed it or remained neutral. Gompers said those leaders were "men who were clothed with responsibility as well as authority" over railway workers, so it made sense to hear their views.

In fact, the AFL leader had been trying to get the brotherhoods, with their thousands of members, to join his federation for years. Gompers considered them more in line with orthodox trade unionism, even if their success in battles with the railroads had been limited. He was even willing to overlook their exclusion of African Americans, despite the fact that the AFL was nominally free of discrimination. Each brotherhood had potential power because of its members' particular skills. The tens of thousands of unskilled laborers who had rushed to join the American Railway Union had no leverage—they could be replaced too easily.

Peter M. Arthur, the conservative head of the Brotherhood of Locomotive Engineers, said he could not attend. Edgar E. Clark, leader of the Order of Railway Conductors, flatly refused to come. The Brotherhood of Locomotive Firemen's Frank W. Arnold and Patrick H. Morrissey of the Brotherhood of Locomotive Trainmen did show up at the meeting and weighed in with their view of the situation.

As things got under way, Charles Dold, representing a committee from the city's cigar makers, proposed that the AFL fully support the general strike in Chicago and across the country. He emphasized the enormity of the situation. It was not a question of union organizing, he said, but "one of capital and labor." He knew the American Federation of Labor could settle the dispute if member unions joined the general strike. He was equally sure that the group would be held responsible for the boycott's failure if they did not.

Gompers questioned him. If the AFL did not enter the fray, would the general strike, which had gotten off to a feeble start, decide the matter? No, Dold admitted, that would mean certain defeat. How would a vastly larger number of workers joining the battle compel George Pullman to submit? Dold, grasping for an answer, insisted that "united action would accomplish it." Gompers said nothing.

In his autobiography, Gompers admitted that he had come to Chicago with little hope that the situation could be salvaged. An unprecedented nationwide strike of all workers in the middle of a depression smacked more of fantasy than reality.

Members of the AFL council hotly debated the question but reached no decision. After additional discussion, the group agreed to send a telegram to President Cleveland suggesting that the urgency of the situation required his presence in Chicago. They envisioned a summit meeting that would put pressure on Pullman and the railroads to relent and submit the matter to arbitration.

Most of the afternoon was spent drafting this message to Washington. They stressed the seriousness of the matter and urged the president to use his influence to end this grave industrial crisis in a fair manner. Cleveland did not bother to respond.

With the question of the general strike still unresolved, they invited Eugene Debs, free on bail after his arrest, to speak to the conference after supper. The men filed out of the room at five and returned three hours later. The pastel light of a summer evening washed the sky and the air was still thick with the day's heat.

Debs rose to address the conference. Gompers described his demeanor as "calm, dispassionate." What he had to say was stunning. He proposed that Samuel Gompers serve as go-between to deliver a message from the American Railway Union to the General Managers' Association. The message was a "proposition as a basis of settlement."

The union men pricked up their ears. They had expected from Debs an impassioned plea that the trade unions join the general strike. But now the lanky young man was saying that ARU members would "agree to return to work at once in a body, provided they shall be restored to their former positions without prejudice."

Calmly, dispassionately, Eugene Debs was conceding defeat. He added the proviso that the railroads would be justified in denying employment to any worker who had been convicted of a crime during the strike, "if any there be."

He was sure the strike would not be for naught. "Sacrifices . . . will have their compensation." The lessons learned from the experience "will prove a blessing of inestimable value in months and years to come." It was hard for AFL delegates to discern either the lesson or the blessing.

All the forces of labor, Debs said, should be mustered now to save the jobs of union members. If the GMA rejected the terms he had put forth on behalf of the ARU, then a general strike must be called and fought to the bitter end.

The astonished delegates thanked Debs for his contribution. Gompers told him he would call him later to let him know the outcome of their deliberations. Debs returned to his hotel.

The entire tone of the meeting changed. It was clear that the ARU was throwing in the towel. The railroad men were no longer concerned with the boycott or with the fate of the Pullman employees. They wanted their jobs back. The AFL delegates put the question of pursuing a general strike aside. They offered to send a member to petition the GMA, but only if Debs went along. It was a half-hearted gesture, since the managers had made clear they would never agree to meet Dictator Debs. The board voted to contribute a thousand dollars to a legal defense fund for Debs and the other ARU officers. They knew the men would need it.

Gompers later said, "The conference regarded the proposition made by the American Railway Union as a declaration that this strike had been lost."

The delegates appointed a committee to draw up a statement setting forth the AFL position on the crisis. "The heart of Labor everywhere throbs responsive to the manly purposes and sturdy struggle of the American Railway Union," they asserted. The suppression of the strike showed "the immense forces held at the call of corporate Capital for the subjugation of Labor."

But strikes should be "entered only as a last resort." They pointed out that the press had "maliciously misrepresented matters." They condemned the railroads for cloaking themselves in law while their monopolistic practices flouted legality. They took a parting shot at George Pullman, describing him as "the most consummate type of avaricious wealth absorber, tyrant and hypocrite of this age."

They recognized the ARU boycott as "an impulsive, vigorous protest against the gathering, growing forces of plutocratic power and corporation rule." They expressed sympathy for the railroad workers but "disclaimed the power to order a strike of the working people of the country." It was the sense of the conference "that a general strike at this time is inexpedient, unwise, and contrary to the best interests of the working people." They recommend that the members of any trade unions now on strike return to work.

∽

In the immediate aftermath and in later recounting of the events of that July, many commentators tried to saddle Samuel Gompers with the failure of the Pullman boycott. Debs himself, who would veer ever further from Gompers's conservative brand of unionism, thought of him as a traitor who delivered "one of the final blows that crushed the strike." He declared that Gompers and the trade unionists "not only did no good, but did great harm. The whole capitalist press exulted over the decision of Mr. Gompers and his colleagues."

It was true that newspapers praised Gompers for "saving the people of this country from a most far-reaching and bloody revolution." But the labor leader explained that supporting a general strike in a lost cause would have been unfair to wage earners, and that "such a course would destroy the constructive labor movement of the country."

Debs had made the right decision in calling off the strike. People were dying in this contest and the odds of success had shrunk to zero. Gompers had regarded the struggling ARU in the same way that Debs had initially looked at the Pullman strikers. Debs, puffed up by his Great Northern victory and overflowing with sympathy for the oppressed factory workers, had been unable to prevent his union from diving into the struggle to the aid of their brothers. Gompers refused to do the same. Another man drowning would achieve nothing.

When the meeting at Briggs House finally broke up at one thirty in the morning, Samuel Gompers telephoned Debs at his hotel. He was informed that Debs had retired and asked not to be disturbed.

PART IV

July 13, 1894–
October 20, 1926

24

The Poor Striker

On Thursday night, July 12, as the AFL representatives were meeting in Chicago, labor supporters crowded into a mass meeting at the Cooper Union in New York City. "Eugene V. Debs is battling in the cause of humanity," a speaker exclaimed. "The time will come when all Americans will adjudge Debs right and our present Federal judiciary wrong."

Reformer Henry George stood up to insist that "the most vociferous shouters for law and order are they whose official actions have violated law and incited to disorder."

Frank Foster, the editor of a labor newspaper, promised that "George Pullman is but of today, Olney is but of today, and Grover Cleveland is but of today. But the cause of labor . . . and the cause of American citizenship are for now and all time to come."

In Washington, Grover Cleveland had that day announced that as soon as the disorders were over, he would appoint a commission to investigate the issues raised by the strike. He would create the body under the Arbitration Act of 1888, which he had signed into law during his first term. The legislation was the first to give the government an official role in labor relations and was specifically aimed at railroad companies. It provided for the voluntary arbitration of disputes as well as the appointment of temporary commissions to analyze strikes and other labor problems.

Cleveland was invoking the second provision. The act's title led many to believe that he was finally demanding arbitration of the Pullman strike. A Knights of Labor official who met with the president called his decision "a great victory for the labor organizations and everything the A.R.U. has fought for." Eugene Debs said that he was gratified and hoped the move would bring "a speedy settlement of the existing conflict." But the commission's task was to start an investigation after the dust settled and report its findings to the president, nothing more.

⁓

The next morning, Friday, July 13, George Pullman, together with company lawyer Robert Lincoln, arrived in a blisteringly hot New York City from the Thousand Islands. The two men had slept comfortably through the night aboard a sleeping car made by Pullman's rival, the Wagner Palace Car Company. Lincoln, then fifty years old, had long been friendly with George Pullman and was serving both as a company employee and as Pullman's personal legal adviser.

After breakfasting at the Murray Hill Hotel, Pullman, looking tanned but careworn, proceeded to his office. He spent the day compiling a detailed rehash of his dispute with his employees.

"The deplorable events of the last few weeks have not been caused by the Pullman Company taking an obstinate stand," he obstinately insisted. He proceeded once again to reduce the entire dispute to dollars and cents.

The boycott, he declared, had nothing to do with the discontent of his employees anyway—it was a way for the unions to target the railroads, which happened to have had contracts with his company. He believed his employees were loyal but had been duped by outside interests who wanted to establish gambling dens and brothels in Pullman. The workers went on strike "under the excitement of their recruiting into the new organization."

"What is the demand concealed under the innocent sounding word arbitration?" He answered his own question: "Arbitration always implies acquiescence."

⁓

In Chicago, Mayor John Patrick Hopkins received a visit from Eugene Debs and James Sovereign of the Knights of Labor to talk about the future of the still-sputtering strike. Debs seemed to imply that Cleveland's proposed commission somehow settled the matter. Arbitration had been decreed. Now the railroads needed to do their part by taking back the men on strike. As soon as they did so, the union would call off the boycott. That was his offer.

Hopkins agreed to carry Debs's message to the general managers. He and Alderman John McGillen went to the Rookery and presented what the press was calling the "terms of surrender" to GMA chairman Everett St. John. While they were there, strike strategist John Egan showed up and read over the proposal. St. John said he could take no action until the managers met to discuss the matter.

Hopkins pressed him. He urged a settlement that would leave laboring men "in good humor." He explained that unless the strike was officially declared off, some hotheads might persist in rioting or committing acts of vandalism. He pointed out that a quick resolution was in the interest of the state, which was paying $18,000 a day to keep the militia in Chicago.

Throughout the day, other railroad managers came by individually. Each looked over Debs's offer with twinkling eyes. Egan decided they need not meet as a body. At seven that evening, Debs's proposal was returned to the mayor. A polite note explained that the managers could not receive or consider any communication from Debs or the American Railway Union. They had decided that scorn was a better tactic than conciliation.

"It doesn't make any difference to the members of this association," Egan stated, "whether Mr. Debs declares the strike on or off."

❧

On Saturday, July 14, a *Chicago Tribune* headline announced: DEBS' STRIKE DEAD. It was not quite true, but the flood of turmoil had crested and was definitely receding. Marshal John Arnold dismissed five hundred deputized men from duty in Chicago.

Sioux City was quiet. Workingmen in Peoria celebrated the peace with a parade. In Decatur, Illinois, the strike was over. The Wabash line was moving all trains. Men were returning to work in Fargo.

Produce was now abundant in Chicago markets. Wholesaler outlets were crowded with country buyers who had not been able to reach the city for weeks. Business at theaters was picking up.

With no declaration from Debs, the strike still limped along in the hinterlands. A train was dynamited in Oakland. An explosion a few miles west of Missoula, Montana, blew off the front of a locomotive. Strikers let loose a train of thirty cars on an incline in Indianapolis. Picking up speed, it slammed into the Home Brewing Company stables, slaughtering numerous horses.

People continued to die. A New York express train on the Big Four line was wrecked at Fontanet, Indiana, on Friday morning. Both the engineer and fireman were killed in the crash after a vandal broke a lock and threw open the switch.

In Sacramento, troops provoked by stone throwers fired shots, killing one striker and wounding another. ARU organizer Harry Knox was arrested there for conspiracy in the fatal wreck at the trestle on Wednesday. He claimed he was innocent, but the confession of another man purportedly implicated him.

Soldiers guarding the Northern Pacific line outside St. Paul saw a man pouring oil on a trestle. When he ran, they shot him dead. A man tampering with railroad property in Hope, Idaho, met the same fate.

The overriding concern of many of the strikers was no longer to harass the railroads but to get their jobs back. The general managers knew they could not operate without taking back many of their old men, but they ordered that "no men will be discharged to make room for applicants." Strikebreakers had been promised permanent jobs. In many cases they had gone to work at peril to their safety amid the riots. Some regarded them as cowardly scabs, others as heroic defenders of public order.

Scores of penitent strikers were lining up at railroad offices. Managers turned many away. Some of those who did find work had spent their careers climbing slowly up the railroad hierarchy, starting with a long stint as a fireman, then spending more years as a freight engineer before reaching the exalted position of passenger engineer at $150 a month. Now they would have to start over, perhaps driving a switch engine for half the money.

༖

Eugene Debs redoubled his activity and seemed genuinely surprised when the general managers rejected his peace terms out of hand. He looked frantically for signs of hope and found them. Two days after his offer was scorned he declared, "We will win our fight in the West because we are better organized there. There is brawn and energy in the West. Men there are loyal, fraternal and true." But while the strike was taking longer to wane in Montana, Utah, and California, the trajectory there was the same as it was in the rest of the country.

If the West was not the key, then something—perhaps a general strike—might still save the day. He wired a friend in Terre Haute: "Pay no attention to newspaper rumors. Indications of settlement by tomorrow but no strike off yet."

Snatching at every positive sign, he seemed to lose sight of the somber reality. The Northern Pacific, he said, was "tied up as stiff as a petrified whale." In fact, federal troops were opening the line along its entire length. "The Northwestern will not be turning a wheel tonight," Debs asserted. He toyed with a scheme for new leaders to take over management of the strike while the indicted ARU directors would "enter the field to spread the gospel of unionism."

Still interpreting President Cleveland's call for an investigatory commission as an initiative to arbitrate the strike, he said the gesture was pointless. The boycott was already over. "There is no dispute to be settled."

"What will become of the original issue?" a reporter asked him.

The Pullman strike would be dealt with later, Debs answered. "It has got beyond the specific issue which started this great movement." Like so many, he had lost sight of Thomas Heathcoate, Jennie Curtis, and the others at the Pullman shops. Their strike was still going on. For them, nothing had been resolved.

Debs's desperate faith was shared by the other ARU directors. Louis Rogers told a mass meeting of supporters that the boycott was not over. He seemed to imagine that the union had emerged victorious. "We started out with a demand for arbitration and we have won our point," he said. "All that is left for us to do is to put our men back in the places they left." He told the audience that the press was falsifying news of the strike's collapse. The men at the rally shouted their enthusiasm.

General Miles was equally unable to realize that the cataclysm had run its course. He continued to raise dire prospects if his troops were pulled out of Chicago. Anarchists, he was sure, were "plotting methods of destruction, plunder and terror." On July 16, Secretary of War Lamont had to remind him of the danger of "overstaying our welcome."

∽

The activity by Debs and all the ARU directors to sustain the crumbling boycott came to a halt on Tuesday, July 17. They received word at union headquarters that the government was now charging them with violating the omnibus injunction. By continuing to communicate with and urge on their members after the injunction was issued, they had put themselves in contempt of court. Federal authorities ordered them to appear at 10:00 a.m. to answer the charge.

Debs, Howard, Keliher, and Rogers walked into the federal building with three counselors, including Stephen S. Gregory, one of the city's most prominent lawyers. U.S. Attorneys Thomas Milchrist and Edwin Walker were waiting with a lawyer from the Santa Fe Railway, the company that was making the formal complaint against the four men. Judge Grosscup, who would preside over the case, was out of town. Milchrist laid the facts before federal judge William Seaman, and he issued warrants for contempt.

"We will test the question," Debs said, "as to whether men can be sent to jail without trial for organizing against capital."

Seaman scheduled a hearing on the case for the following Monday and set bail at $3,000 for each man. In a surprise move, the men refused to post bond. As he was led away to jail, Debs said they were forgoing bail to demonstrate to what lengths corporate power would go. "I would rather be a free man behind prison bars," Debs said, "than a slave under the sunlight."

Having plotted his strategy in advance, Debs had written his parents to prepare them for news of his incarceration. The next day they wired him: "Stand by your principles, regardless of consequences. Your Father and Mother."

Debs's wife, Kate, and one of his sisters came from Terre Haute to visit him in jail. A reporter described Kate as "a graceful woman of strong physique. Her head is adorned with dark, short, wavy hair, and her black eyes snap as she discusses the questions at issue." Another paper noted "sparklers of about a carat and a quarter each on her left hand." She told reporters that she believed in the principles of the American Railway Union and supported her husband's stand.

Some claimed that Debs and the others had gone to jail to depict themselves as martyrs. Debs said, "The poor striker who is arrested would be thrown in jail; we are no better than he." Jail also offered a respite from the relentless duties of running the boycott. Rogers frankly admitted, "I am getting a rest such as I have not had for weeks."

The accommodations in the ancient Cook County Jail were grim. The decrepit facility was chronically overcrowded, the more so with vandals and rioters arrested during the strike stuffed into cells. Bedbugs and other vermin left prisoners scratching. The rustling of rats interrupted sleep. Through a window, the ARU directors could see the site of the gallows where the innocent men accused in the Haymarket bombing case had been hanged. A jailer showed them the bloodstained rope "by way of consolation." As he did everywhere he went, Debs made friends among the thieves, vagrants, and drunks who crowded the jail. His supporters sent him food, flowers, and cigars, all of which he shared freely with his fellow inmates.

The following Monday, the defendants appeared before Judges Grosscup and Woods. The question was whether the union directors had called their members out on strike and had continued to direct their activities after the injunction was issued. Making the contempt charges stick was crucial to the government's strategy. The criminal case was more serious, but to prove a criminal conspiracy required hard evidence and reliable witnesses. It also depended on a potentially fickle jury. The contempt case left the matter entirely to the discretion of the two judges. If the government won there, Edwin Walker wrote to Olney, injunctions would become permanent weapons and "there would be no more boycotting and no further violence, in aid of strikes."

One of the pillars of Debs's defense was the contention that the American Railway Union left all strike decisions to its local unions. Debs could advise, but he could not order. The boycott was the "free, voluntary and peaceable action of the employees." In addition, the lawyers pointed to Debs's continual reminders to his men not to commit violence or break any law, only to withhold their labor if they chose to do so.

To counter this argument, the federal attorneys again hauled out the slew of telegrams that had been sent from ARU headquarters, many of them under Debs's signature. The messages gave the impression that Debs was trying his best to guide the activities of the strikers, not just acceding to their decisions.

To Litchfield, Illinois: "Take action to have all classes of employees withdrawn from service. Pledge full support for all, whether members or not."

To Fort Wayne, Indiana: "Call out all loyal employees."

To Peoria, Illinois: "Withdraw from the service immediately."

The sheer numbers of wires in this tone suggested his active role. The government would also make much of a telegram to a union man in South Butte, Montana, that advised: "Save your money and buy a gun." Was this the encouragement of violence? The union produced a letter as proof that the catchphrase had been added by a secretary who was simply sharing a private joke with a former colleague.

More to the point was a wire sent to strikers at the Union Stock Yard that they should allow a train to come through to pick up rotting animal carcasses, which were threatening public health. Before receiving this instruction, the men had not allowed the train to proceed; afterward, they did. That clearly showed Debs's power to order the men to act. Prosecutors even produced his courtesy telegram allowing the passage of Mrs. Stanford in California as evidence of his dictatorial power.

The hearing went on for two days, then assistant prosecutor Edwin Walker fell ill—from the summer heat and, he said, the proximity of the unwashed strikers who crowded the courtroom to watch the proceedings. The two judges decided to postpone the matter until September. They tacked on an additional $7,000 bail for each defendant. This time, the men posted bond and went free.

Debs returned to his home in Terre Haute. Kate barred all visitors. Hollowed out by fatigue and stress, her husband spent most of the next two weeks in bed.

‍✑

On July 15, the Sunday before Debs's arrest on the contempt charge, the Illinois National Guard troops at Pullman had staged a field day. A crowd of several thousand friends and supporters came to the model town for the spectacle. The men lined up in their dress uniforms to march behind the town band. The parade was a welcome diversion after two months of tense waiting.

The warlike atmosphere of the past weeks had dissolved. Residents handed soldiers bouquets of flowers. Seven hundred visitors took dinner with the officers at the Hotel Florence. More dined with the troops in their camp. A thousand people, many of them wearing white ribbons, attended an outdoor religious service conducted by the militia chaplain.

The strikers were still wary. Thomas Heathcoate said, "I don't believe the strike has been declared off." He was waiting to hear from ARU officials. One man denounced Debs. "If he has given up the fight what are we going to do? We will be worse off than we were before."

On Tuesday, July 17, with Chicago suffering the worst heat of the summer, notices were tacked up on the gates of the Pullman shops: "These works will be opened as soon as the number of operatives taken on is sufficient to make a working force in all departments."

Vice President Wickes made it clear the company was ready to take back former employees and even to investigate their grievances. "I have always told the men I was ready to talk with them," he said to reporters. "I have the kindest of feelings toward them." The news flew through Pullman and Kensington. Scores of idle workmen stood in groups discussing the development. Union men appealed to their comrades to stand firm.

As the company began to accept applications, First Regiment soldiers and a large force of police stood by. Hundreds of men swallowed their pride and asked for their jobs back. To do so, they had to surrender their union membership cards and sign a "yellow dog" contract stating that they would not rejoin the ARU or any other union. They agreed to accept their old wages and their old rents. Numerous unemployed men also made the journey to Pullman in hope of getting work.

Strike leaders like Heathcoate knew they would not be welcome and did not bother to apply. Theodore Rhodie, a veteran employee of Pullman, also declined the offer. "Because," he said, "when a man asks me to give up my principles, my rights as an American citizen, he might just as well ask me for my life."

The factory departments opened gradually. Dissension continued in the community as union stalwarts watched friends and neighbors give up the struggle and rejoin the workforce. By the end of August, the company had hired nineteen hundred former workers and eight hundred new men.

During the drawn-out process of restarting the plant, continuing hardship pressured the men to accept the company's terms. The arson and violence during the strike's climax had drained public sympathy and dried up contributions to the workers' relief fund. Now as the boycott faded, appeals went unheeded. During July, the Scandinavian Painters Union No. 194 contributed $15 to the relief fund; a local of the Cigar Makers International Union gave $50. Individuals subscribed a dollar or two. The relief committee sponsored a picnic at South Chicago that raised $600. It was a pittance for the sixteen hundred destitute families.

Few of the strikers had any savings left. Shoes and clothing were wearing thin. Many families lacked sufficient food. When the factory finally opened, it operated with fewer employees, leaving more than a thousand of the old men still jobless. The relief committee begged a ton of flour from the Chicago Trade Council. Men living on black bread and coffee, short of car fare, had to walk the fourteen miles to central Chicago to seek work. On August 17, Pullman residents appealed to Governor Altgeld. "Starvation stares us in the face."

George Pullman had finally returned from his sojourn in the East. He kept busy at the downtown Pullman Building and avoided the public eye. A visitor reported him "very quiet, worn out by the strike." Governor Altgeld wrote to him directly, pleading with him to contribute to the relief of the residents of his model town. Many had "practically given their lives to you." Even if they were foolish to strike, Altgeld wrote, they had "served you long and well and you must feel some interest in them."

The state, the governor reminded Pullman, had paid out more than $50,000 to protect the company's property. Should the people of Illinois be asked to pay the cost of his employees' relief as well?

Visiting the town, the governor found alarming conditions. The relief committee had made its last distribution: two pounds of oatmeal and two of cornmeal per family. "The men are hungry and the women and children are actually suffering," Altgeld wrote to George Pullman. "I assume that . . . you will not be willing to see them perish."

The company president replied that he did not "doubt that there are many cases of need," but he denied all responsibility. The men were destitute because they had left their jobs. He would do nothing to relieve the suffering they had brought on themselves.

Finally, Altgeld issued a proclamation to the state calling on "all humane and charitably disposed citizens to contribute what they can" to a relief committee. Some Chicago newspapers also started fund drives. The people of Illinois, struggling through the depression themselves, responded generously to the emergency. Enough donations of clothing, provisions, and money came in to allow Pullman families to again receive weekly allotments.

George Pullman's final outburst of meanness was never forgotten. He had triumphed in the great dispute that had cost the city, state, and nation so much. All knew that the trouble was rooted in his stubborn willfulness. Now he turned a blind eye to hungry, desperate people.

Only a year earlier, Pullman had been hailed as a visionary, an idealist, and a great benefactor of workingmen. Now he was widely seen as a petulant and selfish plutocrat without a soul.

25

Everything Was at Stake

THE STRIKE WAS OVER, BUT FOR MANY OF THE STRIKERS, THE ordeal would go on. Some were lucky—the Illinois Central Railroad took back two-thirds of the employees who had gone out. The Rock Island line rehired all but 450 of 4,500 strikers. But the managers of many other roads were adamant that those who struck would never work again. They tried to identify the men who had been active in the boycott and bar them from further employment.

With the ongoing depression and rampant unemployment, the managers had no trouble filling positions. The Pullman's Palace Car Company, although it took many of its Chicago employees back, rehired only sixty strikers in St. Louis, none in Ludlow, Kentucky.

The corporations made liberal use of the blacklist to ruin men's lives. Rather than circulate an actual list, the managers often required clearance papers from the man's last employer. These would specify the circumstances that had ended his tenure. If a prospective employee could not show a paper, a simple inquiry would reveal if he had been a troublemaker at his previous job. Henry Huntington of the Southern Pacific established a policy of hiring no union men, but kept it secret so as not to arouse public resentment.

In an era when all jobs were scarce, many of the strikers found themselves permanently blocked from earning a middle-class wage. The U.S. Strike Commission would estimate that three-quarters of railroad strikers did not get their jobs back, although some probably found work under assumed names.

⌇

On July 26, with Eugene Debs and the other ARU officers entangled in federal charges and the strike fading, Grover Cleveland decided it was time to establish the investigative commission. He recruited fifty-four-year-old Carroll D. Wright, the first U.S. commissioner of labor, for the job. Ten years earlier, Wright had accompanied a delegation of state labor commissioners on a tour of Pullman's model town and come away favorably impressed. Two additional pro-labor men filled out the panel.

For Cleveland, the commission was an opportunity for political fence-mending. A report sympathetic to workers would soften the harshly anti-labor image that his own actions had created.

On August 15, the board met in the ornate chambers of the U.S. District Court in Chicago. For the next two sweating weeks, the commissioners listened to more than a hundred witnesses and pored through stacks of documents related to the strike. A historian called the seven-hundred-page report they submitted in November "the most thorough examination of a labor disturbance in American history."

Eugene Debs, refreshed after his rest in Terre Haute, was his usual talkative self when he appeared before the commission on Monday, August 20. He gave a detailed account of the strike's origins. He swore that before the Pullman workers walked out, he had been "particularly anxious" to avoid a strike.

Yet when he visited the town of Pullman personally, he said, he had been moved by the workers' plight. Wages and expenses were "so adjusted that every dollar the employees earned found its way back into the Pullman coffers" in the form of excessive rent. He was determined to "right the wrongs."

His account hinted at how Debs's natural sympathy and exuberance seduced him down a path whose destination was disaster. At the ARU convention in June he had followed his head and resisted the delegates' rush to call a boycott, but his heart was on the side of the strikers.

Debs excoriated General Miles for his alleged statement that he had "broken the backbone of the strike." The general's role was only to maintain law and order. "But the fact is," Debs said, "he was in active alliance with the general managers." Ultimately, he explained, "the strike was broken up by the Federal courts of the United States, and not by the Army."

He went on to contend that at the peak of the havoc, he and the ARU directors had decided to call off the boycott, the sole proviso being that the railroads accept the men back. "It was in the crisis when everything was at stake, where possibly it might have eventuated in a revolution."

Debs did not want a revolution. And it may be that a sense of events barreling out of control had convinced him to call off the action. But his recollection that this had happened "about the 6th day of July, if I am not mistaken," was indeed mistaken. The violence had reached a crescendo on Friday, July 6, with widespread arson in Chicago. Disturbances had continued across the country during that weekend. But it was not until the next Thursday, July 12, after the failure of the general strike, that Debs had asked Samuel Gompers and his colleagues at the Briggs House meeting to present peace terms to the managers.

It did not really matter. The commissioner asked when the railroad boycott was actually called off. Sticking to his insistence that he was merely a servant of the members, Debs said that the strike could only be cancelled by a vote of the locals. He had called a special ARU convention three weeks after the Briggs House meeting. The delegates had officially called off the boycott on August 2.

The commissioners asked Debs, as they did most witnesses, what he thought were the solutions to the country's industrial problems. What measures would prevent future strikes?

He pointed to labor-saving machinery and "unrestricted foreign immigration" as leading causes of falling wages and joblessness. In Pennsylvania, he pointed out, miners had been displaced after the corporations had sent agents to Europe to import "the most vicious element of European countries." The unemployment that resulted from this importation of cheap labor, he said, was "where the Coxey army comes from."

Going deeper, Debs complained that venal courts had handed enormous advantages to the corporations. Samuel Gompers, who testified earlier, had made a similar point. He noted that laws about conditions in tenements, laws prohibiting sweatshops, laws requiring pay to be handed out at least every two weeks, even laws dictating that wages be paid in "lawful money" rather than scrip, all had been voided by the federal courts, which had declared them unconstitutional. The Constitution, with its eighteenth-century bias toward property rights, did not have enough flexibility for the industrial age. An Illinois law prohibiting women and children from working more than eight hours a day was then being challenged in court by business interests.

"No matter what may be said about the freedom of contract under our Constitution," Debs declared, "no man has a right to sell himself into slavery."

One of the remedies repeatedly raised during the hearing was government ownership of the railroads. Debs recycled an applause line he had used at the ARU convention. "To avert railroad strikes," he said, "I would propose this: 'That Government ownership of railroads is decidedly better for the people than railroad ownership of Government.'"

Debs weighed in on what he thought was a bigger issue. "I believe," he said, "in a cooperative commonwealth as a substitute for the wage system." If industry were organized into workers' cooperatives, he thought, those who produced the wealth would receive their fair share.

Debs took the phrase from an influential book by the Danish immigrant Laurence Gronlund, who had popularized the insights of Karl Marx. Citing the contradictions of capitalism, Gronlund had in *The Cooperative Commonwealth* imagined a system in which national wealth would be distributed more equitably.

Chairman Wright asked if a commonwealth was not "another name for State socialism?"

"No, sir, I do not call myself a socialist," Debs insisted. "My idea, is to secure harmonious relations, there must be kindness and mutual confidence as a basis."

Flames had scorched the rail yards, brickbats had flown, men had hurled bombs and wrecked trains, bayonets and gunfire had inflicted wounds and death, yet none of it had shaken Eugene Debs's bedrock notion that harmony and cooperation, trust and solidarity were not only possible but essential. Kindness, that most fragile of human attributes, had to be the foundation of national healing.

৩

August 27 was a humid, eighty-degree scorcher in Chicago, but the galleries of the high-ceilinged courtroom were packed. During the afternoon session, George Pullman sat down in front of the commissioners to give his version of the recent upheaval. His haughty demeanor, his superficial deference, his frequent deflection of questions to subordinates, his unflappable self-righteousness, all set a pattern for the corporate chief executives who, down the years, would find themselves being grilled by public officials.

Asked why he had created the model town, he read a prepared answer. "Working people are the most important element which enters into the successful operation of any manufacturing enterprise," he said. The town was an attempt to attract "the best class of mechanics."

He wanted to eliminate "baneful influences," citing saloons and brothels and "other bad places." That, he said, was what explained his refusal to allow employees to buy their homes—they might use them for wicked pursuits.

Yes, he had intended the town to earn a "reasonable" 6 percent return, but it never had. During the past two years, the return was only 3.82 percent.

The commissioners dug in to what they called the "phenomenal success" of the Pullman's Palace Car Company. "I don't know just what you mean by 'phenomenal,'" Pullman averred. They cited total dividends paid over twenty-six years of more than $28 million at an annual rate of 8 and sometimes 12 percent. The company currently retained an additional $25 million in undistributed earnings. That very year, in spite of the depression and strike, the firm had earned more than $5.2 million on revenues of $9.6 million, a 54 percent rate of profit. Pullman conceded the truth of these accomplishments.

But when it came to paying his men, he said simply: "The wage question is settled by the law of supply and demand."

The commissioners pressed him. Given the firm's financial success, should the company not have "borne some losses for employees who had been working for a long time?"

That would have amounted to giving the employees a gift, Pullman said, and he was not about to hand out gifts. "It was simply a matter of business."

He was asked if the company had ever divided any of its profits with its employees. "The Pullman Company," he answered, "divides its profits with the people who own the property."

The commissioners tried another approach. "Would it not have been a good business investment to have paid those men a little more wages and had the works continue?"

The implication was clear. Although George Pullman swore by "business principles," his inflexibility had caused his own company, the rail-roads, and the country to incur enormous losses. He groped for an answer. It would not have been a good business investment, he said, because "the wages had been fixed."

"Who fixed them?"

"They were to work at an agreed scale."

"They were forced to?"

"No, they were not forced."

"They had to take that or quit?"

"Exactly."

A commissioner suggested that a lack of bread and meat might compel a man to work for less money.

"Then," Pullman replied, "I would say it was agreed."

Pullman parried in the same opaque manner questions about "what is known to workmen as the living wage."

Pullman said that his employees' claim that before the strike they were not receiving a living wage was not true "because they are working for it now." Their strike broken, their union membership canceled, the men had taken what they could get. They were living on it, therefore it must be a living wage.

The commissioner naturally tried to delve into the question of why Pullman had so adamantly refused to arbitrate.

"It was the principle involved," Pullman said. "We must be the parties to decide whether we were willing to continue the manufacturing business at a loss." To arbitrate would have been "a piece of business folly."

He went on to explain that the question of whether the shops would be operated at a loss was "impossible for the company, as a matter of principle, to submit to the opinion of any third party."

"You use the expression, 'Impossible to be submitted.' Why is it impossible?"

"Because it would violate a principle."

"What principle?"

"The principle that a man should have the right to manage his own property."

Carroll Wright would later observe that "stubbornness in men is often claimed, by those having it, as a virtue, as a principle."

At a number of points during his testimony, George Pullman's apparent lack of knowledge of his own property went beyond an executive's habit of delegating responsibility. He repeatedly deferred to Thomas Wickes about fundamental details of the business.

With wages the central issue of the strike, Pullman was unable to tell what the average wage had been in 1893 or what the company had reduced it to the following year. He was unsure of the extent to which the men work by the day or were paid for piecework. Although he said he was the one who would have decided about reducing rents in the town, he did not know the details of the leases or exactly who maintained the buildings.

"Are you at the town of Pullman much?" he was asked.

"Not much."

His version of how the strike had come about was that in spite of the good tendencies inculcated by his model town, "outside influences were brought to bear." When business had slumped after the world's fair, the American Railway Union had organized those workers he had been forced to lay off. He did not explain how men who were already separated from the company could initiate a strike.

Raising one last point, the commissioners asked: When wages were reduced for the workers, were the salaries of executives, superintendents, and foremen also cut? They were not. Why not?

"Because it is not easy for the manager of a corporation to find men to fill the positions." If a company executive had worked there twenty-five years, Pullman said, "it don't lie with me to go to him and say to him, 'I am going to reduce your salary $1,000' because he will quit."

"You might reduce your own, perhaps, but not theirs."

"I might, if I chose, but the difference that it would make on the cost of a car would be so infinitesimal and fractional that it would not be worth considering."

Should he not have reduced his own pay out of fairness and justice?

"We cannot," Pullman murmured, "do everything at once."

After his testimony, Pullman returned to his mansion and spent the next four days in bed, laid low by exhaustion and nervous depression.

∽

The commissioners, in the voluminous report they sent to the government, called the strike "epochal," an event that had shifted the landscape of industrial America. Their conclusions made labor supporters cheer and capitalists wrinkle their noses.

They saw that the problems of the railroads had their roots in the fact that "the rapid concentration of power and wealth . . . has greatly changed the business and industrial situation." The competition that was supposed to make corporations self-regulating had been extinguished by monopolies and collusive agreements. If the government did not actually take over the railroads, the commissioners stated, it "must restrain corporations within the law."

George Pullman, instead of being a forward-thinking leader, was backward in his methods. "The Pullman Company," the commissioners stated, "is behind the age." The aesthetic features of his model town, they said, "have little money value to employees, especially when they lack bread." His workers had no interest or responsibilities in the company-owned town. The library and theater were not amenities for them but window-dressing for elite visitors. "The air of business" that pervaded the place excluded the men from management of their own affairs while away from the job. "Men, as a rule, even when employees, prefer independence to paternalism in such matters."

As for Pullman's refusal to arbitrate, the report blandly stated that a "different policy would have prevented the loss of life and great loss of property and wages." In the opinion of the commissioners, if George Pullman had shown good faith, he would have "relieved the harshness of the situation, and would have evinced genuine sympathy with labor in the disasters of the times."

The General Managers' Association came in for criticism as well. The organization was an example of "the persistent and shrewdly devised plans of corporations to override their limitations." Given the GMA's own dubious legality, its refusal to recognize and deal with the American Railway Union was "arrogant and absurd."

The report went easier on the union, declaring: "There is no evidence before the commission that the officers of the American Railway Union at any time participated in or advised intimidation, violence, or destruction of property."

The commission's recommended solutions looked forward to the coming Progressive Era. They suggested a permanent U.S. strike commission to look into all major labor disputes. A government mechanism to facilitate voluntary arbitration would be an important advance. They said unions should be required to write bans on violence into their by-laws. Because strong rather than weak unions were conducive to labor peace, the government should encourage companies to recognize labor organizations. They said that the yellow-dog contracts that barred employees from union membership should be illegal. Mentioned in passing were restrictions on immigration, compulsory arbitration, pensions for workers, and statutes that limited hours of work and fixed a minimum wage.

These measures, none of them very radical, were intended to ease the cruelest of the effects of industrialization. Some would find favor soon. Others would have to wait forty years until they were enacted as part of Franklin Roosevelt's New Deal. Commissioner Wright even suggested a need to reexamine "socialist" proposals and to "apply some of the features involved in them" to railroad labor.

The commissioners recognized that the strike had deep roots. The nation had long neglected the problems that industrialization had inflicted on American society. "Much of the real responsibility for these disorders," they wrote, "rests with the people themselves and with the Government for not adequately controlling monopolies and corporations, and for failing to reasonably protect the rights of labor and redress its wrongs."

John Dewey, while acknowledging that labor had lost the strike, wrote that "if I am a prophet, it really won." The Pullman boycott was an "exhibition of what the unions might accomplish, if organized and working together." He thought the few thousand freight cars burned were a cheap price "to get the social organism thinking."

Never before had working people shown the true—and to some frightening—power of solidarity. Alarmed government officials, with all their resources, had joined with corporations and the press to quell the uprising. But only barely.

In defeat, the railroad workers had taught America a lesson. The powerful show of strength by the American Railway Union had planted the seed of reform and left the traditional railroad brotherhoods with new muscle. Eugene Debs had shown workers that if they organized and consolidated their forces, they could indeed gain the power to "demand and command."

Even Samuel Gompers, who had harbored many doubts about Debs's strategy, said that a lost strike was a "warning to the employing class generally that the working men will not go down further, that any attempt to force them down will be very expensive."

In 1898, with the support of none other than Richard Olney, Congress passed the Erdman Act, which wrote into law some of the recommendations of the Strike Commission that had examined the Pullman boycott. The law spelled out the right of railroad workers to unionize, banned yellow-dog contracts in that industry, and created a federal board to facilitate voluntary arbitration of railroad labor disputes. Strike Commission chairman Carroll Wright called it "practically a bill of rights for labor." This early reform envisioned a new role for government as mediator and regulator. The law was necessary, one senator said, to deal with both "the tyranny of capital" and "the unjust demands of labor organizations."

Congress had already enacted a law to improve the safety of railroad workers. By 1900, automatic couplers, air brakes, and other measures became mandatory on all roads. The rate of accidents and injuries declined precipitously.

Railroad workers would enjoy collective bargaining and systematic arbitration a generation earlier than other industrial workers. Mediation would head off more than sixty strikes over the next decade and a half. The membership of the railroad brotherhoods soared and workers gained new clout in negotiations with employers. They did not, however, loosen their racist opposition to African American members. It was not until after the Civil Rights Act of 1964 that black workers would gain full access to railroad jobs.

Reacting to the Strike Commission report, Eugene Debs said the corporations "might as well try to stop Niagara with a feather as to crush the spirit of organization in this country." He welcomed the commission's conclusions as fair and impartial, a "vindication" of the American Railway Union.

Debs had testified that his union was "stronger to-day, numerically and in every other way, than it ever was since its organization. We are adding to our memberships every day." But the massed forces of Capital were not done with the ARU or with Debs himself.

26

Strikes and Their Causes

Clarence Darrow said he had never met a "kindlier, gentler, more generous man than Eugene Debs." He described Debs as the "bravest man I ever knew. . . . He had the courage of the babe who had no conception of the world or its meaning."

Darrow shared a similar background with the labor leader. A product of small-town Ohio, he had, like Debs, largely educated himself. Darrow became a lawyer and settled in Chicago. Both men were ambitious. Darrow, a protégé of John Peter Altgeld, had served a stint as corporate counsel of the City of Chicago, then gained a prestigious position with the Chicago & North Western Railway.

Like Debs, Darrow had grown more radical in his views as he grew older. He decided that corporate law was a form of "servitude," a "bum profession . . . utterly devoid of idealism." In 1894, he stepped away from his lucrative job and began a full-time career defending the underdog. Joining the team of lawyers who would try to keep Debs and his fellow ARU directors from going to prison, Darrow became the chief antagonist of Richard Olney.

The attorney general had declared that "no man should be allowed to play the part Debs did last summer and go unwhipped of justice." No punishment that Debs was likely to incur, Olney said, "will be commensurate with his offense."

On September 5, 1894, Darrow joined Stephen Gregory and the ARU's original lawyer, William Erwin, for the first of two trials. Judge

William Woods would decide whether Debs and ARU directors Howard, Keliher, and Rogers had been guilty of contempt of court in defying the July 2 injunction. The hearing took place in the courtroom of the U.S. Seventh Circuit Court of Appeals in Chicago's new Monadnock Building. Every seat was taken and fifty spectators stood.

Over the next few weeks, U.S. Attorneys Milchrist and Walker called a parade of witnesses, mostly railroad supervisors and detectives, to prove that Debs was indeed the dictator of the strike. Fully nine thousand telegrams had gone out under Debs's name. Copies were hauled into court and everyone waited impatiently while Western Union manager E. M. Mulford sorted through them to find specific wires. The government presented in more detail the evidence from the preliminary hearing: the endless directives to the locals, the joking "buy a gun" wire, Debs's power to clear animal carcasses from the stockyards, his intervention on behalf of Mrs. Stanford.

The defense team surprised onlookers by calling no witnesses and introducing no evidence. The lawyers had decided to save their ammunition for the criminal conspiracy trial, which was now scheduled to be heard in January. That charge bore heavier penalties—two years in prison—and a greater onus of guilt. They did not want to tip their hand.

But Darrow did not miss the chance to take some jabs at the prosecutors. Thomas Milchrist had said he never knew "four more dastardly criminals . . . than these men." Darrow noted that "there are various kinds of cowards. It was not brave of this man Milchrist to stand in court . . . and heap vituperation on these men who cannot reply." He referred to Milchrist as a "puppet in the hands of the great railroads corporations." Reporters said they saw Milchrist "turn red in the face."

Woods took his time deciding the case and crafting a suitably grandiloquent opinion. Finally, on December 14, he began to intone his decision to a crowded courtroom. He spoke for an hour before it became clear that he was going to find the defendants in contempt. If the men "advise workmen to go upon a strike, knowing that violence and wrong will be the probable outcome, neither in the law nor on morals can they escape responsibility." The Sherman Antitrust Act, he said, gave the government sufficient jurisdiction even though Congress had not directed it "at organizations of labor in any form."

Before banging his gavel, he sentenced Debs to six months in jail, the other directors to three months. Because of crowding in the Cook County

Jail, they would serve their sentences in Woodstock, the rural seat of McHenry County sixty miles to the northwest. The men reported to the Woodstock courthouse on January 8. Debs wrote his parents: "Would you believe it? The sheriff Mr. Eckert is an alsacian and a noble man. The daughters treat me with the greatest kindness." He went on to reassure them that "my disgrace is doing much to arouse public conscience. No disgrace attaches to the family. You need not blush."

౿

The men spent sixteen days in Woodstock. On January 24, 1895, they were released on bail in order to return to Chicago for their trial on the criminal conspiracy charge. Along with another dozen alleged conspirators, they were to face Judge Grosscup in federal district court.

For the defense, Gregory questioned how Edwin Walker could sit at the prosecutors' table when he was a paid employee of the Chicago, Milwaukee & St. Paul Railroad. The government's case, Darrow said, was a "club to defeat the effort that was being made to better the condition of workingmen and women."

The spontaneous lawlessness accompanying the boycott could not have been the product of a conspiracy, the defense asserted. ARU members had tried to keep trains without Pullman cars running, but the general managers had shut down the nation's rail lines by adding Pullmans unnecessarily.

Debs took the stand in his defense. Expecting to see the wild-eyed "dictator" they had been reading about in the papers, the jurors were surprised by a witness who looked and spoke more like a small-town banker. He presented his side of the story in cogent detail.

Darrow, always a master of courtroom drama, achieved a coup when he produced excerpts from the minutes of General Managers' Association meetings—how he had obtained them was not revealed. They showed the managers plotting with detectives to take strikers' names and making plans to reroute trains to annoy the public. Their frank goal was to utterly destroy the American Railway Union. The real conspiracy, he said, had been mounted in these secret conclaves, not in the open meetings of the ARU.

George Pullman, whom Darrow described as "that man whose name is odious wherever men have a drop of blood," played a bit part in the trial. Remembering his unpleasant grilling before the Strike Commission, he panicked when a process server appeared at his office with a sub-poena to appear as a witness in the conspiracy trial. Pullman ducked out the back door, hurried to the train station, and left Chicago. He never did testify, nor was he held in contempt of court.

"There is something wrong in this country," Debs noted, when "judicial nets are so adjusted to catch minnows and let the whales slip through."

By that time, the trial was in limbo. It became clear that Darrow intended to counter the charges by putting the general managers on trial and exposing their collusion with the government. The illness of a juror gave Judge Grosscup an excuse to call an abrupt halt to the trial. Convinced the case was going their way, defense attorneys suggested appointing a new juror and reading him the previous evidence. Grosscup, exchanging meaningful glances with the prosecutors, refused. He dismissed the jury and initiated a series of delays. The government, unwilling to pursue a losing battle, finally dismissed the charges.

But the conviction for contempt stood and the resulting jail sentence still loomed.

❧

It was Debs's good fortune that the partner of his lawyer Stephen Gregory happened to be James Harlan, the son of Supreme Court Justice John Marshall Harlan. The elder Harlan agreed to hear the defense team's application for relief in the contempt case. Although he refused to ascribe a flaw to Judge Woods's opinion, he did decide that there was enough question about the justice of the procedure to merit a review.

The writ of habeas corpus that he issued was the narrow crevice that Debs's case slipped through to gain a hearing from the full Supreme Court. The nation's highest tribunal would weigh in on the key issues of the strike. Was the injunction a proper weapon to use in the case of a labor dispute? Had the executive branch and the courts overstepped their authority? Did the collusion of Olney with the railroad managers put the government's actions beyond the letter or spirit of the law?

To help argue the case, Gregory and Darrow recruited eighty-one-year-old Lyman Trumbull, a legal heavyweight who would lend needed gravitas to the defense arguments. Trumbull had been a U.S. senator from Illinois and was famously the author of the Thirteenth Amendment abolishing slavery.

On Monday, March 25, the U.S. Supreme Court justices filed into the Old Senate Chamber in the Capitol, the semicircular room where the court had met since 1860. The chamber was packed, the gallery above crowded with the type of working people who rarely listened in on the proceedings. The customary decorum was frequently interrupted by grumbles and cheers as the lawyers argued the case known as *In re Debs*.

Trumbull led off the first day of arguments. In a sonorous voice, he declared that "refusing to work for a railroad is no crime" even if it delayed the mail or slowed interstate commerce. "A lawful act and not done for the purpose, it is no offense." Government should not use its civil writs simply to protect private property. If strikers committed crimes, they should be charged with crimes, not entangled in the injunction net, where trial by jury was denied them. Stephen Gregory expanded on Trumbull's argument. The liberty of Americans was at stake, he said.

The finale came the next day. It was unusual for the U.S. attorney general to supersede the solicitor general and argue a case personally before the Supreme Court. But Richard Olney had shaped the government's anti-strike strategy from the beginning and he was determined to see it through.

Olney scanned the faces of the workingmen who looked down from the gallery. Raised amid wealth, he embraced the social Darwinism that ratified his life of privilege. "Man is by nature a fighting animal," he had said. The victors deserved the spoils, including the twenty-six-room summer house on the coast in Falmouth that he enjoyed in addition to his Boston mansion. He took personally the threat Debs posed to America's wealthiest citizens.

Knowing that the case for criminal conspiracy was unlikely to yield a conviction, he badly needed a victory here. He elected to shift the argument away from the Sherman Antitrust Act as the basis for the court's authority. He declared that act to be "an experimental piece of legislation." He wanted to place the government's use of injunctions to break strikes on a firmer foundation—the Constitution itself.

Olney argued that Judge Woods had "decided rightly enough but upon the wrong ground." He emphasized the government's "absolute" constitutional authority over interstate commerce and mail delivery. No legislation was needed. If the Supreme Court justices accepted his reasoning, they would slam a permanent lid on disruptive strikes.

He swept aside the notion that the defendants were not responsible for the destruction and disorder that the strike had caused. They must be, he said, unless "a man can wantonly touch the match to powder and yet be blameless because not rightly realizing the ensuing devastation." The justices gave Olney their "closest attention," the *Chicago Tribune* reported, without once interrupting for a question.

Clarence Darrow addressed the court last. With the face of a blacksmith, he regarded the courtroom from beneath his perpetually skeptical eyebrows. His baritone voice bottomed in gravel, he explained that his clients were not criminals. They had acted on the purest motives. Olney, with all his abstract arguments, had left out the crucial human element.

Darrow insisted that the government had no authority to issue an omnibus injunction. The Sherman Antitrust Act made no mention of labor strikes. The defendants had not broken the law. They had not even violated the injunction. The telegrams showed them urging men to exert a right and to avoid violence. The men were justified in leaving their jobs because "to deprive workingmen of this power would be to strip and bind them and leave them helpless as the prey of the great and strong."

"Strikes are deplorable," he said, "and so are their causes."

Darrow, speaking in the spirit of Eugene Debs, dug down toward the fundamental issue. Laborers were free men, "but freedom does not consist alone in political rights, or in theories of government, or in theories as to man's relation with the state." Freedom was not obedience or deference or simple order.

Darrow made the case that solidarity was a necessary component of freedom, that liberty could not be separated from community. Labor organizations were based on the common interest of workingmen and on the idea that an injury to one is the concern of all.

The railroad men had laid down the implements of their labor "not because their own rights have been invaded, but because the bread has been taken from the mouths of their fellows." Their right to strike was "the right to consider each other 'brother.'" To deny that right "would leave each individual worker completely isolated and unaided to fight his battle alone against the combined capital."

Richard Olney later said that the pleadings of the defense lawyers had not impressed him. He scoffed at the fact that they had resorted "to heated declamations about individual liberty."

The fate of Eugene Debs and his fellows, to some extent the fate of the American labor movement, was left for nine black-robed men to decide. When the arguments were over, Olney invited Clarence Darrow and the other defense lawyers to his home for dinner. The fierce advocates for labor soon found themselves trading pleasantries and sipping fine wines with the government attorneys, Chief Justice Melville Fuller, Secretary of War Daniel Lamont, and their wives. A memorable scene.

❦

The men had to wait until May 27, 1895, for the unanimous decision of *In re Debs*. The petition was denied. The judgment of the lower court stood.

Justice David J. Brewer explained the reasoning of the court. He was a Republican and a staunch supporter of corporate power. He first took up the question of whether the government had the authority to prevent impediments to interstate commerce and to the prompt delivery of the mail. Yes, he wrote, "the strong arm of the national government may be put forth to brush away" all such obstructions. He agreed with Olney that those powers derived directly from the Constitution. The government could "execute on every foot of American soil the powers and functions that belong to it," by physical force if necessary.

What was more, the "power of a court to make an order carries with it the equal power to punish for disobedience of that order." To seek an injunction was not a usurpation of power but a decision to submit the question to the "peaceful determination of judicial tribunals."

The thinking behind the decision was influenced by men like Brewer's uncle, Justice Stephen J. Field, who had sat on the Supreme Court for more than thirty years. Born during the presidency of James Monroe, Field still thought of America as a place where business owners could form contracts with their employees as equals and where the courts had to protect private property from taxation by kings or their modern equivalents.

Field's thinking had prompted the same Supreme Court to invalidate a modest federal income tax passed by Congress. The ruling was based on a constitutional technicality, but the justices asserted they were warding off an attack on property by "mere force of numbers." Democracy was suspect. The justices were in more accord with what a dissenting opinion called the "sordid despotism of wealth." That same year, the court would declare that the American Sugar Refining Company was not subject to the provisions of the Sherman Antitrust Act, even though it controlled 98 percent of the nation's sugar market. The following year, in *Plessy v. Ferguson*, the court would make racial segregation the law of the land.

After the Debs decision, five state governors said the court had "flagrantly usurped jurisdiction first to protect corporations and perpetuate their many abuses, and, second, to oppress and destroy organized labor." Oregon governor Sylvester Pennoyer said, "Our government has been supplanted by a judicial oligarchy."

To the editors of the *Chicago Tribune*, the decision was "a notice to all Anarchists and other disturbers of the peace that the hands of the General Government are not fettered." Attorney General Olney would later brag that the court "took my argument and turned it into an opinion."

Eugene Debs thought the decision "left the law so biased that, in cases involving strikes, at least, a man could be sent to prison without trial by jury." He declared that "every Federal Judge is now made a Czar."

In June 1895, Debs and his fellow ARU directors reported to the Woodstock jail to serve out the remainder of their sentences. "I shall go into history right," Debs declared.

27

The Common Heartbeat

GEORGE PULLMAN HAD WON. HIS CAR SHOPS WERE OPEN. HIS employees had returned to work on his terms. But the victory left a residue of bitterness in Pullman's heart. He could not understand the ungratefulness of his workers. He could not understand the Strike Commission's harsh verdict about his paternalism and his refusal to arbitrate. How had he, the unlucky victim of a series of circumstances, been transformed into a villain?

His friends remained cordial, although many whispered behind his back that he could have avoided the whole damn catastrophe. Mark Hanna, an Ohio businessman and politician, thought Pullman was giving capitalists and Republicans a bad name. At the height of Pullman's intransigence, Hanna had supposedly blurted, "A man who won't meet his men halfway is a God-damned fool."

Bertha Palmer, the wife of retail and real estate tycoon Potter Palmer, was the doyenne of Chicago society, but she sympathized with put-upon workers and had helped organize Chicago's seamstresses. She crossed George Pullman off her guest list.

If anything, Grover Cleveland faced an even more dismal prospect than Pullman in the autumn of 1894. Voters blamed the Democrats for the ongoing misery of the depression as well as for the months of national anxiety generated by the coal miners' strike, the Coxey armies, and finally the disastrous Pullman crisis. With his heavy-handed actions during the strike, Cleveland had alienated working people, a key faction of his party. Congressional Democrats had stuck by him and would be the first to pay the price.

Democrats had held the House of Representatives by 94 seats when Cleveland took office. After the election of 1894, they found themselves with a 161-seat deficit. This stunning reversal, the greatest turnaround in American political history, was capped two years later by the election of Republican William McKinley. His party would hold the presidency and both houses of Congress until 1910.

⤳

In August 1896, three prospectors found a nugget of yellow metal in a stream near the Klondike River of Canada's Yukon Territory. The news set off a gold rush of insane proportions. A hundred thousand would-be prospectors trekked north. The influx of precious metal and the frenzy of spending to find it were factors in finally getting the U.S. economy back on its feet.

At the Pullman works, orders began to creep upward and the workers even received a modest pay raise. Work became more regular. Company managers instituted a policy of surveying employees who were leaving the company to ask about any dissatisfaction. They systematically analyzed complaints.

But the town of Pullman, one resident said, "was never the same after the strike." As late as 1900, men who had taken different sides refused to speak to each other. The company gradually withdrew support from social activities. There were no more bicycle races. The athletic clubs declined. Lake Vista, which had beautified the main entrance to the plant, was filled in. Most of the town's parks and the playing fields were converted to industrial uses. The theater was closed, the sewage farm abandoned. Lawns went unmowed. Flowers became scarce.

In 1898, the Supreme Court of Illinois ruled that the Pullman's Palace Car Company had exceeded its corporate charter, which did not allow the firm to operate a company town. Within a decade, the model town was sold off, its residents freed from company control. Marshall Field, for one, was relieved. He had never thought that George Pullman's vision was anything but a mirage.

Pullman had steered his company through the worst depression in the nation's history, fighting for each scarce contract to build cars. At sixty-five, he lacked the resilience of his earlier years. Yet he could not relinquish his intense work pace. Ever the businessman, he plunged into the high-stakes stock manipulation and deal making that accompanied the Gilded Age merger mania. He teamed up with other Chicago investors in attempts to corner the market in both crackers and matches. He was always tired, often irritable, frequently ill, and plagued by daily headaches. The memory of the strike would not leave him.

ᕲ

For Jane Addams, as for many Americans, the crisis had been a life-altering trauma. "During all those dark days of the Pullman Strike," she later wrote, "the growth of class bitterness was most obvious." The events of 1894 evoked in her, who had made such an effort to remedy the wrongs of industrialism, the "paralyzing consciousness that our best efforts were most inadequate."

She did her best to find a meaning in the disquieting events. Unlike the Strike Commission, she did not focus on wage rates, the price of water in the model town, or the legal technicalities of the dispute. Instead, she considered what she called the social dimension of the great upheaval.

As an advocate of reform and a selfless proponent of helping others, she had much in common with Eugene Debs. She wrote of her hope for "the larger solidarity which includes labor and capital" based on a "notion of universal kinship."

The strike forced her to see how America was split between its professed ideals and the brutal practicality of the marketplace. "Are you content that greed . . . shall rule your business life," she asked the country's upper classes, "while in your family and social life you live so differently?"

In her speeches and writings about the strike, she wondered why George Pullman, a man who had "spent a million of dollars on a swamp to make it sanitary for his employees, should refuse to speak to them for ten minutes." She wanted to know why he "should grow hard and angry when they needed tenderness and help."

Addams saw that Pullman was not a thoughtless plutocrat but a figure of tragedy. He was King Lear, who, after deciding to hand his realm to his daughters, demanded professions of love; who, in spite of his generosity, could not bring himself to relinquish control.

George Pullman, Addams wrote, was a man who had "heaped extraordinary benefits upon those toward whom be had no duty." But he was a humanitarian who "loved the people without knowing them." Only a recognition of shared humanity could bridge the great class divide that the strike and boycott had made so clear.

"We must learn to trust our democracy," she wrote, "giant-like and threatening as it may appear in its uncouth strength and untried applications." She hoped for a gradual but deep shift in Americans' view of themselves and of their fellow citizens. Hoped that they could find what she called "the rhythm of the common heartbeat."

∽

In January 1897, two and a half years after the great strike, Hattie Pullman recorded an "unhappy scene" with George before leaving for a dinner party. "These sudden thunder storms out of a clear shine," she told her diary, "are getting pretty hard to endure." That June the Pullmans celebrated their thirtieth wedding anniversary. Hattie gave George a sterling silver toilet set. She received nothing in return. Not long afterward, her husband selected his burial plot in Chicago's Graceland Cemetery.

The couple quarreled again that summer at their seaside estate. George returned to Chicago by himself in early October to attend a company board meeting. The city was blanketed by an unseasonable heat wave, which left Pullman fatigued and out of sorts. He nevertheless took the president of the Pennsylvania Railroad and some other executives on a tour of his factory. He sent Hattie a brief telegram on October 17: "Letter rec'd am entirely alone miss you very much am not very well."

Before he went home from work on October 18, Pullman finalized the endowment of a hospital bed for indigent children. He made the bequest in the name of his new grandson and namesake, Florence's son, George Mortimer Pullman Lowden. He completed a letter for the infant to read when he was older. The bed would be available for "any sick child whom you may choose," he wrote. "I hope your life may be successful, and that you will always remember that good actions speak louder . . . than spoken words."

Late that night, the sixty-six-year-old Pullman felt a weight on his chest. One of the buildings he had moved in his youth, a towering hotel, had slipped from its foundation. It was pressing down on him. Crushing him. He could not signal his workmen to lift the burden. He had no breath left to whistle.

∽

Much would be made about the elaborate precautions taken in the design of George Pullman's final resting place. Following his wishes, workmen labored into the night to prepare an underground concrete vault. Then a lead-lined coffin wrapped in tar paper and covered in hot asphaltum. Iron rails bolted across the top. More concrete.

"The body of George M. Pullman," the *Chicago Tribune* noted, "will lie undisturbed for as long as time shall last."

Solon Beman, the architect who had designed the buildings in the model town eighteen years earlier, devised a monument for the sleeping-car king: a single Corinthian column supporting nothing but sky.

After Pullman's death, Robert Lincoln became the president of the Pullman's Palace Car Company. He stripped away the remnants of the old-fashioned, one-man proprietorship that had remained under George Pullman and installed a modern bureaucratic management system. He also oversaw the absorption in 1899 of the Wagner Palace Car Company, the firm's last major rival. Pullman now stood alone as a producer of sleeping cars.

The reading of George Pullman's will added one last paradox to the reputation of this paradoxical man. His $17,500,000 estate was massive by the standards of the time. He was generous to his daughters but stinted his wife and allotted his sons only a yearly stipend. The boys, then twenty-two, had always failed to live up to their father's expectations.

Hattie was not having it. She asserted her dower rights to carve out a larger legacy, mostly so that she could support her sons. The twins lived off her during their short, dissipated lives—both were dead within eight years of their father's passing.

On the other hand, one of George Pullman's largest bequests went to the town of Pullman. He left $1.25 million to underwrite the Pullman Free School of Manual Training, a vocational institute for the children of town residents and Pullman employees. The *Tribune* said the gift "takes rank with the most liberal and useful ever made to a Chicago institution." The school was finally built in 1915 and taught skills to both boys and girls until 1949.

Asked about Pullman's demise, Eugene Debs offered a simple eulogy: "He is on equality with toilers now."

28

True to Man

ON NOVEMBER 22, 1895, AN EARLY WINTER STORM BROUGHT eight inches of snow to Woodstock, Illinois. During the morning, Gene Debs and his brother, Theodore, borrowed a horse and sleigh to go around town and say goodbye to the local people Gene had met and befriended during his six-month stay in the county jail.

In June, Debs and seven other American Railway Union officers had resumed their punishment for disobeying the federal injunction. All but Debs had left Woodstock in August when their three-month sentences were completed. When Debs walked free, the final curtain would descend on the Pullman crisis.

The small jail extended from the back of Sheriff George Eckert's home next to the courthouse. The prisoners had taken their meals with him and his family and played football in the backyard. Organizers all, they kept to a strict schedule of exercise, reading, and discussions of the issues facing the labor movement. Debs received hundreds of visitors and was so overwhelmed by the stacks of incoming mail that he had to hire a secretary.

Debs's wife, Kate, spent time in Woodstock while he was there. Like her husband, she impressed the town's residents. A reporter noted her "dignified manner and yet with a charming air which attracts a stranger at once." His account described her "unbounded faith in her famous husband" and observed that she was well read on the subjects pertaining to

Gene's work and could "hold her own remarkably well in a talk on economics."

In January, Debs had been interviewed by the intrepid *New York World* reporter Nellie Bly. He told her of his support for women's rights and said he did not profess any religion except that of the golden rule. She noted his blue eyes and gold-rimmed glasses. "He smiles frequently," she reported. He told her he had two pets, Fay, an Irish setter, and a canary named Sweetie.

While in jail, Debs assembled a scrapbook of documents related to the Pullman boycott. He wrote to Richard Olney for a copy of his Supreme Court argument. He held no animus against the man who had put him behind bars.

Victor Berger, an Austrian immigrant who had become a leader of the strong socialist movement in Milwaukee, visited Debs at Woodstock. He "delivered the first impassioned message of socialism I had ever heard," Debs later remembered, "the very first to set the wires humming in my system." Berger left him a copy of Karl Marx's *Das Kapital*.

Debs soaked up ideas from other books detailing socialist and utopian visions. He also reread the works of his namesakes, Victor Hugo and Eugène Sue. He kept a copy of Shakespeare's plays handy—he could recite much of *Julius Caesar* and *Romeo and Juliet* from memory. He studied textbooks on rhetoric. His highest ambition, he told Nellie Bly, was to be a great orator.

⸏

At 5:00 p.m. on that snowy November day, a train from Chicago arrived in Woodstock carrying three hundred Debs supporters and a brass band. The band marched around the large town square playing "Annie Laurie," while Debs devotees "wept and cheered and laughed and cried." They waved flags, sipped from flasks of whiskey, shouted themselves hoarse. Soon everyone piled back onto the special train with Debs in tow.

GO WILD OVER DEBS, the *Tribune* reported.

After a raucous two-hour ride to Chicago, they were greeted by a crowd of at least a hundred thousand people packing Union Station and the streets outside. When Debs appeared on the rear platform of the arriving train, pandemonium erupted. The uproar echoed through the train shed. Men gripped by hysteria screamed and beat on their neighbors. They lifted Debs onto their shoulders. Union men and police pushed against the sea of humanity in an effort to clear a way. Debs declined the carriage that awaited him and said he would walk to the auditorium. Under a heavy rain, the band and an enormous crowd followed Debs down Wells Street through the slush.

They reached Battery D Armory on Michigan Avenue, not far from the site of the federal military encampment in Lake Front Park during the summer of the previous year. Every square inch of the auditorium was filled. Messengers bearing congratulatory telegrams had to be handed over the heads of the crowd so they could deliver them to Debs on the podium. Calls for "Debs! Debs! Debs!" rocked the building.

The muckraking journalist Henry Demarest Lloyd introduced the ARU leader as "the most popular man among the real people today." The man of the hour stood to address the crowd.

"Manifestly, the spirit of '76 still survives," Debs intoned to begin his oration. He complained that convicted of no crime he had been jailed in "flagrant violation of the Constitution." The decision by the Supreme Court had placed every citizen "at the mercy of any prejudiced or malicious federal judge."

If the plutocrats were ever to reach heaven, he said, they would "wreck every avenue leading to the throne of the infinite" and would "debauch heaven's supreme court to obtain a decision that the command 'thou shalt not steal' is unconstitutional."

Through his secular sermon, he kept coming back to the theme of liberty. He extolled the freedom guaranteed by the Declaration of Independence and promised to every man and woman as a divine birthright.

But though guaranteed, liberty had to be fought for. It was, he said, "for those only who dare strike the blow."

Only through reliance on a pliant federal judiciary had the railroad managers defeated the men of the American Railway Union united in solidarity with each other. He pointed with scorn to this "exhibition of the debauching power of money which the country had never before beheld."

"What is to be done?" he asked. Every person had to answer the call. "You cannot do your duty by proxy." By stepping up to play a role, each man would receive the reward that Debs himself had gained. "Not only will you lose nothing but you will find something of infinite value, and that something will be yourself."

Workingmen must use the ballot to "rescue American liberties from the power of the vandal horde." The crowd cheered.

"The people are aroused," Debs declared. "Agitation, organization and unification are to be the future battle cries of men who will not part with their birthright."

He ended the speech with a quote from abolitionist poet James Russell Lowell: "He's true to God who's true to man."

გ

As he headed home to Terre Haute the next day, Debs found his wrist swollen to twice its normal size from the orgy of handshaking. He quickly discovered that the American Railway Union was in trouble. Many locals had been destroyed. In the wake of the strike, the blacklist was depriving ARU members of employment wherever they went.

Debs set off on a speaking tour to help rebuild the union. Although not personally liable for the organization's $22,000 debt, he took on the moral obligation to make it good. It took him nineteen years to pay off every penny.

Everywhere he traveled, he was shadowed by railroad detectives. At a hotel in Providence, Rhode Island, he held a secret midnight meeting with local organizers in his hotel room. The next day, all of them were fired from their jobs. In Alabama, he signed up 111 new members. The company fired eighteen of them and gave the others ten days to turn in their union cards. And so it went.

Yet Debs insisted the signs were encouraging. He had become the personification of the defiant workingman. Now that the threat of anarchy had receded, many remembered that he had been vilified by the rapacious railroad companies, libeled by the press, and persecuted by an overreaching government. He was the man who had been jailed for his sincere beliefs.

Everywhere he went, he was met with adulation. Every speech drew a crowd. Debs's sparkling, cutting oratory set fire to the imagination of his listeners. Many vividly recalled their souls leaping in response.

During the 1896 presidential election, Debs backed the Great Commoner, William Jennings Bryan, who merged the Populist and Democratic tickets. Bryan railed against the corporations, whom he called "imperious, arrogant, and compassionless." He represented the ordinary people who "work-worn and dust-begrimed . . . make their sad appeal."

Bryan's radical ideas were ahead of their time. His emphasis on fair treatment for labor, regulation of business monopolies, and the stabilization of markets for farmers set a path toward the progressive reforms of the coming century, but McKinley beat him handily.

After he saw that Bryan was unable to "blunt the fangs of the money power," Debs gave up on traditional party politics. "I have been a Democrat all my life," he said, "and I am ashamed to admit it."

On January 1, 1897, he declared himself a socialist. Bryan's defeat proved that the ballot in itself would not emancipate the wage slave. The economic system had become too corrupt, too "cannibalistic, with men set one against another." The stark issue, he proclaimed, was "Socialism vs. Capitalism. I am for Socialism because I am for humanity."

Debs would later promote the story that he had experienced a dramatic conversion to socialism during his time in the Woodstock jail. In fact, he had, step by step, grown more radical over the years.

When the government had intervened to cripple the ARU, Debs began to see that deeper change was required. "In the gleam of every bayonet and the flash of every rifle," he would later write, "*the class struggle was revealed.*" Society itself needed to be remade.

"Money constitutes no proper basis for civilization," he declared. "The time has come to regenerate society—we are on the verge of a universal change." It was the faith he would espouse for the rest of his life.

Debs's socialism was a deeply American creed. He found the principles of community, solidarity, and fairness in the Declaration of Independence and the Constitution. He saw himself as a "revolutionary patriot." He insisted that the industrial malaise was the result of a counterrevolution fabricated by business interests in the form of corporations. Americans' independence was in danger of being snuffed out by wage slavery and gross inequality.

The American Railway Union did not regain its feet after the strike. Over the next few years, Debs transformed the organization into the Social Democratic Party, then simply the Socialist Party.

No socialist in American history ever attained the stature of Eugene Debs. During the summer of 1900, he agreed to run for president of the United States under the party's banner. Socialism, he insisted, was the true patriotism.

People loved to hear him talk. His long orations drew rapt crowds.

But on election day, few of his listeners cast their votes for him. He lost resoundingly, even in Terre Haute.

Why was his message applauded, then rejected? For one thing, he underestimated his opponents. The men he called plutocrats were not blind followers of the gospel of capital, but shrewd, adaptable players in the economic arena. Socialists offered a glorious vision; capitalists held out the prospect of a ten-cent raise. Socialists stood on principle; capitalists compromised and curried favor with both major parties. Socialists represented a risky upheaval of the familiar; capitalists enticed the public with luxuries ranging from electric lights to Pullman cars. The nation's citizens wanted pie, all right, but they didn't want it in the sky.

Yet many of the ideas promoted by socialists became, over time, quite palatable to American tastes. As the outmoded political shibboleths of the Victorian era faded, programs like unemployment insurance, a government-backed old-age pension, reduced working hours, voting rights for women, and international arbitration to prevent war acquired widespread favor.

Debs's medicine was too strong for many. "The capitalist politician tells you how intelligent you are to keep you ignorant," he proclaimed. "I tell you how ignorant you are to make you desire to be intelligent." Yet he never relinquished hope. He was sure "the whole plutocratic crew" were skating on thin ice. "Socialism is not just a theory," he insisted, "it is a destiny."

His voice aroused many. "I heard him speak in San Francisco in 1912," said the poet Witter Bynner, "and was moved by the kind of appeal he made to his audience; not the appeal of a politician desiring power or corralling votes, but a vivid and humane passion for the betterment of his species."

For Debs, the Pullman boycott remained the golden moment of solidarity when it seemed that all might be different. He wrote that he was prouder of his participation in the "grandest industrial battle in history . . . than of any other act of my life." The vivid experience remained the high point, the peak from which he had glimpsed his own destiny and the future of his country.

"The Debs of fable lighted a fire in the car yards of Chicago," the essayist Horace Traubel observed. "The Debs of fact lighted an idea in the dangerous shadows of the republic."

∽

The 1904 presidential election was a reunion of sorts for veterans of the Pullman upheaval. Debs ran again as a socialist. Both Richard Olney and Nelson Miles made futile attempts to gain the Democratic nod to face Republican incumbent Theodore Roosevelt. The young hero of San Juan Hill easily won the general election. Debs improved his showing from four years earlier, garnering four hundred thousand votes, about 3 percent of the total.

In 1905, working with western miners like Big Bill Haywood, Debs helped found the Industrial Workers of the World, another attempt at a militant, all-inclusive union. The Wobblies welcomed workers of all trades and all races. A delegate at the founding convention said that the Pullman boycott, "in spite of the fact that it apparently ended in Woodstock jail, is not ended yet, but is going on today."

Debs soon abandoned the IWW. He could not abide the group's tactic of "direct action," the type of sabotage and violence that he had always seen as self-defeating for the labor movement. "The American workers are law-abiding," he said.

He ran for president on the Socialist ticket again in 1908, traveling the country on a train dubbed the Red Special. On one campaign swing he logged nine thousand miles and made 187 speeches in twenty-five days. Children waved red flags in his honor. At a rally in New York's Madison Square Garden, fifteen thousand supporters applauded him for more than twenty minutes before they allowed him to speak. He garnered less than 3 percent of the popular tally and no electoral votes. Republican William Howard Taft, who during the strike had hoped that enough men would be killed to make an impression, won the presidency.

Debs was a prophetic socialist. He was never a theorist. He read and studied, but he always found the truth of his beliefs written in the faces of working people. No other radical voice ever rang out so clearly in America. His mission was to convince and inspire. He drove his message home with what to some was fanaticism and to others faith.

For a generation and more, Debs remained what his biographer Nick Salvatore called "the most visible and dynamic opponent of the new corporate order." He warned audiences that "the world only respects as it is compelled to respect." Workers had to have regard for themselves first, had to desert the politicians of the major parties, who took them for granted. They had to reject the cozy collaboration with bosses that satisfied the leaders of trade unions.

In 1912, Debs made his fourth run for the White House. There were indications that socialism was finally gaining traction. Backed by Debs's relentless cheerleading and strategizing, party membership had doubled since 1909 and socialists had become a force in some state and local elections. "Comrades, this is our year," Debs proclaimed. He received more than nine hundred thousand votes, 6 percent of the total.

It was the high-water mark for socialism in America. Afterward, Debs became a voice crying in the wilderness. In 1916 he ran to represent Terre Haute in Congress. Now nearly sixty-one, he joined the contest with his usual energy, touring the district by automobile. He lost.

ᔢ

During World War I, political repression swept the country. Socialists began to disappear into American prisons. It became a crime to "willfully utter . . . any disloyal, profane, scurrilous, or abusive language about the form of the Government of the United States." Debs protested. During a speech in Canton, Ohio, he told listeners that "the master class has always declared the wars; the subject class has always fought the battles."

It was a principled stand, but an unpopular one. A U.S. attorney had this heresy transcribed by a stenographer and charged Debs with denigrating the war effort. "American institutions are on trial here," Debs declared in court. A jury convicted him of treason for speaking out.

At his sentencing in September 1918, he summed up his life's view and shaped an enduring motto. "Years ago I recognized my kinship with all living beings," he said. "While there is a lower class, I am in it, and while there is a criminal element I am of it, and while there is a soul in prison, I am not free." The judge gave him ten years.

Some thought it shameful that members of the same railroad brotherhoods that Debs had helped build forty years earlier now transported him to prison. Debs said he was glad to be carried "by union men, not by scabs, what more could I ask."

Ten years in a maximum-security prison was hard time for a sixty-three-year-old. "An awful loneliness has gripped me," he wrote. He later told a biographer that he had yearned for his "beloved little community of Terre Haute, where all were neighbors and friends." At least the "profit pirates" could not destroy "our sweet and priceless memories."

During his time in prison, Debs wrote to a friend: "I had a strange dream last night. I was walking by the house where I was born—the house was gone and nothing left but ashes . . . only ashes—ashes!" He had done so much, inspired so many, yet what had he accomplished that would last? It was, for the indomitable Debs, an uncharacteristic flash of heartbreak.

He was not done. In 1920, he agreed to run one more time for president of the United States. He would campaign as "Convict Number 9653." He again received more than nine hundred thousand votes from across the country, this time without ever leaving his prison cell. After the election, supporters signed petitions and demonstrated at the White House, urging his release.

In December 1921, the new president, Warren G. Harding, commuted the sentences of Debs and twenty-three other political prisoners. Debs had served two years and eight months. As he walked out of the federal prison in Atlanta on Christmas Day, he heard a familiar, heartening roar. It was the cheering from the twenty-three hundred inmates who had been won over by the friendship, the principled stance, the boundless heart of this man who never lost sight of the tragedy of working people and their longing for dignity.

During the heyday of Debs's politicking, a Yiddish speaker remembered crowds of Jewish immigrants chanting for "Deps! Deps!" "His words made men cry," the man noted, "even when they were not fully understood." Immigrants mounted his picture in their homes. A reporter who watched Debs address a crowd in New Orleans wrote that his listeners did not care so much what he said. "They cared that he cared for them."

Even a sophisticate like New York journalist Heywood Broun, who dismissed rhetorical excess as bunk, admitted that "that old man with the burning eyes actually believes that there can be such a thing as the brotherhood of man. And that's not the funniest part of it. As long as he's around I believe it myself."

He would not be around much longer. In the spring of 1926, he and Kate took a trip to Bermuda, their first long vacation since their honeymoon forty years earlier. Gene caught a cold on the way home. In September he entered a sanitarium. While he was there, he suffered a heart attack. He died on October 20, 1926, at the age of seventy-one.

29

Solidarity

THE PULLMAN BOYCOTT WAS THE MOST CONSEQUENTIAL labor conflict of the nineteenth century, the last credible threat of a nationwide general strike, the last time workers seriously imagined overturning the industrial order and establishing a more equitable society.

It was a power struggle rooted in American values. The players were marked by traits thought to be typical of Americans—self-reliance and impatience, invention and resolve, endless longing, stubborn dignity. For all the destruction, killing, and hatred it evoked, the many thousands who were involved on both sides joined the battle with an eager fervor and the love of a good fight that were also deeply American.

The system of government in the United States has often been deemed an experiment. We have repeatedly put to the test the question of whether our creed rests on a foundation of individualism and private property or of solidarity grounded in equality and mutual sympathy. During the great railroad conflict of 1894, these two ideals collided violently. A resolution could not be found then. It eludes us to this day.

∾

In practical terms, the Pullman crisis and the destruction of the American Railway Union were bad news for unions. Although railroad workers saw gains in succeeding years, the strike was followed by three decades of setbacks and retrenchment for the labor movement as a whole. America's privileged classes had been stunned by the scope of the strike and were determined never to approach the ragged edge of anarchy again. Workers' organizations were no match for determined capitalists and a government armed with the power of the injunction. Almost any sign of radical action brought violent repression.

Yet the wake-up call of the great sympathy strike did contribute to the dawning of the Progressive Era. The nation took steps along a path mapped out by middle-class reformers like Jane Addams and John Peter Altgeld. Even Richard Olney admitted after the strike that "the mass of wage-earners can no longer be dealt with by capital as so many isolated units. . . . Organized labor now confronts organized capital."

As years passed, the federal government moved to dismantle the trusts and holding companies that enforced the most egregious monopolies. Cities established new standards for tenement housing. Legislation limited child labor and rectified some unsafe working conditions. Congress passed a Workmen's Compensation Act in 1902, the first minimum wage law ten years later. Arbitration and collective bargaining were used more frequently to resolve conflict.

More substantial gains for American laborers arrived during the New Deal of the 1930s. The rise of industrial unions in the automobile, steel, and other industries—organizations similar to the American Railway Union—aided by a fundamental shift in federal labor laws, ushered in a golden age for workers. By the early 1950s, the proportion of unionized employees reached nearly 35 percent of the nonagricultural labor force. The unions' clout boosted wages and benefits for members and for non-union laborers as well. Over the fierce opposition of corporations, pressure from unions helped push through programs ranging from Social Security to Medicare.

Beginning in the 1980s, a sea change swept over the American workplace. Deindustrialization, which had accelerated through the 1970s, was presenting working people with problems parallel to those that had accompanied the industrialization of the nineteenth century. The country's institutions were ill prepared to deal with the social disruption and loss of jobs brought on by the steady decline in manufacturing. Unemployment in the early 1980s shot up to levels not seen since the Great Depression. Corporations shuttered plants. Capitalists shifted their investment to low-wage countries overseas. Non-union jobs, especially in service industries, paid employees far less than positions protected by organized labor.

With the election of Ronald Reagan, the federal government adopted an increasingly pro-business stance. In August 1981, Reagan fired and permanently blacklisted eleven thousand air traffic controllers, who had struck for more pay. His action signaled an open season on labor unions. The gains for workers resulting from nearly a century of struggle were threatened.

Americans debated in different terms the same issues that had raged in the 1890s. Did workers have a right to organize? Was labor a mere commodity subject to the law of supply and demand? Should those who invested brains and sweat and time in an enterprise have a say in how it was run? Or was all power in the workplace to be retained by capitalists? The nation struggled to resolve the conflict between what Samuel Gompers had called "autocracy in the shop and democracy in political life."

～

In May 1981, eighty-seven years after Pullman workers laid down their tools and walked off the job, a railcar rolled out of a modern factory only a few blocks from the brick buildings of the old Pullman shops. It was a bi-level sleeping car, a Superliner, part of an order of equipment for Amtrak, the entity that now operated all of the nation's long-distance passenger rail service.

The railroad boom, which had lasted until the middle of the twentieth century, was long over. Automobiles and airplanes had replaced trains. The classic Pullman car had become an artifact of old movies.

The manufacturing arm of George Pullman's company had, under the name Pullman-Standard, come to dominate the entire railcar-making business in the United States. The previous year, it had been bought out for $600 million by a diversified conglomerate known as Wheelabrator-Frye. The Pullman operation became a victim of mergers, spin-offs, and leveraging—financial maneuvering that would have impressed George Pullman. Citing "restrictive labor contracts," the new owners decided to close down much of the company's railcar business. This would be the last Pullman car ever made.

Stunned workers had begun a "save-our-jobs" campaign in an attempt to stem the inevitable. They proposed legislation that would make it il-

legal for companies to pull out of a community without softening the
transition for workers and residents. They lobbied for more spending on
mass transit. Neither the company nor the government heeded their
pleas.

They had no options. The mood in the nation had turned against
unions. Eugene Debs's advice to working people that they should abandon the major parties, build their own political power, widen their solidarity, and pursue fundamental changes in society now took on a
prophetic ring.

Instead, bureaucracy and corruption within unions had demoralized
the labor movement. The racial exclusion and misogyny that Debs had
preached against had sapped the organizations' vitality. Workers found
themselves powerless in the face of ever larger and more efficient corporate employers and a hostile government.

During our own time, which some call the New Gilded Age, workers are beset by trends that would have sounded familiar to the strikers
of 1894. More than half the states have, at the behest of business interests, passed "right to work" laws intended to cripple labor organizing.
Union representation has withered to less than 7 percent of private-sector
workers. Wages have stagnated, benefits evaporated. The spread of the
"contingent workforce"—employees converted to contract workers—has
allowed corporations to duck state and federal laws regarding the minimum wage, overtime, and benefits. Demeaning and abusive treatment
of employees, wage theft, and neglect of workplace safety rules have in-
fected many industries.

The workers at Pullman-Standard in 1981 found themselves facing
a situation that another generation of Pullman employees had warned
against, one that those workers were afraid would go on forever. It was
the creative, destructive dynamic of unregulated capitalism. Rooted in
human greed, it was spreading around the globe, lifting up some, dashing down others, creating wealth beyond imagining for a few, forcing
many more into economic and spiritual poverty. It was what the Pullman workers had called "the dance of skeletons bathed in human tears."

The workers who put the finishing touches on the last Pullman car
were the men and women of the Eugene V. Debs Local of the United
Steelworkers of America. When they completed their work, they attached a brass plaque announcing the car's name: the George M. Pullman. Then they laid down their tools and their jobs disappeared forever.

Notes

PART I

1 Boss Town

3   *"Uncle Jumbo"*: Welch, 280.
3   *"rule themselves"*: Currey, vol. 3, 35.
4   *"My mind was dazzled"*: Trachtenberg, 218.
4   *"civilizing strides"*: Books of the Fairs, 5.
5   *"fever of rapid"*: Ibid., 16.
5   *"Americans take to"*: Wolmar, 51.
6   *"Here of all her"*: Miller, "The White City."
6   *"Compared to the bustle"*: Martin, *Railroads Triumphant*, 54.
7   *"The old nations"*: Burg, 40–41.
7   *"cynosure and cesspool"*: Miller, "The White City."
7   *"grease so thick"*: Ibid.
7   *"solid stink"*: Pierce, 311.
7   *"the very Mecca"*: Buder, 29.
7   *"the culminating product"*: Pullman's Palace Car Company, 2.
8   *"Chicago asked"*: Brands, 33.
8   *"under a sham"*: Trachtenberg, 215.
9   *"The free lands"*: Turner, 219.
9   *"penniless beginner"*: Fink, *The Long Gilded Age*, 16.
9   *"the seedbed"*: Douglas, 206.
10   *"brandishing war-clubs"*: Bancroft, 878.
11   *"people are in a state"*: Steeples and Whitten, 27.

2 Our Cause Is Just

13   *"this wonderful age"*: St. Paul Daily Globe, June 10, 1893, 8.
13   *"Tod has been p-s-ing"*: Martin, *James J. Hill*, 404.
13   *"The floor might have passed"*: Steeples, 33.
14   *"The most remarkable day"*: New York Times, May 6, 1893, 5.
16   *"it would be a fitting"*: Martin, *James J. Hill*, 404.
17   *"Our cause is just"*: Chicago Tribune, February 10, 1893, 3.
17   *"debasing greed"*: Salvatore, 88.

18 "*Labor can organize*": Ginger, *The Bending Cross*, 92.
19 "*The time was*": Wiebe, 8.
19 "*more friends than any man*": Ginger, *The Bending Cross*, 93.
19 "*organized railway labor*": Debs, "About the Unions."
20 "*take whatever steps*": Martin, *James J. Hill*, 411.
21 "*break the chains*": Salvatore, 120.
21 "*they have violated*": Ginger, *The Bending Cross*, 103–4.
22 "*to go over the Great Northern*": Richard White, 426.
22 "*somewhat awkward*": Page Smith, 521.
23 "*If the other organizations*": Salvatore, 120.
24 "*in which the employees*": Richard White, 428.
25 "*gave the strikers nineteen-twentieths*": Debs, *Letters*, vol. 1, 68.
25 "*For the first time*": St. Paul Daily Globe, May 2, 1894, 2.
26 "*The greatest tribute*": Ginger, *The Bending Cross*, 106.

3 More Than a Joke

27 "*It will not be long*": Brecher, 82.
28 "*They may be wrong*": Schwantes, 56.
30 "*I am the Great Unknown*": Ibid., 44.
30 "*a manifestation of*": Studenski, 221.
30 "*it doesn't hurt me*": Brands, 161.
30 "*leaves a trail of*": Schwantes, 147.
30 "*Is there anything foolish*": Rezneck, 334.
31 "*a symptom of*": Howard, 692–3.
31 "*idle, useless*": Ibid., 697.
31 "*There is no telling*": Schwantes, 167.
31 "*The evils of*": Howard, 689.
32 "*We ain't too good*": Schwantes, 234.
32 "*I'm not afraid*": Ibid., 131.

4 A Heart for Others

34 "*one of the completest*": Indianapolis News, May 2, 1894, 1.
35 "*What has occurred tonight*": Salvatore, 125.
37 "*The locomotive was my*": Gamst, 245.
37 "*I have a little company*": Salvatore, 18.
38 "*I still believe*": Ginger, *The Bending Cross*, 17.
38 "*kept one clean sheet*": Taillon, 22.
38 "*the ceaseless danger*": Ginger, *The Bending Cross*, 19.
38 "*took nerve, coordination*": Wolmar, 197.
39 "*There are too many things*": Ginger, *The Bending Cross*, 20.
40 "*rugged honesty, simple*": Ibid., 21.
40 "*the obligation that*": Taillon, 50.
41 "*is absolutely adored*": Salvatore, 47.
42 "*perfect social equality*": Locomotive Firemen's Magazine 4, 273 (1880).
42 "*Our fundamental principle*": Salvatore, 58.
44 "*The strike is the weapon*": Ibid., 81.
44 "*the white savage*": Fogelson, 30.
45 "*I have a heart*": Ginger, *The Bending Cross*, 82.
45 "*only clear cut victory*": Salvatore, 125.

5 The Commercial Value of Beauty

47 "*promenaded in all*": Leyendecker, 22.
49 "*He was one of those rare*": Carnegie, 161.
49 "*pitched in pretty deep*": Leyendecker, 63.

49   *"people are always"*: Miller, *City of the Century*, 230.
49   *"Like sleeping on"*: Wolmar, 182.
51   *"He will feel his position"*: Buder, 209.
53   *"that there will be no"*: Central Pacific Railroad Photographic History Museum.
53   *"I have always held"*: Gilbert, 155.
54   *"Capital will not invest"*: Carl Smith, 184.
54   *"we shall see great"*: Buder, 45.
54   *"commercial value of"*: Ibid., 43.

6 Well-Wishing Feudalism

56   *"We have never had"*: Hirsch, 29.
56   *"all pervading air"*: Buder, 102.
56   *"What is seen in a walk"*: Gilbert, 135.
56   *"High honor is due"*: Ely.
57   *"simply as a matter"*: Emerson, 339.
57   *"a needless air of"*: Ely.
57   *"where not one single"*: Ibid.
57   *"seeing families settle"*: Rousiers, 181.
57   *"Nobody regards Pullman"*: Buder, 82.
58   *"It was not intended"*: Carwardine, 20.
58   *"always enter or leave"*: Lindsey, 70.
58   *"looked at but dared"*: Buder, 66.
58   *"It is not the American"*: Ely.
60   *"We made all the carpets"*: United States Strike Commission, 435.
60   *"educational tool in"*: Montgomery, 129.
60   *"The wages he pays out"*: United States Strike Commission, 88.
61   *"One man has a pay check"*: Carwardine, 69.
61   *"I have known men"*: United States Strike Commission, 425.
62   *"It was only the friends"*: Ibid., 418.
62   *"talk to the men as though"*: Ibid., 436.
62   *"the tyrannical and abusive"*: Carwardine, 77.
62   *"George is feeling very"*: Buder, 154.
63   *"he was always quick"*: Ibid., 5.

7 Armies

64   *"If these tramps"*: Schwantes, 120.
65   *"a dangerous mob sentiment"*: Ibid., 154.
65   *"Public sympathy strongly"*: Ibid., 152.
66   *"How in hell do you expect"*: Ibid., 149.
66   *"thoughtfully replaced"*: Ibid., 174.
67   *"met with enthusiasm"*: Anaconda Standard, April 25, 1894, 1.
67   BLOOD FLOWS: New York Times, April 26, 1894, 1.
69   *"questions of ethics"*: Schwantes, 165.
69   *"Such a fantastic aggregation"*: Campbell et al., 80.
70   *"lean on the government"*: Studenski, 221.
71   *"Up these steps"*: Dray, 193.
71   *"I appreciate"*: Schwantes, 168.
71   *"Twenty million people"*: Prout, 325.
71   *"Clubbing may subdue"*: Schwantes, 181.
72   *"They had a right"*: Ibid., 183.

8 The Works Are Closed

73   *"the sunny street"*: Teaford, 19.
74   *"I never knew a man"*: Buder, 31.

74 *"one of the most frigid"*: Miller, *City of the Century*, 228.
74 *"about as hot"*: Buder, 31.
74 *"I have no other interest"*: Wagenknecht, 87.
77 *"work for lower wages"*: Buder, 151.
77 *"we will stand by it"*: *Chicago Tribune*, May 10, 1894, 1.
78 *"Mr. Pullman, we want"*: Ibid.
78 *"Is there a man here"*: Ibid.
79 NO STRIKE JUST NOW: Ibid.
79 *"the committee was received"*: Newberry Library, "Report of a Meeting Held Under the Auspices of the American Railway Union."
80 *"of the same impudent"*: Chicago History Museum, "Report, May 10, 1894."
83 *"It is so long since"*: *Chicago Tribune*, May 12, 1893, 1.
83 *"most unpleasant surprise"*: Ibid., 6.
83 *"The boys were bound"*: Ibid., 1.
84 *"And on that proposition"*: Lindsey, 126.

PART II

9 Nothing to Arbitrate

87 *"codfish, coal oil"*: *Locomotive Firemen's Magazine* 11, 8 (1887).
88 *"I am with you heart"*: Stead, 177.
88 *"I believe a rich"*: Lindsey, 124.
88 *"it will be the duty"*: Boase, 89.
89 *"as quiet as a New"*: Papke, 21.
90 *"specious interest in"*: Menand, 373.
91 *"We are sunk under a mass"*: Knight, 285.
91 *"It is merciful and necessary"*: Badger, 39.
92 *"at a time when mistakes"*: Lindsey, 125.
93 *"there is nothing needed"*: Buder, 171.
93 *"left in the cold"*: Ibid.
94 *"There is danger in extremes"*: Debs, "President's Keynote."
95 *"a window behind which"*: Knight, 314.
96 *"we had made a beginning"*: Ibid.
96 *"It was impossible to come"*: Schneirov et al., *The Pullman Strike*, 135.
96 *"that broad conscience"*: Ibid., 136.
96 *"unrest, discontent, and fear"*: Knight, 314.
98 *"blackest man with the whitest"*: Tye, 25.
98 *"Everything is in the line"*: *Locomotive Firemen's Magazine* 11, 9 (1887).
98 *"by nature adapted faithfully"*: Wolmar, 186.
99 *"I am not here to advocate"*: Arnesen, 29.
99 *"would not 'brother' the negro"*: Taillon, 58.
99 *"if we do not admit the colored man"*: Arnesen, 29.
99 *"It is not the colored man's fault"*: Ibid.
100 *"a different story of the strike"*: Ibid., 30.

10 Dance of Skeletons

101 *"Twenty thousand souls"*: United States Strike Commission, 87.
102 *"We are born in a Pullman"*: Ginger, *Altgeld's America*, 149.
102 *"when a man is sober"*: Ginger, *The Bending Cross*, 113.
102 *"We go into the market"*: Kaufman, 40.
102 *"And so the merry war"*: United States Strike Commission, 88.
103 *"Many a time"*: Carwardine, 78.
103 *"We ask you to come"*: Lindsey, 129.
103 *"monumental monster"*: *Chicago Tribune*, June 16, 1984, 3.

104   *"The situation with regard"*: United States Strike Commission, 92.
104   *"The forces of labor must unite"*: Debs, "President's Keynote."
105   *"Unless the Pullman Palace Car"*: United States Strike Commission, 94.
106   *"likely to precipitate a"*: Chicago Tribune, June 24, 1894, 1.
107   *"sensational developments"*: Chicago Tribune, June 27, 1894, 2.
107   *"Look out for tomorrow"*: Ibid.

11 The Crisis Has Come

109   *"If the railroad companies"*: Chicago Tribune, June 27, 1894, 2.
109   *"the Illinois Central, Chicago"*: Dray, 201.
109   *"We do not wish to interfere"*: Chicago Tribune, June 27, 1894, 2.
109   *"be postponed and our"*: W. Thomas White, 25.
110   *"There will be no settlement"*: Ibid.
111   *"who say they are bound to quit"*: Chicago Tribune, June 29, 1894, 8.
112   *"I think there is no necessity"*: Eggert, Railroad Labor Disputes, 157.
113   *"The fight is on"*: New York Times, July 1, 1894, 1.
113   *"Strike situation very serious"*: Leyendecker, 225.
113   *"My anxiety is very great"*: Buder, 141.
113   *"This trouble has now outgrown"*: Chicago Tribune, June 29, 1894, 7.

12 We Mean Business

116   *"Though the people support"*: Beatty, 195.
116   *"no harm shall come to"*: Ibid., 194.
116   *"under-government, from the failure"*: Clark, 39.
117   *"The corporation plunders"*: Beatty, 305.
118   *"problems of management"*: Lindsey, 115.
118   *"I regard the Pullman Company"*: Carwardine, 63.
119   *"We mean business"*: Chicago Tribune, June 29, 1894, 1.
120   *"Portly officials"*: Lewis, 223.
120   *"we will coax them"*: Chicago Tribune, July 1, 1894, 2.
121   *"We have organized to resist"*: New York Times, June 29, 1894, 1.
121   *"I think we should get men"*: Deverell, 70.
122   *"in reality it will be a struggle"*: Lindsey, 136.

13 Not a Wheel Moving

123   *"my nerves were more thrilled"*: Menand, 295.
125   *"I can see no good reason"*: San Francisco Call, July 1, 1894, 6.
125   *"dignity of labor while excluding"*: Adelman et al., 613.
126   *"The starvation of a nation"*: Menand, 300.
126   *"Mr. Pullman is not being considered"*: Chicago Tribune, July 1, 1894, 5.
126   *"assumed the proportions of"*: New York Times, June 29, 1894, 1.
126   *"to starve the people"*: Chicago Tribune, June 30, 1894, 1.
126   *"We have in our power"*: Chicago Tribune, June 29, 1894, 8.
129   *"Mr. Pullman's bouillon"*: Chicago Tribune, July 1, 1894, 3.
129   *"I appeal to the striking men"*: New York Times, June 30, 1894, 1.
130   *"I do not see how the police"*: Chicago Tribune, July 1, 1894, 5.
130   *"law or anarchism"*: Schwantes, 196.
130   *"so-called railroad kings"*: Ibid.
130   *"a man of brains"*: Edwards, 202.
131   *"Deputations of little girls"*: Labor, 71.
131   *"These men"*: Schwantes, 271.
132   *"This movement"*: Ibid., 133.
132   *"These men who feel"*: Ibid., 260.

14 Disaster Threatens

134 *"for once will feel"*: Chicago Tribune, July 1, 1894, 1.
135 *"The ultimate disaster"*: New York Times, July 1, 1894, 1.
135 *"not shown any disposition"*: Schwantes, 162.
136 *"raised truculence"*: Welch, 143.
137 *"The government might with"*: Salvatore, 131.
137 *"It has seemed to me that if"*: Barnard, 287.
137 *"advisable not merely"*: Ibid.
138 *"all regular mail trains"*: United States Department of Justice, 58.
139 *"I feel that the true way"*: Barnard, 287.
139 *"because they refused to turn"*: Lindsey, 280.
140 *"waging an active war in Colorado"*: Ibid., 168.
142 *"bladder-belly bosses"*: Chicago Tribune, July 1, 1894, 4.
142 "LAW IS TRAMPLED ON": Chicago Tribune, June 30, 1893, 3.
143 "GREATEST STRIKE IN HISTORY": New York Times, July 1, 1894, 1.

15 To a Standstill

144 *"emotional intellectual"*: Salvatore, 66.
145 *"I have always been partial"*: Karsner, 106.
145 *"an artist, adventurer"*: Sandburg, 214.
145 *"There's nothing 'at's patheticker"*: Young, 15.
145 *"And there's 'Gene Debs"*: Riley, 374.
145 *"the strikers have shown"*: Chicago Tribune, July 2, 1894, 9.
146 *"We want to win as"*: Salvatore, 133.
146 *"fought to a standstill"*: Lindsey, 144.
146 *"practically a network"*: United States Strike Commission, xliv.
148 *"Pay no attention to rumors"*: Lindsey, 245.
148 *"stupidly managed"*: Deverell, 65.
149 *"the passenger depot"*: San Francisco Call, July 3, 1894, 1.
149 *"This looks more like a fair"*: Deverell, 73.
149 *"Peace officers here are"*: Ibid.
151 *"an earnest individualist"*: National Cyclopaedia, 253.
151 *"any act whatever"*: United States Supreme Court, 572.
152 *"Gatling gun on paper"*: New York Times, July 3, 1894, 1.
152 *"so broad and sweeping"*: Papke, 42.

16 Ragged Edge

153 *"if strike not settled"*: Winston, 554.
153 *"conspirators and lawless"*: Lindsey, 144.
154 *"force which is overwhelming"*: Barnard, 287.
154 *"the belligerent invasion"*: Eugene E. Leach, 214.
154 *"neurasthenia and dipsomania"*: Chicago Tribune, July 8, 1894, 3.
155 *"a seething mass of smells"*: Buder, 184.
155 *"cold-hearted, cold-blooded"*: Lindsey, 318.
155 *"More dangerous and menacing"*: New York World, July 3, 1894, 1.
155 *"almost everyone on Halsted Street"*: Schneirov, Labor and Urban Politics, 338.
156 *"marks him peculiarly"*: Shaw, 87.
157 *"from among those"*: Altgeld, 21.
157 *"I will be a dead man"*: Dray, 207.
157 *"to encourage again the spirit"*: New York Times, June 28, 1893, 4.
157 *"a typical German anarchist"*: Barnard, 18.
157 *"I have reason to fear"*: Ibid., 291.
158 *"A standing military force"*: Madison, vol. 2, 992.
159 *"I do not understand"*: Lindsey, 246.

161   *"nobody wanted to be the first"*: Chicago Tribune, July 3, 1894, 1.
161   *"in all his dignity was rolled"*: Barnard, 289.
161   *"literally fell over one another"*: Chicago Tribune, July 3, 1894, 1.
161   *"I command you in the name"*: Ibid.
161   *"I am here at Blue Island"*: Barnard, 289.
162   *"Congratulate you upon the legal"*: United States Department of Justice, 65.
162   *"more threatening and far"*: Eggert, Richard Olney, 142.
163   *"a number of baggage cars"*: Barnard, 289.
163   *"Believe that no force"*: Ibid.
163   *"be the judge on questions"*: Eggert, Richard Olney, 142.
164   *"We have been brought"*: Lindsey, 245.

PART III

17 We Shall Have Debs

167   *"They're regulars, Theodore"*: Salvatore, 133.
167   *"destroying property, the stigma"*: Lindsey, 174–5.
168   *"the mania of owning things"*: Whitman, 56.
169   *"No one cared to take the risk"*: Chicago Tribune, July 5, 1894, 2.
170   *"should not be scattered or divided"*: Connelly, 287.
170   *"to protect federal property"*: Ibid.
170   *"quieter than a blue law Sunday"*: Chicago Tribune, July 5, 1894, 2.
171   *"he preserves his customary calmness"*: New York Times, July 5, 1894, 2.
171   *"The story of the origin"*: Ibid.
172   *"The first shot fired"*: Lindsey, 175.
172   *"It is corporation greed"*: New York Times, July 5, 1894, 2.
172   *"The subject has now passed"*: Lindsey, 171.
172   *"It has now become a fight"*: Salvatore, 131.
173   *"Every man who has trampled"*: Chicago Tribune, July 5, 1894, 3.
173   *"with the sullen defiance"*: Cozzens, 450.
173   *"I have never heard of a more brutal"*: Wooster, 194.
173–74   *"for display or for picnic purposes"*: Chicago Tribune, July 5, 1894, 3.
174   *"like a flock of frightened sheep"*: New York Times, July 5, 1894, 1.
174   *"not so much to quell a riot"*: Dray, 210.
174   *"thugs, thieves, and ex-convicts"*: Ibid., 211.
175   *"It was hoped the presence of the troops"*: Chicago Tribune, July 5, 1894, 1.
175   *"Mr. Debs where the hair is short"*: Ibid.
176   *"Where's my fireman"*: Ibid., 2.
176   *"No act of violence or mob action"*: Frank A. Leach.
176   *"You will fire low, and fire to kill"*: Deverell, 75.
177   *"to go over to the scene of the strife"*: Sacramento Daily Union, July 5, 1894, 1.
177   *"Don't you know that we were raised"*: Richard White, 445.
178   *"soldiers and strikers were wandering"*: Ibid.
178   *"first instance of this sort"*: New York Times, July 5, 1894, 8.

18 Strike Fever

180   *"A grave crisis is before Chicago"*: Chicago Tribune, July 6, 1894, 2.
181   *"extraordinary coolness of the men"*: Indianapolis Journal, July 6, 1894, 1.
181   *"if Miles would do less talking"*: Eggert, Richard Olney, 146.
181   *"or you would not have taken"*: Barnard, 295.
182   *"Federal troops were sent to Chicago"*: New York Times, July 6, 1894, 2.
182   *"involves some startling conclusions"*: New York Times, July 7, 1894, 1.
182   *"I neither transcended my authority"*: Barnard, 307.
182   *"the especial representative"*: Chicago Tribune, July 7, 1894, 4.

182 *"a sausage-maker from Wurttemberg"*: Barnard, 299.
184 *"amid the wildest enthusiasm"*: *New York Times*, July 6, 1894, 2.
184 *"acted as a kind of wet blanket"*: *New York Times*, July 5, 1894, 2.
184 *"the most efficient protection"*: Nevins, 620.
184 *"There is no glory shooting"*: Lindsey, 199.
185 *"guards or custodians of private"*: Ibid., 200.
185 *"utterly unable to cope"*: *New York Times*, July 6, 1894, 2.
185 *"The police and the soldiers"*: Ibid.
186 *"California fruits are now"*: Ibid., 1.
186 *"this idea of shooting down"*: Deverell, 82.
186 *"Deputy United States Marshals have"*: *New York Times*, July 6, 1894, 3.
186 GOV. WAITE ON: Ibid.
186 *"entirely of their own accord"*: Ibid., 2.
187 *"want of the actual necessaries"*: *Chicago Tribune*, July 6, 1894, 2.
187 *"the spectacle of Mr. Pullman fanned"*: *New York Times*, July 6, 1894, 2.
187 *"A million of men stand ready"*: *Durham Globe*, July 6, 1894, 4.
187 *"an instrument of oppression"*: *New York Times*, July 6, 1894, 2.
188 *"neither make nor accept any"*: *Chicago Tribune*, July 6, 1894, 5.
189 *"There was no regret"*: Miller, *City of the Century*, 550.
190 *"O, it's all over"*: *Chicago Tribune*, July 6, 1894, 7.

19 Pandemonium

191 *"Alarm becoming general among"*: United States Department of Justice, 73.
191 *"the dominant characteristic"*: Badger, 36.
191 *"All America"*: Miller, "The White City."
191 *"the very sight of a bluecoat"*: Salvatore, 132.
192 MOB WILL IS LAW: Lindsey, 311.
192 *"will be fired upon"*: Miller, *City of the Century*, 545.
192 *"war of the bloodiest"*: Lindsey, 311.
192 *"are not strikers, most of them"*: Foner, *History of the Labor Movement*, 270.
193 *"none of the wild howlings"*: *Chicago Tribune*, July 7, 1894, 1.
193 *"We have it upon reliable authority"*: Debs et al., *Organized Labor's Demands*, 5.
194 *"were armed and paid by"*: Barnard, 312.
194 *"they caught men in the act"*: Ibid., 313.
195 *"feast of famine"*: W. Thomas White, 29.
196 *"the pliant tools of the codfish"*: Ibid., 33.
196 *"If it takes the entire army"*: Menand, 300.
197 *"a battle for supremacy between"*: Ibid., 57.
197 *"I am running this town"*: Ibid., 61.
198 *"strike upon any railroad"*: United States Department of Justice, 72.
198 *"We have assurance"*: *Chicago Tribune*, July 7, 1894, 2.
199 *"any gentlemen of standing"*: Ibid., 5.
199 *"Let Mr. Pullman agree"*: *Chicago Tribune*, July 8, 1894, 12.
199 *"a general cessation"*: *Chicago Tribune*, July 7, 1894, 1.
200 *"You had all better get on"*: Ibid., 4.
200 *"The fight is on, and our"*: Ibid., 2.
200 *"moving mass of shouting"*: Brands, 154.

20 Day of Blood

202 *"Capital has combined to enslave"*: Lindsey, 268.
202 *"Blood has been spilled"*: John H. Smith.
204 *"shied a stone at the soldiers"*: *Chicago Times*, July 8, 1894, 5.
205 *"not inclined to be merciful"*: *Chicago Tribune*, July 8, 1894, 1.
205 IS A DAY OF BLOOD: Ibid.

206 "Terrible scenes at Chicago": Steinway.
206 "Civil war is imminent": Chicago Tribune, July 8, 1894, 3.
207 "roughs from Chicago": Clark, 147.
207 "They were firing directly at us": Miller, City of the Century, 545.
208 "I would like to know by what authority": Lindsey, 260.
208 "Federal troops shooting citizens": Ibid.
208 "It will be necessary for the military": Tuchman, 456.

21 I, Grover

209 "I am so worn out and tired": Chicago Tribune, July 9, 1894, 5.
209 "Pullman could have": New York Times, July 9, 1894, 2.
209 "Let [the employees] return to us": Chicago Tribune, July 9, 1894, 5.
209 "only two roads are making any": Chicago Tribune, July 8, 1894, 10.
210 "He will not be arrested": Ibid.
210 "I consider our position impregnable": Ibid.
210 "quietest day that the neighborhood": New York Times, July 9, 1894, 2.
210 "Relic hunters and camera-snappers": Chicago Tribune, July 9, 1894, 8.
210 "bloomer girl much in evidence": Ibid.
211 "The pulse of the great strike": New York Times, July 9, 1894, 1.
211 "may have a bad effect on the mob": Chicago Tribune, July 8, 1894, 2.
211 "from the ravage and persecution": Ibid., 10.
212 "If you want to save united labor": Chicago Tribune, July 9, 1894, 1.
212 "If this fight is won": Chicago Tribune, July 10, 1894, 2.
213 "I, Grover Cleveland, President": Chicago Tribune, July 9, 1894, 1.
213 "amounts to the same thing": Ibid.
214 "with the wine of special privilege": Chicago Inter Ocean, July 9, 1894, 5.
214 "We have not come to the bridge": Chicago Inter Ocean, July 8, 1894, 4.
214 "The Pullman Company has taken": Chicago Inter Ocean, July 10, 1894, 2.

22 Watching a Man Drown

215 "a serious mistake has been made": Chicago Tribune, July 11, 1894, 1.
216 "open war against the state": Lindsey, 312.
216 "We will win": Chicago Tribune, July 10, 1894, 4.
216 "cheerful and hopeful": Ibid.
216 "He has ten hopes to your one hope": Traubel, 40.
218 "in behalf of the community": New York Times, July 10, 1894, 1.
219 "A crisis has been reached": New York Times, July 11, 1894, 2.
219 "a remodeling of the Government": New York Times, July 10, 1894, 3.
219 "The question": Chicago Tribune, July 10, 1894, 5.
220 "make an effort to bring order": New York Times, July 10, 1894, 3.
220 "disperse and retire peaceably": Ibid.
221 "rioters or anarchists have": Wooster, 199.
222 "the opportunities of life": New York Times, July 11, 1894, 1.
222 "The arrest will not deter": Chicago Tribune, July 11, 1894, 1.
222 "It is no longer a question of right": Ibid., 7.
223 "As to whether they will be criminally": Chicago Tribune, July 12, 1894, 1.
224 "their Springfields leveled threateningly": San Francisco Call, July 12, 1894, 1.
225 "orderly and law-abiding": Chicago Tribune, July 11, 1894, 2.
225 "I for one will die rather than submit": Ibid., 5.
225 "To strike now": Ibid., 2.

23 Last Resort

226–27   "it was not expected that all": Chicago Tribune, July 12, 1894, 1.
227 "develops the more subtle qualities": Gompers, 7.

227 "one of the most brainy men": Salvatore, 102.
227 "disruptive movement": Ibid., 126.
228 "I would make an injury": Ibid., 136.
228 "go slow on Chicago meeting": Foner, History of the Labor Movement, 272.
229 "men who were clothed with responsibility": Salvatore, 125.
229 "one of capital and labor": Taft, 78.
230 "calm, dispassionate": United States Strike Commission, 191.
230 "proposition as a basis of settlement": Taft, 79.
230 "Sacrifices . . . will have their": Ibid., 80.
231 "The conference regarded the proposition": United States Strike Commission, 191.
231 "The heart of Labor everywhere": Debs et al., Organized Labor's Demands, 10.
232 "one of the final blows that crushed": Salvatore, 136.
232 "saving the people of this country": Foner, History of the Labor Movement, 273.
232 "such a course would destroy": Salvatore, 136.

PART IV

24 The Poor Striker

235 "Eugene V. Debs is battling in the cause": New York Times, July 13, 1894, 6.
236 "a great victory for the labor": San Francisco Call, July 13, 1894, 1.
236 "The deplorable events": Chicago Tribune, July 14, 1894, 1.
237 "terms of surrender": Ibid.
237 "in good humor": Ibid.
237 "It doesn't make any": Ibid.
238 "no men will be discharged": Chicago Tribune, July 12, 1894, 1.
239 "We will win our fight ": Lindsey, 235.
239 "Pay no attention to newspaper": Chicago Tribune, July 14, 1894, 1.
239 "tied up as stiff as a petrified": Chicago Tribune, July 15, 1894, 1.
239 "enter the field to spread": Ibid.
239 "There is no dispute to be settled": Ibid., 2.
239 "We started out with a demand": Ibid., 1.
239 "plotting methods of destruction": Wooster, 200.
240 "We will test the question": Chicago Tribune, July 18, 1894, 8.
240 "I would rather be a free man": Ibid.
240 "Stand by your principles": Debs, Debs: His Life, 66.
240 "a graceful woman of strong": Chicago Tribune, July 19, 1894, 1.
240 "sparklers of about a carat": Salvatore, 141.
241 "The poor striker who is arrested": Lindsey, 282.
241 "there would be no more boycotting": Ibid., 285.
241 "free, voluntary and peaceable action": Ibid., 287.
242 "Take action to have all classes": Chicago Tribune, July 18, 1894, 8.
242 "Save your money and buy a gun": Kersten, 71.
243 "I don't believe the strike": Chicago Tribune, July 14, 1894, 1.
243 "These works will be opened": Chicago Tribune, July 19, 1894, 1.
243 "I have always told the men": Chicago Tribune, July 17, 1894, 1.
243 "Because," he said, "when a man asks": United States Strike Commission, 438.
244 "Starvation stares us in the face": Lindsey, 339.
244 "very quiet, worn out by the strike": Leyendecker, 231.
244 "practically given their lives to you": Burns, 301.
244 "The men are hungry and the women": Lindsey, 340.
244 "doubt that there are many cases of need": Barnard, 327.
244 "all humane and charitably disposed": Ibid.

25 Everything Was at Stake

247 "*the most thorough examination*": Buder, 187.
247 "*particularly anxious*": United States Strike Commission, 129.
247 "*so adjusted that every dollar*": Ibid., 130.
247 "*broken the backbone*": Ibid., 144.
248 "*It was in the crisis when everything*": Ibid., 146.
248 "*about the 6th day of July*": Ibid., 145.
248 "*unrestricted foreign immigration*": Ibid., 170.
249 "*No matter what may be said*": Ibid.
249 "*To avert railroad strikes*": Ibid., 163.
249 "*I believe,*" he said, "*in a cooperative*": Ibid., 170.
250 "*Working people are the most important*": Ibid., 529.
250 "*I don't know just what you mean by*": Ibid., 545.
250 "*The wage question is settled*": Ibid., 557.
250 "*borne some losses for employees*": Ibid., 554.
250 "*divides its profits with the people*": Ibid.
250 "*Would it not have been a good*": Ibid., 565.
251 "*the wages had been fixed*": Ibid.
251 "*what is known to workmen*": Ibid., 566.
251 "*It was the principle involved*": Ibid., 553.
251 "*impossible for the company*": Ibid., 556.
251 "*stubbornness in men is often*": Wright, 143.
252 "*Are you at the town of Pullman*": United States Strike Commission, 538.
252 "*Because it is not easy*": Ibid., 567.
253 "*the rapid concentration of power*": Ibid., xlvii.
253 "*The Pullman Company*": Ibid., xxvii.
253 "*different policy would have prevented*": Ibid., xlii.
253 "*the persistent and shrewdly*": Ibid., xxxi.
253 "*There is no evidence before the commission*": Ibid., xlv.
254 "*apply some of the features involved*": Schneirov, *Labor and Urban Politics*, 341.
254 "*Much of the real responsibility*": United States Strike Commission, xlvi.
254 "*if I am a prophet, it really*": Menand, 297.
254 "*warning to the employing class*": Carwardine, xli.
255 "*practically a bill of rights for labor*": Rezneck, 337.
255 "*might as well try to stop Niagara*": Lindsey, 358.
255 "*stronger to-day, numerically*": United States Strike Commission, 175.

26 Strikes and Their Causes

256 "*kindlier, gentler, more generous*": Lindsey, 107.
256 "*bum profession . . . utterly*": Kersten, 45.
256 "*no man should be allowed to play*": Eggert, *Richard Olney*, 165.
257 "*four more dastardly criminals*": Papke, 48.
257 "*advise workmen to go upon a strike*": Ibid., 49.
258 "*Would you believe it*": Ibid., 50.
258 "*club to defeat the effort*": Ibid., 55.
258 "*that man whose name*": Kersten, 73.
259 "*There is something wrong*": Papke, 56.
260 "*refusing to work for*": Lindsey, 295.
260 "*Man is by nature*": Papke, 66.
260 "*an experimental piece*": Ibid., 72.
260 "*decided rightly enough*": Ibid., 67.
261 "*closest attention*": Ibid., 72.
261 "*to deprive workingmen*": Kersten, 77.
261 "*Strikes are deplorable*": Lindsey, 295.

261 *"but freedom does not consist"*: Trachtenberg, 233.
261 *"the right to consider"*: Ibid., 232.
261 *"to heated declamations"*: Ibid., 78.
262 *"the strong arm of"*: United States Supreme Court, 158.
262 *"mere force of numbers"*: Wiebe, 93.
262 *"sordid despotism of wealth"*: Beatty, 203.
263 *"flagrantly usurped jurisdiction"*: Ibid.
263 *"a notice to all Anarchists"*: Papke, 78.
263 *"left the law so biased"*: Ibid., 79.
263 *"I shall go into history"*: Dray, 214.

27 The Common Heartbeat

264 *"A man who won't meet"*: Lindsey, 319.
265 *"was never the same after"*: Buder, 206.
266 *"During all those dark"*: Addams, *Twenty Years*, 139.
266 *"paralyzing consciousness"*: Knight, 88.
266 *"the larger solidarity"*: Ibid., 328.
266 *"Are you content that"*: Ibid.
266 *"spent a million of dollars"*: Elshtain, 167.
266 *"heaped extraordinary"*: Ibid.
267 *"We must learn to trust"*: Knight, 330–31.
267 *"the rhythm of the common"*: Addams, "The Modern Lear."
267 *"These sudden thunder"*: Leyendecker, 254.
267 *"Letter rec'd am entirely"*: Chicago History Museum.
267 *"any sick child whom"*: *Chicago Tribune*, October 20, 1894, 1.
268 *"The body of George M. Pullman"*: *Chicago Tribune*, October 24, 1894, 1.
268 *"takes rank with the most"*: *Chicago Tribune*, October 31, 1897, 32.
268 *"He is on equality"*: Lindsey, 342.

28 True to Man

269 *"dignified manner"*: Ginger, *The Bending Cross*, 176.
270 *"He smiles frequently"*: Bly.
270 *"delivered the first impassioned"*: Papke, 86.
270 *"wept and cheered and laughed"*: Ginger, *The Bending Cross*, 176.
270 GO WILD OVER: Dray, 224.
271 *"the most popular man"*: Cashman, 626.
271 *"Manifestly, the spirit"*: Salvatore, 153.
272 *"imperious, arrogant"*: Beatty, 363.
273 *"blunt the fangs"*: Coletta, 170.
273 *"I have been a Democrat"*: Dray, 22.
273 *"cannibalistic, with men"*: Papke, 87.
273 *"In the gleam of every bayonet"*: Carl S. Smith, 237.
273 *"Money constitutes"*: Papke, 87.
274 *"The capitalist politician"*: Debs, *Debs: His Life*, 448.
274 *"Socialism is not just"*: Salvatore, 193.
274 *"I heard him speak"*: Le Prade, 22.
274 *"grandest industrial"*: Debs, *Debs: His Life*, 204.
274 *"The Debs of fable"*: Traubel, 40.
275 *"in spite of the fact"*: Foner, *History of the Labor Movement*, 278.
275 *"The American workers"*: Debs, *Debs: His Life*, 353.
275 *"the most visible"*: Salvatore, 232.
275 *"the world only respects"*: Ibid., 230.
276 *"Comrades, this is"*: Watson, 133.
276 *"any disloyal, profane"*: Debs, *Letters*, vol. 3, 6.

276 *"the master class"*: Ginger, *The Bending Cross*, 358.
276 *"American institutions"*: Salvatore, 295.
276 *"Years ago I recognized"*: Ibid.
276 *"by union men"*: Ibid., 316.
276 *"An awful loneliness"*: Ibid., 300.
276 *"beloved little community"*: Ibid., 22.
277 *"I had a strange dream"*: Ibid., 315.
277 *"His words made men"*: Ibid., 232.
277 *"that old man with the burning"*: Ibid., 225.

29 Solidarity

279 *"the mass of wage-earners"*: Schneirov, *Labor and Urban Politics*, 341.
280 *"autocracy in the shop"*: Beatty, 279.
280 *"restrictive labor contracts"*: Chicago Tribune, January 20, 1981, 44.
281 *"the dance of skeletons"*: United States Strike Commission, 88.

Bibliography

Addams, Jane. "The Modern Lear." *So Just: Speeches on Social Justice.* http://www.sojust.net
/speeches/addams_lear.html (accessed February 20, 2018).
———. *Twenty Years at Hull-House.* Urbana: University of Illinois Press, 1990.
Adelman, William J., et al. "The Pullman Strike: Yesterday, Today and Tomorrow." *John Marshall Law Review* 33 (Spring 2000): 583–638.
Aldrich, Mark. *Death Rode the Rails: American Railroad Accidents and Safety, 1828–1965.* Baltimore: Johns Hopkins University Press, 2006.
Alexander, Benjamin F. *Coxey's Army: Popular Protest in the Gilded Age.* Baltimore: Johns Hopkins University Press, 2015.
Altgeld, John Peter. *Our Penal Machinery and Its Victims.* Chicago: Jansen, McClurg, 1884.
Anaconda Standard. Anaconda, MT, 1894.
Arnesen, Eric. *Brotherhoods of Color: Black Railroad Workers and the Struggle for Equality.* Cambridge, MA: Harvard University Press, 2001.
Badger, Reid. *The Great American Fair: The World's Columbian Exposition and American Culture.* Chicago: N. Hall, 1979.
Bancroft, Hubert Howe. *The Book of the Fair: An Historical and Descriptive Presentation.* Chicago: Bancroft, 1893.
Barnard, Harry. *Eagle Forgotten.* New York: Bobbs-Merrill, 1938.
Beatty, Jack. *Age of Betrayal: The Triumph of Money in America, 1865–1900.* New York: Alfred A. Knopf, 2007.
Bly, Nellie. "Nellie Bly in Jail." *The Archive: Historic American Journalism.* https://thegrandarchive.wordpress.com/nellie-bly-in-jail/ (accessed February 20, 2018).
Boase, Paul H., ed. *The Rhetoric of Protest and Reform, 1878–1898.* Athens: Ohio University Press, 1980.
Books of the Fairs. New York: New York Public Library. Microfilm, reel 121, item 3.
Boorstin, Daniel J. *The Americans: The Democratic Experience.* New York: Random House, 1973.
Brands, H. W. *The Reckless Decade: America in the 1890s.* New York: St. Martin's Press, 1995.
Brecher, Jeremy. *Strike!* Boston: South End Press, 1997.
Buder, Stanley. *Pullman: An Experiment in Industrial Order and Community Planning, 1880–1930.* New York: Oxford University Press, 1967.

Burg, David F. *Chicago's White City of 1893*. Lexington: University Press of Kentucky, 1976.

Burns, W. F. *The Pullman Boycott: A Complete History of the Great R. R. Strike*. St. Paul: McGill, 1894.

Campbell, Randolph B., et al. *Our Nation's Heritage*, vol. 2. New York: American Heritage Custom Publishing, 1999.

Carnegie, Andrew. *Autobiography of Andrew Carnegie*. New York: Houghton Mifflin, 1920.

Carwardine, William H. *The Pullman Strike*. Chicago: Charles H. Kerr, 1994.

Cashman, Sean Dennis. *America in the Gilded Age: From the Death of Lincoln to the Rise of Theodore Roosevelt*. New York: New York University Press, 1993.

Central Pacific Railroad Photographic History Museum. http://www.cprr.org/Museum /Trans-Continental/index.html (accessed February 16, 2018).

Chandler, Alfred D., ed. *The Railroads, the Nation's First Big Business: Sources and Readings*. New York: Harcourt, Brace and World, 1965.

Chicago History Museum. *Pullman-Miller Family Papers*.

Chicago Inter Ocean. Chicago, IL, 1894.

Chicago Times. Chicago, IL, 1894.

Chicago Tribune. Chicago, IL, 1893–1894; 1981.

Clark, Judith Freeman. *America's Gilded Age: An Eyewitness History*. New York: Facts on File, 1992.

Coletta, Paolo Enrico. *William Jennings Bryan*, vol. 1. Lincoln: University of Nebraska Press, 1964.

Connelly, Donald B. *John M. Schofield and the Politics of Generalship*. Chapel Hill: University of North Carolina Press, 2006.

Cooper, Jerry M. *The Army and Civil Disorder: Federal Military Intervention in Labor Disputes, 1877–1900*. Westport, CT: Greenwood Press, 1980.

Cozzens, Peter. *The Earth Is Weeping: The Epic Story of the Indian Wars for the American West*. New York: Alfred A. Knopf, 2016.

Currey, J. Seymour. *Chicago: Its History and Its Builders*. Chicago: S. J. Clarke, 1918.

Debs, Eugene V. "About the Unions." *Railway Times* 1 (January 1, 1894). https://www .marxists.org/archive/debs/works/1893/931200-debs-abouttheunion.pdf (accessed February 19, 2018).

———. *Debs: His Life, Writings and Speeches*. Girard, KS: Appeal to Reason, 1908.

———. *Letters of Eugene V. Debs*. Urbana: University of Illinois Press, 1990.

———, et al. *Organized Labor's Demands*. New York: Morning Advertiser, 1894.

———. "President's Keynote Address" (June 12, 1894). https://www.marxists.org/archive /debs/works/1894/940612-debs-keynoteaddress.pdf (accessed February 17, 2018).

D'Eramo, Marco. *The Pig and the Skyscraper: Chicago: A History of Our Future*. New York: Verso, 2002.

Deverell, William. *Railroad Crossing: Californians and the Railroad, 1850–1910*. Berkeley: University of California Press, 1993.

Douglas, George H. *All Aboard: The Railroad in American Life*. New York: Paragon House, 1992.

Dray, Philip. *There Is Power in a Union: The Epic Story of Labor in America*. New York: Doubleday, 2010.

Durham Globe. Durham, NC, 1894.

Edwards, Rebecca. *New Spirits: Americans in the "Gilded Age," 1865–1905*. New York: Oxford University Press, 2015.

Eggert, Gerald G. *Railroad Labor Disputes: The Beginnings of Federal Strike Policy*. Ann Arbor: University of Michigan Press, 1967.

———. *Richard Olney: Evolution of a Statesman*. University Park: Pennsylvania State University Press, 1974.

Elshtain, Jean Bethke. *The Jane Addams Reader*. New York: Basic Books, 2002.

Ely, Richard T. "Pullman: A Social Study." *Harper's* 70 (February 1885). http://urbanplanning
.library.cornell.edu/DOCS/pullman.htm (accessed February 16, 2018).

Emerson, Jason. *Giant in the Shadows: The Life of Robert T. Lincoln.* Carbondale: Southern
Illinois University Press, 2012.

Fink, Leon. *The Long Gilded Age: American Capitalism and the Lessons of a New World Order.*
Philadelphia: University of Pennsylvania Press, 2015.

———, et al., eds. *Workers in Hard Times: A Long View of Economic Crises.* Urbana: University of Illinois Press, 2014.

Fogelson, Robert M. *America's Armories: Architecture, Society, and Public Order.* Cambridge,
MA: Harvard University Press, 1989.

Foner, Philip Sheldon. *The Great Labor Uprising of 1877.* New York: Monad Press,
1977.

———. *History of the Labor Movement in the United States.* New York: International Publish-
ers, 1947.

Fraser, Steve. *The Age of Acquiescence: The Life and Death of American Resistance to Organized
Wealth and Power.* New York: Little, Brown, 2015.

Gamst, Frederick C. "Labor Hero Eugene V. Debs." *Journal of Transportation Law, Logistics,
and Policy* 74 (Second Quarter 2007): 241–69.

Gilbert, James Burkhart. *Perfect Cities: Chicago's Utopias of 1893.* Chicago: University of
Chicago Press, 1991.

Ginger, Ray. *Altgeld's America: The Lincoln Ideal Versus Changing Realities.* New York:
Funk and Wagnalls, 1958.

———. *The Bending Cross: A Biography of Eugene Victor Debs.* New Brunswick: Rutgers University Press, 1949.

Gompers, Samuel. *Seventy Years of Life and Labour: An Autobiography.* New York: A. M. Kelley,
1967.

Gould, Lewis L. *The Progressive Era.* Syracuse: Syracuse University Press, 1974.

Hirsch, Susan E. *After the Strike: A Century of Labor Struggle at Pullman.* Urbana: University
of Illinois Press, 2003.

Howard, O. O. "The Menace of 'Coxeyism.'" *North American Review* 158, no. 451 (June 1894):
687–705.

Howe, Irving. *Socialism and America.* San Diego: Harcourt Brace Jovanovich, 1985.

Indianapolis Journal. Indianapolis, IN, 1894.

Indianapolis News. Indianapolis, IN, 1893–1894.

Karsner, David. *Talks with Debs in Terre Haute.* New York: New York Call, 1922.

Kaufman, Bruce E. *Hired Hands or Human Resources? Case Studies of HRM Programs and
Practices in Early American Industry.* Ithaca: ILR Press, 2010.

Kersten, Andrew. *Clarence Darrow: American Iconoclast.* New York: Hill and Wang, 2011.

Knight, Louise W. *Citizen: Jane Addams and the Struggle for Democracy.* Chicago: University
of Chicago Press, 2005.

Labor, Earle. *Jack London: An American Life.* New York: Farrar, Straus and Giroux, 2013.

Leach, Eugene E. "Chaining the Tiger: The Mob Stigma and the Working Class, 1863–1894."
Labor History 35, no. 2 (Spring 1994): 187–215.

Leach, Frank A. "The Great Railroad Strike of 1894." Library of Congress. http://www.loc
.gov/teachers/classroommaterials/presentationsandactivities/presentations/timeline
/riseind/railroad/strike.html (accessed February 19, 2018).

Leonard, John. "Mr. Debs, My Darling." *Nation* 269, no. 16 (November 15, 1999): 23–28.
https://www.thenation.com/article/mr-debs-my-darling (accessed February 16, 2018).

Le Prade, Ruth, ed. *Debs and the Poets.* Pasadena: Cal. U. Sinclair, 1920.

Lewis, Lloyd. *Chicago: The History of Its Reputation.* New York: Harcourt, Brace, 1929.

Leyendecker, Liston E. *Palace Car Prince: A Biography of George Mortimer Pullman.* Niwot:
University Press of Colorado, 1992.

Lindsey, Almont. *The Pullman Strike: The Story of a Unique Experiment and of a Great Labor
Upheaval.* Chicago: University of Chicago Press, 1942.

Locomotive Firemen's Magazine.

Mack, Adam. *Sensing Chicago: Noisemakers, Strikebreakers, and Muckrakers.* Urbana: University of Illinois Press, 2015.

Madison, James. *The Papers of James Madison.* New York: J. and H. G. Langley, 1841.

Madsen, Axel. *The Marshall Fields.* New York: J. Wiley, 2002.

Martin, Albro. *James J. Hill and the Opening of the Northwest.* New York: Oxford University Press, 1976.

———. *Railroads Triumphant: The Growth, Rejection, and Rebirth of a Vital American Force.* New York: Oxford University Press, 1992.

McMurry, Donald Le Crone. *Coxey's Army: A Study of the Industrial Army Movement of 1894.* Seattle: University of Washington Press, 1968.

Menand, Louis. *The Metaphysical Club.* New York: Farrar, Straus and Giroux, 2002.

Miller, Donald L. *City of the Century: The Epic of Chicago and the Making of America.* New York: Simon and Schuster, 1996.

———. "The White City." *American Heritage* 44, no. 4 (July/August 1993). https://www.americanheritage.com/content/white-city (accessed February 16, 2018).

Montgomery, David. *The Fall of the House of Labor: The Workplace, the State, and American Labor Activism, 1865–1925.* New York: Cambridge University Press, 1987.

The National Cyclopaedia of American Biography, vol. 15. New York: James T. White, 1916.

Nevins, Allan. *Grover Cleveland: A Study in Courage.* New York: Dodd, Mead, 1933.

Newberry Library, Chicago, IL. *Pullman Company Archives.*

New York Times. New York, NY, 1893–1894.

New York World. New York, NY, 1894.

Pacyga, Dominic A. *Chicago: A Biography.* Chicago: University of Chicago Press, 2009.

Papke, David Ray. *The Pullman Case: The Clash of Labor and Capital in Industrial America.* Lawrence: University Press of Kansas, 1999.

Pierce, Bessie Louise. *A History of Chicago, Vol. 3: The Rise of a Modern City, 1871–1893.* New York: Knopf, 1937.

Prout, Jerry. "Coxey's Challenge in the Populist Moment." Ph.D. diss., George Mason University, 2012.

Pullman's Palace Car Company. *The Story of Pullman.* Chicago: Blakely and Rogers, 1893. https://archive.org/stream/storyofpullman00worl/storyofpullman00worl_djvu.txt (accessed March 28, 2018).

Rezneck, Samuel S. "Unemployment, Unrest, and Relief in the United States During the Depression of 1893." *Journal of Political Economy* 61, no. 4 (August 1953): 324–45.

Riley, James Whitcomb. *The Complete Poetical Works of James Whitcomb Riley.* New York: Bobbs-Merrill, 1937.

Rondinone, Troy. *The Great Industrial War: Framing Class Conflict in the Media, 1865–1950.* New Brunswick: Rutgers University Press, 2011.

Rousiers, Paul de. *American Life.* Paris, New York: Firmin-Didot, 1892.

Sacramento Daily Union. Sacramento, CA, 1894.

St. Paul Daily Globe. St. Paul, MN, 1893–1894.

Salvatore, Nick. *Eugene V. Debs: Citizen and Socialist.* Urbana: University of Illinois Press, 1982.

Sandburg, Carl. *The Letters of Carl Sandburg.* New York: Harcourt, Brace and World, 1968.

San Francisco Call. San Francisco, CA, 1894.

Schneirov, Richard. *Labor and Urban Politics: Class Conflict and the Origins of Modern Liberalism in Chicago, 1864–97.* Urbana: University of Illinois Press, 1998.

———, et al., eds. *The Pullman Strike and the Crisis of the 1890s: Essays on Labor and Politics.* Urbana: University of Illinois Press, 1999.

Schwantes, Carlos A. *Coxey's Army: An American Odyssey.* Lincoln: University of Nebraska Press, 1985.

Shaw, Albert. "Post-Election Reflections." *Review of Reviews* 15 (January–June 1897): 88–92.

Smith, Carl S. *Urban Disorder and the Shape of Belief: The Great Chicago Fire, the Haymarket Bomb, and the Model Town of Pullman.* Chicago: University of Chicago Press, 1995.

Smith, John H. *Diaries.* Signature Books Library. http://signaturebookslibrary.org/gaining -statehood/ (accessed February 19, 2018).

Smith, Page. *The Rise of Industrial America: A People's History of the Post-Reconstruction Era.* New York: McGraw-Hill, 1984.

Stead, W. T. *Chicago To-day: The Labour War in America.* New York: Arno Press, 1969.

Steeples, Douglas W., and David O. Whitten. *Democracy in Desperation: The Depression of 1893.* Westport, CT: Greenwood Press, 1998.

Steinway, William. *Diary, 1861–1896.* Smithsonian. http://americanhistory.si.edu /steinwaydiary/diary/?view=transcription&show_anno=true&page=2292 (accessed February 19, 2018).

Studenski, Paul. *Financial History of the United States.* New York: McGraw-Hill, 1963.

Taft, Philip. *The A. F. of L. in the Time of Gompers.* New York: Harper, 1957.

Taillon, Paul Michel. *Good, Reliable, White Men: Railroad Brotherhoods, 1877–1917.* Urbana: University of Illinois Press, 2009.

Teaford, Jon C. *The Twentieth-Century American City: Problem, Promise, and Reality.* Baltimore: Johns Hopkins University Press, 1986.

Trachtenberg, Alan. *The Incorporation of America: Culture and Society in the Gilded Age.* New York: Hill and Wang, 1982.

Traubel, Horace. "Debs." *Conservator* 14, no. 2 (May 1903): 40.

Truer, Tamara C. "Eugene V. Debs, James J. Hill and the Great Northern Railway Strike." *Ramsey County History* 25, no. 1 (1990).

Tuchman, Barbara W. *The Proud Tower: A Portrait of the World Before the War, 1890–1914.* New York: Macmillan, 1966.

Turner, Frederick Jackson. *The Frontier in American History.* Tucson: University of Arizona Press, 1986.

Tye, Larry. *Rising from the Rails: Pullman Porters and the Making of the Black Middle Class.* New York: Henry Holt, 2004.

United States Department of Justice. *Appendix to the Annual Report of the Attorney General of the United States for the Year 1896.* Washington, DC: Government Printing Office, 1897.

United States Strike Commission. *Report on the Chicago Strike of June–July, 1894.* Washington, DC: Government Printing Office, 1894.

United States Supreme Court. *In re Debs,* 158 *U.S.* 564 (1895). https://supreme.justia.com /cases/federal/us/158/564/ (accessed February 18, 2018).

Wagenknecht, Edward. *Chicago.* Norman: University of Oklahoma Press, 1964.

Watson, Bruce. *Bread and Roses: Mills, Migrants, and the Struggle for the American Dream.* New York: Viking, 2005.

Welch, Richard E. *The Presidencies of Grover Cleveland.* Lawrence: University Press of Kansas, 1988.

White, John H. *The American Railroad Passenger Car.* Baltimore: Johns Hopkins University Press, 1978.

White, Richard. *Railroaded: The Transcontinentals and the Making of Modern America.* New York: Norton, 2011.

White, W. Thomas. "Montana and the Pullman Strike of 1894: A Western Response to Industrial Warfare." Master's thesis, University of Montana, 1970.

Whitman, Walt. *The Works of Walt Whitman.* New York: Funk and Wagnalls, 1968.

Wiebe, Robert H. *The Search for Order, 1877–1920.* New York: Hill and Wang, 2001.

Winston, A. P. "The Significance of the Pullman Strike." *Journal of Political Economy* 9, no. 4 (September 1901): 540–61.

Wolmar, Christian. *The Great Railroad Revolution: The History of Trains in America*. New York: Public Affairs, 2012.

Wooster, Robert. *Nelson A. Miles and the Twilight of the Frontier Army*. Lincoln: University of Nebraska Press, 1993.

Wright, Carroll D. "The Significance of the Recent Labor Troubles in America." *International Journal of Ethics* 5 (1895): 137–47.

Young, Marguerite. *Harp Song for a Radical: The Life and Times of Eugene Victor Debs*. New York: Alfred A. Knopf, 1999.

Index

Adams, Henry, 8, 15, 33
Addams, Jane, 90–92, 95–96, 129, 134, 155, 266–267, 279
air brakes, 39, 255
Altgeld, John Peter, 134, 163, 256
  deployment of state troops, 28, 157–158, 184–185
  dispute with Cleveland over federal troops, 181–183, 191
  family and background of, 156–157
  legacy of, 279
  "Our Penal Machinery and Its Victims," 156–157
  pardon of Haymarket prisoners, 157
  reformer, 88, 156–157, 279
  request for relief for Pullman residents, 244–245
  and United Mine Workers of America work stoppage, 27–28
  and World Columbian Exposition, 11
Amalgamated Association of Iron and Steel Workers, 45
Amalgamated Clothing Cutters, 219
American Civil War, 5, 8, 18, 31–33, 36, 39, 173, 210
American dream, 9
American Federation of Labor (AFL), 46, 133, 144, 199, 214
  and ARU boycott, 187
  Briggs House meeting of labor organizations, 220, 228–232, 248
  Executive Council, 220, 228–231
  founding of, 71
  New Orleans general strike, 198
  and railroad brotherhoods, 227–229
  recommendation against general strike, 231
American frontier, 6, 8–9, 41, 47
American Railway Union (ARU)
  boycott decision, 106–107
  boycott deliberations, 94–95, 103–107
  boycott's first days, 108–114
  Briggs House meeting of labor organizations, 220, 228–232, 248
  first national convention, 93–105, 247
  and General Managers' Association, 119–120, 135–137, 253, 258
  and Great Northern strike, 21–26, 27, 35, 45–46, 64, 75, 88, 96, 104, 120–121, 129, 146, 201, 232
  membership guidelines, 46
  organizing meeting, 16–18
  Pullman employees as members, 46, 63, 87
  purpose of, 76, 79, 117
  and race, 96–100, 125
  significance of, 254, 278–279
  Strike Commission on, 253, 255
  structure and hierarchy of, 147, 216–217, 241–242
  transformed into Socialist Party, 273
American Sugar Refining Company, 262–263
anarchism, 130, 157
  anarchy as distinct from, 114
  and assassination attempt against Frick, 45
  and assassination of Carnot, 105, 155
  Eugene Debs accused of, 23
  Eugene Debs on, 98
  and Haymarket Square bombing, 44, 157
  and red scare, 44

anarchy, 154, 164, 170, 190, 199, 272
  anarchism as distinct from, 114
  newspapers' use of the term, 67, 114, 155, 186
Anslyn, William, 194
Arbitration Act (1888), 235
Armour, Philip, 18, 74, 126
Arnold, Frank W., 229
Arnold, John W., 139, 160–163, 169–170, 221–222, 237
Arthur, Peter M., 229
Atchison, Topeka & Santa Fe Railway, 6, 46, 109, 124, 135, 159, 221, 240

Bach, Martea, 208
Baker, Ray Stannard, 30
Baldwin, Barry, 149, 176–178
Baltimore & Ohio Railroad, 109, 125, 127, 128, 183, 192, 206
Barrett, Miles, 112
Bellamy, Edward, 8
Beman, Solon, 268
Berger, Victor, 270
Berkman, Alexander, 45
Bettrich, Marguerite. See Debs, Marguerite "Daisy" (née Bettrich)
Big Four (Cleveland, Cincinnati, Chicago & St. Louis Railway), 82–83, 238
Bissell, Wilson, 211, 225
Bloodless Battle of the Depot, 176–178
Bly, Nellie, 156, 270
Borden, Lizzie, 16
Boston & Maine Railroad, 135
brakemen, 17, 20, 38, 41, 107, 110, 112, 124, 217, 221
Brennan, Michael, 130, 147, 174
Brewer, David J., 262
Brotherhood of Locomotive Engineers, 229
Brotherhood of Locomotive Firemen, 17, 19, 22, 34, 40–45, 112, 229
Brotherhood of Sleeping Car Porters, 100
brotherhoods. See railroad brotherhoods
Broun, Heywood, 277
Browne, Carl, 29–31, 69–71
Bryan, William Jennings, 272–273
Buchanan, Jasper Johnson, 70
Buffalo switchmen's strike (1892), 44
Burlington Railroad (Chicago, Burlington & Quincy Railroad) 44, 109, 135, 208
Burlington strike (1888), 44
Butte Miners' Union, 65, 67
Bynner, Witter, 274
Byrnes, Thomas, 31

Campbell, W. H., 207
Canadian Pacific Railway, 12, 119
Cantwell, Frank T. "Jumbo," 32

capitalism, 8, 9, 24–25, 87, 94, 117, 133, 217, 232, 249, 252, 264, 273–274, 279–281
Carnegie, Andrew, 7, 18, 45, 48–49
Carnegie Steel Company, 45
Carnot, Nicolas Léonard Sadi, 105, 155
Carter, "General" Henry, 32
Carwardine, William, 61
Case, Charles Whipple, 21
Central Transportation Company, 48–49
Chicago, Burlington & Quincy Railroad (Burlington Railroad), 44, 109, 135, 208
Chicago, Illinois
  Building Trades Council, 199, 225
  failure of general strike, 226
  Great Chicago Fire, 180, 189
  Haymarket Square bombing, 43–44, 130, 153, 157, 198, 241
  newspaper accounts of, 7
  Pullman Building, 59, 74, 75, 92, 144, 173, 202, 218, 244
  riots, 167–173, 192–206
  as "Rome of the railroads," 6
  stockyards, 95, 126–127, 155, 170–171, 174–175, 180, 183–185, 192–194, 200, 203, 205, 221, 242, 257
  Trades and Labor Assembly, 133–135, 187
  See also Pullman, Chicago; World's Columbian Exposition
Chicago, Milwaukee & St. Paul Railroad, 137, 258
Chicago, Rock Island & Pacific Railroad, 112, 130, 133, 140, 183, 246
Chicago & Alton Railroad, 53
Chicago & North Western Railway, 64, 109, 141–142, 256
Chicago Civic Federation, 91, 95
Chicago Great Western Railway, 109, 119, 124, 138
Chicago Hussars, 221
Chicago Typographical Union, 188
Cigar Makers International Union, 244
Civil Rights Act (1964), 255
Clark, Edgar E., 229
Clark, Sam, 224
Cleveland, Cincinnati, Chicago & St. Louis Railway (Big Four), 82–83, 238
Cleveland, Grover
  background and political career, 115–116
  and Coxeyism, 31, 68, 70, 71, 94
  election of 1884, 115
  election of 1888, 89, 116
  election of 1892, 116
  and Great Northern strike, 23–24
  Labor Day bill signed by, 111

and midterm elections of 1894, 264–265
opening of World's Columbian Exposition,
    3, 11, 189
and panic of 1893, 14–15, 29
pro-business stance of, 115–116, 118
and Pullman strike, 230, 235
and U.S. Strike Commission, 235–237, 239,
    246–247, 255, 264, 266
coal mining
    anthracite, 28, 193, 210
    bituminous, 27
    coal miners' strike (1894), 27–28, 64, 223,
        264
    and Pullman strike, 160, 213, 225
Cole, Thomas, 141
Columbian Exposition. See World's
    Columbian Exposition
conductors, 17, 21, 40–41, 44, 97–98, 110,
    123, 195, 221, 229
Constitution, United States, 117, 181–182,
    248–249, 259–260, 262, 271, 273
couplers
    automatic, 39, 255
    link-and-pin, 38–39
Coxey, Jacob, 29–32, 69–72, 127, 132
    arrest and trial for walking on public lawn,
        71–72
    background of, 29
    origins of Coxey's Army, 29–32
Coxey's Army (protest march), 28–32, 69–72,
    132, 136, 150, 159, 196
    as Commonweal of Christ, 28, 69, 71
    contingent armies, 28–33, 64–69, 124,
        130–131, 196
    deployment of federal troops against,
        68–69, 136, 159
    Eugene Debs on, 248
    injunctions against, 68, 136, 150
    newspaper accounts of, 28–30, 67, 69–70,
        132
    and train stealing, 67–69, 196
Crofton, Robert E. A., 169–171, 174
Curtis, Jennie, 62, 75, 77, 80, 82, 90, 102–104,
    239

Darrow, Clarence S., 137, 157, 223, 256–259,
    261–262
Debs, Eugene "Gene"
    arrest of, 222–223, 225, 230
    ARU boycott decision, 94–95, 103–106,
        108–109
    at ARU national convention, 93–96,
        98–100, 103–105
    at ARU organizing meeting and
        recruitment, 17–20
    background and family of, 35–39
    at Briggs House meeting, 230–232

and Brotherhood of Locomotive Firemen,
    17, 19, 22, 34, 40–45, 112
and Chicago riots, 167–173, 192, 193,
    198–200, 206
conspiracy trial, 258–259
contempt trial, 256–258
criticism of, 210, 216
death of, 277
editor of Locomotive Firemen's Magazine,
    41–42, 87, 98, 145
general strike discussions, 187–188,
    198–199, 212–213, 218–223, 226–227,
    229–232, 236–243
and Great Northern strike, 21–26, 34–35
imprisonment for treason, 276–277
In re Debs (Supreme Court case), 259–263
influences on, 39–46
newspaper accounts of, 111, 121, 127,
    129–130, 135, 142–143, 154–155, 175,
    192, 216–217
order of contempt against, 197–198
political career, 40–41
presidential campaigns, 275–276, 277
Pullman compared with, 9–10, 47
and Pullman strike, 63, 81, 87–90,
    186–187, 201–202, 206
Samuel Gompers compared with,
    227–229
U.S. Strike Commission testimony,
    247–249, 255
visit to Pullman (town), 87–90
at World's Columbian Exposition, 9
Debs, Jean Daniel (father of Eugene), 35–36
Debs, Katherine "Kate" (née Metzel, 34, 43,
    45, 155, 240, 242, 269, 277
Debs, Marguerite "Daisy" (née Bettrich,
    mother of Eugene), 35–36, 39
Debs, Theodore, 22, 43, 144, 167, 222–223,
    269
deindustrialization, 279–280
Denver & Rio Grande Railroad, 125
Dewey, John, 123, 254
dignity, 18, 26, 41, 51, 81, 98, 125, 215, 217,
    277, 278
Dimond, William H., 176, 178
Dold, Charles, 229
Douglass, Frederick, 10

Egan, John, 12, 119, 121, 124, 126, 130, 146,
    147, 153–154, 169–170, 172, 198, 203,
    209–210, 237
eight-hour labor movement, 43–44, 94, 113,
    249
Ely, Richard, 55–59
Emerson, Ralph Waldo, 5
Erdman Act, 255
Erwin, William, 256

Federalist Papers, 158
Field, Marshall, 12, 18, 74, 153, 265
Field, Stephen J., 262
Finn, J. D., 66–68
Firemen (locomotive), 36–38, 40–42, 44, 99, 105, 110,
    Brotherhood of Locomotive Firemen, 17, 19, 21, 22, 34, 40–45, 112, 229
    and Great Northern Railway strike, 21
    Locomotive Firemen's Magazine, 41–42, 87, 98, 145
    and Pullman strike, 123–124, 174, 176, 184, 193, 195, 199, 221
    recruited for ARU, 20–21
    work of locomotive firemen, 36–37
Fleischer, Charles, 207–208
Flemming, Annie, 207
Flower, Roswell P., 15
Foster, Frank, 235
Frick, Henry Clay, 45, 216
Fry, "General" Lewis C., 31–32
Fuller, Melville, 262
Fulton, Robert, 55

Gage, Lyman, 91, 95
Gatling gun, 152, 176, 195, 221, 224
Geeting, John F., 223
General Managers' Association (GMA)
    and American Railway Union, 119–120, 134–137, 253, 258
    and ARU boycott, 118–119, 124–125, 146–147, 154
    criticism of, 253, 258
    and federal government, 136–137, 169, 203
    formation of, 117–119
    and omnibus injunction, 151
    policy of no negotiations, 121, 179, 184
    and strike settlement, 230–231, 237
George, Henry, 235
George, J. R., 203–204
Gilbert, James H., 130, 147, 160
Gilded Age, 7, 18–19, 73, 266, 281
gold reserves, 11, 70
gold rush, 49, 265
gold standard, 15, 29
golden spike (Promontory Summit), 5
Gompers, Samuel, 71, 144, 187, 214, 220, 227–232, 248, 254, 280
Gould, Jay, 18, 216
Grant, Frederick Dent, 73
Grant, Julia, 74
Grant, Ulysses S., 73–75
Great Chicago Fire, 180, 189
Great Northern Railway
    dinner in honor of James Hill, 12–13, 16
    strike (1894), 21–26, 27, 35, 45–46, 64, 75, 88, 96, 104, 120–121, 129, 146, 201, 232
    wage cuts, 20–21, 23
great railroad upheaval (1877), 9, 40, 130, 163
Gregory, Stephen S., 240, 256, 258, 259–260
Gresham, Walter, 162, 215, 225
Gronlund, Laurence, 249
Grosscup, Peter S., 151, 162–163, 222–223, 240–241, 258–259

Hailey, M. J., 66–67
Hamilton, Alexander, 54
Hanna, Mark, 264
Harding, Warren G., 277
Harlan, James, 259
Harlan, John Marshall, 259
Harrison, Benjamin, 74, 116
Harrison, Carter, 11, 89
Hartz, Wilson T., 207
Hayes, Rutherford B., 163
Haymarket Square bombing (1886), 43–44, 130, 153, 157, 198, 241
Heathcoate, Thomas, 60–62, 76–77, 80, 83–84, 87, 91, 195, 239, 243
Hemingway, J. B. H., 159
Henrotin, Ellen, 95
Hill, James Jerome, 18–25, 34, 45–46, 60, 96
    dinner in honor of, 12–13, 16
Hogan, James, 21
Hogan, William, 64–69, 124, 196
Homestead strike (1892), 44–45
Hopkins, John Patrick, 89–90, 130, 147, 179, 184–185, 195, 202–203, 213–214, 236–237
Howard, George W., 46, 63, 75–76, 78–83, 91–92, 96, 104–105, 109, 112, 134, 141–142, 191
    arrest and trial, 222, 240, 256–258
    and Great Northern Railway strike, 22
Hugo, Victor, 36, 37, 217, 270
Hull House, 90–91, 129
Hulman, Herman, 39, 41
Huntington, Collis, 121–122
Huntington, Henry, 246

Illinois Central Railroad, 79, 83, 107–110, 119–120, 127, 157, 175, 194, 221, 246
    Diamond Special, 107, 108, 142, 146, 170
Illinois Women's Alliance, 134
In re Debs, 259–263
Industrial Workers of the World, 275

Jaxon, Honoré, 30
Jefferson, Thomas, 44, 158
Jim Crow system, 10. See also race
Journeymen Horse Shoers Union, 213

Kavanaugh, Fanny, 134, 228
Keliher, Sylvester, 109, 179, 222, 240, 257
Kelley, Charles T., 32, 64, 130–131
Keynes, John Maynard, 29
Kipling, Rudyard, 6–7
Kirtland, Cyclone, 30
Knights of Labor, 17, 44, 112–113, 188, 211,
    214, 218, 236–237
Knowles, Hiram, 65, 68, 196
Knox, Harry, 238
Knox, Frank, 177

Ladies' Federal Labor Union, 228
Lally, John, 110
Lamont, Daniel S., 68, 162, 163–164, 196,
    225, 239, 262
Leach, Frank A., 176
Leach, Joshua, 40
L'Enfant, Pierre Charles, 54
Lincoln, Abraham, 9, 53, 97
Lincoln, Mary Todd, 53
Lincoln, Robert Todd, 73–74, 236, 268
Lindholm, E. J., 214
Lloyd, Henry Demarest, 271
Lockwood, B. C., 197
Locomotive Firemen's Magazine, 41–42, 87,
    98, 145
Logan, John, 161
London, Jack, 131

MacVeagh, Franklin, 12
Madison, James, 158
Mair, Thomas I., 203–204
manhood, 35, 41–42, 81, 88, 215
Mann Boudoir Car Company, 59
Markham, Henry, 149, 176
Marshall, Thurgood, 99
Marx, Karl, 249
    Das Kapital, 270
Matthews, Claude, 208
McBride, John, 27, 212–213, 225
McDermott, William, 65–66
McGillen, John, 218–219, 237
McGuire, Peter, 228
McKeen, William Riley, 41
McKinley, William, 265, 273
Merritt, Wesley, 196
Michigan Central Railroad, 194, 206
Middleton, Harvey, 63, 75–77, 80, 195
Milchrist, Thomas, 136–138, 150–151,
    162–163, 191, 197, 222–223, 240, 257
Miles, Nelson, 162–164, 169, 173–174, 176,
    180–181, 184–185, 190, 202–203, 206,
    211, 213, 221, 239, 247–248, 275
Missouri Pacific Railroad, 110, 201
Monroe, James, 262
Morrissey, Patrick H., 229

Mulford, E. M., 222, 257
Murvin, James, 141

National Cordage Company, 13
National Union of Seamen, 212
Nelson, Knute, 23
New Deal, 254, 279
New York Central Railroad, 5, 135
Norris, Frank, 6, 148
Northern Pacific Railway, 20, 65, 109, 124,
    128, 195–197, 238–239

O'Connell, James J., 212
Olney, Richard, 172, 181, 182, 210, 225, 235,
    241, 256, 270, 275, 279
    and ARU boycott, 137–140
    background and career of, 135–136
    and Coxeyism, 31, 65, 68
    Erdman Act supported by, 255
    and Great Northern strike, 24
    and *In re Debs*, 259–263
    and injunctions, 150, 152
    and order of contempt against Eugene Debs,
        197
    on panic of 1893, 11
    "ragged edge of anarchy," 164
    and use of federal troops, 158–160
O'Neill, Edward, 185

Palmer, Bertha, 264
Pan Handle Route (Pittsburgh, Cincinnati,
    Chicago & St. Louis Railroad), 124–125,
    128, 140, 193, 210
panic of 1873, 37
panic of 1893, 11–16, 19–20, 59, 65, 90–91
Pennoyer, Sylvester, 263
Pennsylvania Railroad, 5–6, 48–49, 113, 125,
    221, 267
Perkins, Charles Elliott, 44
Pettigrew, Richard, 12
Philadelphia & Reading Railroad, 10–11
Pillsbury, Charles, 12, 24, 25
Pingree, Hazen S., 174, 209
Pittsburgh, Cincinnati, Chicago & St. Louis
    Railroad (Pan Handle Route), 124–125,
    128, 140, 193, 210
Plains Indians, 173
Plessy v. Ferguson, 263
plutocracy, 11, 16, 32, 95, 112–113, 133, 231,
    245, 266, 271, 274
Porter, Horace, 74
Posse Comitatus Act (1878), 158
Prescott, William B., 212
Progressive Era, 156, 253, 279
Pulitzer, Joseph, 155
Pullman, Albert, 48, 63
Pullman, Florence, 51, 268

Pullman, George Mortimer, 4–5
  background and career of, 47–48
  business skills and strategies, 51–54
  and Carnegie, 48–49
  Chicago Prairie Avenue home of, 7, 73–74,
    107, 202
  and conspiracy trial against Eugene Debs,
    258–259
  death of, 267–268
  and dinner in honor of James Jerome Hill,
    12–13
  Jane Addams on, 266–267
  marriage to Harriett Sanger, 50–51
  New Jersey seashore home of, 74–75, 113,
    171
  and panic of 1893, 14, 19
  refusal to arbitrate, 92, 171, 187, 199, 209,
    211–213, 215–221
  temperament and habits of, 74–75
  Thousand Islands, New York, home, 75,
    209, 219
  U.S. Strike Commission report on,
    249–253
  U.S. Strike Commission testimony, 252
  and World's Columbian Exposition
    financing, 6
  See also Pullman, Illinois; Pullman strike of
    1894; Pullman's Palace Car Company
Pullman, George, Jr., 51, 113
Pullman, Harriett Amelia "Hattie" (née
  Sanger), 5, 50–51, 62–63, 73–74, 113,
  267–268
Pullman, Harriett (George and Hattie's
  daughter), 51, 113, 267, 268
Pullman, Illinois (later Pullman, Chicago)
  Arcade Building, 7–8, 56, 80, 89
  Hotel Florence, 55, 58, 74, 195, 242
  origins of, 53–54
  post-strike conditions, 243–245
  rents, 57–58, 60–61, 76–78, 87, 92, 95–96,
    101, 171, 243, 247, 252
  Supreme Court of Illinois ruling against,
    265–266
Pullman, Sanger, 51
Pullman Building, 59, 74, 75, 92, 144, 173,
  202, 218, 244
Pullman Free School of Manual Training, 268
Pullman-Standard, 280–281
Pullman strike of 1894
  Altgeld-Cleveland dispute over federal
    troops, 181–183
  Blue Island protests, 147, 160–163
  Chicago riots, 183–185, 192–208
  community support for strikers, 88–89
  conspiracy case against Eugene Debs,
    George W. Howard, Sylvester Keliher,
    and Louis W. Rogers, 258–259

contempt case against Eugene Debs,
  George W. Howard, Sylvester Keliher,
  and Louis W. Rogers, 256–258
effects of, 123–139
effects on mail delivery, 137–139
effects on passengers, 127–129, 160, 176
effects on Pullman, 92–93
effects on strikers, 246–247
effects on Union Stock Yard, 126–127
and Erdman Act, 255
federal injunctions against, 150–153,
  159–162, 175–176, 186–187, 196–197,
  210, 240–241, 257, 260–262, 269
federal troops dispatched to, 158–163, 167,
  169–178
In re Debs (Supreme Court case), 259–263
newspaper accounts of, 91–93, 96, 107,
  124–126, 135, 171, 192, 237
notice of, 82
proclamation by Cleveland regarding,
  213–214, 220–221
public opinion of, 121, 128
Pullman's refusal to arbitrate, 92, 171, 187,
  199, 209, 211–213, 215–221
and race, 125
roots of, 254
significance of, 278–282
U.S. Marshals deployed for, 138–140,
  159–163, 174–177, 185–186, 194, 203,
  211
and violence, 129–130, 140–142, 176–178,
  185, 191, 194, 196–197, 202, 206,
  209–210
worker pay, 75–78
worker rights and complaints, 61–62
Pullman's Palace Car Company
  and ARU boycott, 82–83, 94–95, 103–106,
    108–114, 119–128, 133, 136–138, 144,
    159, 161, 177, 195, 197, 223, 258
  and ARU membership, 46, 63, 87
  and capitalism, 87, 117, 264, 274, 281
  and death of Pullman, 268
  Diamond Special, 107, 108, 142, 146, 170
  final car made, 280–281
  first chartered cross-continental train,
    52–53
  foremen, 56, 58, 60, 62, 76–77, 80, 87
  and gilded age, 18–19
  Harper's Weekly article on, 55–59
  journeyman system, 61–62
  layout and structures, 55–57
  luxury and innovation of, 49–53
  Mann Boudoir Car Company acquired by,
    59
  and omnibus injunction, 151
  and panic of 1893, 59
  piecework, 60, 62, 77, 87, 252

Pioneer (sleeping car), 53
porters, 4, 52, 97–100, 125, 224
production factory, 53–55, 59–61, 80–82
promotion and public relations, 52–53
purchased by Wheelabrator-Frye, 280
and rioting, 128, 194, 207
as a service business, 52
Woodruff Sleeping and Parlor Coach
    Company acquired by, 59
and World's Columbian Exposition, 4–5
See also Pullman strike of 1894

race
    and AFL, 229
    and ARU membership, 96, 99, 125
    Civil Rights Act, 255
    and Coxey's Army, 70–71
    and progress, 10
    and Pullman porters, 96–99
    segregation, 263
    and World's Columbian Exposition, 10
railroad brotherhoods, 40–42, 44–46
    and American Federation of Labor,
        227–229
    and American Railway Union, 17, 19–24,
        44–46, 93, 105, 112, 120, 144, 227
    and Briggs House meeting, 228–229
    Brotherhood of Locomotive Engineers, 229
    Brotherhood of Locomotive Firemen, 17, 19,
        22, 34, 40–45, 112, 229
    Brotherhood of Sleeping Car Porters, 100
    effect of Pullman strike on, 254, 255
    and race, 96
Railway Times, 226–227
Randolph, A. Philip, 100
Reagan, John, 19
Reagan, Ronald, 280
Reconstruction, 10, 158
Reed, Harry, 204
Reilly, Patrick, 208
Remington, Frederic, 155
Rhodie, Theodore, 62, 79, 83, 243
Rickards, John E., 68
Riley, James Whitcomb, 145
Rock Island Railroad (Chicago, Rock Island &
    Pacific Railroad), 112, 130, 133, 140,
    183, 246
Rockefeller, John D., 18
Rogers, Louis W., 80, 222, 226–227, 239–241,
    257
Roosevelt, Franklin, 254
Roosvelt, Theodore, 275

Salvatore, Nick, 275
Sandburg, Carl, 145
Sanger, Harriett Amelia. See Pullman,
    Harriett Amelia "Hattie" (née Sanger)

Santa Fe Railway (Atchison, Topeka & Santa
    Fe Railway), 6, 46, 109, 124, 135, 159,
    221, 240
Sargent, Frank, 21, 112
Schofield, John, 11, 31, 68, 162, 170, 181, 196,
    210–211, 225
Seaman, William, 240
Seitor, Victor, 207
Sessions, H. H., 76–77
Sheehan, Timothy, 177–178
Sheridan, Philip H., 73, 153
Sherman, John, 118, 215
Sherman Antitrust Act, 118, 150–152, 257,
    260–263
Sherman Silver Purchase Act, 15
slavery
    abolition of, 96–97, 259
    former slaves hired as Pullman porters, 97
    Fourteenth Amendment, 117
    Thirteenth Amendment, 259
    wage slavery, 21, 90, 112–113, 172, 202,
        240, 249, 273
Smith, Anna Ferry, 32
Smith, John H., 202
Smith, Louis, 30
socialism, 98, 249, 254, 270, 273–276
Socialist Party, 274–276
Southern Pacific Railroad, 6, 121, 124,
    148–149, 186, 246
    Santa Clara County v. Southern Pacific
        Railroad Company, 116–117
Sovereign, James, 112–113, 188, 211, 219,
    236
St. John, Everett, 112, 237
St. Paul, Minneapolis & Manitoba Railway, 12
Stanford, Jane Lathrop, 149–150, 242, 257
Stanford, Leland, 150
Stark, Gerald, 194
Starr, Ellen Gates, 90–91
Stead, William Thomas (W. T.), 96
Steinway, William, 206
Stephenson, George, 55
Stewart, James, 141
Strike Commission, U.S.
    Eugene Debs's testimony, 247–249, 255
    George Mortimer Pullman's testimony,
        249–252, 258–259, 264
    report and findings, 246, 252–255
Studebaker, Peter, 178–179
Sue, Eugène, 36, 270
Swift, Gustavus Franklin, 126, 170
switchmen, 38–39, 44, 106–110, 112, 120,
    122, 125, 141, 185, 199, 201, 217
Switchmen's Mutual Aid Society, 112

Taft, William Howard, 126, 208, 275
Teamsters, 198, 212, 226

Terre Haute & Indianapolis Railroad (later
    Vandalia Railroad), 35–36, 41
Terre Haute, Indiana, 34–35, 39–43, 274,
    276–277
Tod, J. Kennedy, 13
Toland, I. F., 197
Traubel, Horace, 274
Trumbull, Lyman, 259–260
Tuley, Murray F., 209
Turner, Frederick Jackson, 8–9

Udess, Frank, 194
Union Pacific, 6, 201
United Mine Workers of America
    coal miners' strike (1894), 27–28, 64, 223,
        264
    and Pullman strike, 213, 225

Vanderbilt, Cornelius, 19
Victoria, Queen, 59
Victorian era, 4, 41, 51, 144, 274
Vandalia Railroad, 35–36, 41

wage slavery, 21, 90, 112–113, 172, 202, 240,
    249, 273
Wagner Palace Car Company, 236, 268
Waite, Davis H., 139–140, 186
Walker, Edwin, 136–137, 140, 162–163, 169,
    173, 197–198, 203, 210, 240–242,
    257–258
Wall Street, 6, 13–15, 91

Wallace, Lew, 206
Ward, Lester F., 116
Warzowski, Joseph, 206
Weaver, James Baird, 117
West, George, 209
Western Union, 81, 106, 222, 257
Westinghouse, George, 39
White, Stephen Van Cullen "Deacon," 13
Whitman, Walt, 19, 168
Wickes, Thomas H., 63, 75–80, 82, 92,
    102–106, 113, 119, 121, 179, 195,
    218–219, 243, 252
Wilson, A. E., 125
Wisconsin Central Railway, 128
Woodruff, Theodore T., 5
Woodruff Sleeping and Parlor Coach
    Company, 59
Woods, William A., 5
Workmen's Compensation Act (1902), 279
World's Columbian Exposition
    Big Mary (statue of the Republic), 3, 189
    fire of July 5, 1894, 188–190
    opening of, 3–4
    and race, 10
    speech by Eugene Debs, 9
    Transportation Building, 4, 189
    White City, 3, 8, 10–11, 169, 188–190, 193
Wright, Carroll D., 247, 249, 251, 254–255
Wright, J. B., 149

Zepp, Richard, 206